D0167616

"The Mercury Model is an innovative way of creating deeper levels of mutual trust, respect and support between team members. The training clearly shows a team how each of them has unique capabilities and contributions to make. Unlike other development programmes, it has nothing to do with exposing weaknesses. It becomes clear why some individuals find it hard to work together constructively, and this recognition improves relationships as each learns to adapt their messages to suit the other."

Liz Taylor, UK

"Strategic application of the Mercury Model will transform communication across individual and organizational boundaries."

Lewis MacIver, UK

"The Mercury Model has been an eye-opener. It allows you to understand how you communicate and how others communicate, which then allows the communication between yourself and others to be smoother and more effective. Personally, it has given me a greater understanding of myself. I realize why I ask certain questions and I no longer expect others to communicate or respond the same as me, as we all have different styles."

Lynne MacDonald, UK

"I would like to share some thoughts on the importance of what you are doing. Looking at the big picture, it seems that growth or evolution of consciousness is the 'prime directive'. As humans we have become self-conscious, but have become overly identified with the 'receiver', which is the mind. We are in the process of learning to transcend the mind, so that it can become the wonderful tool it was meant to be, instead of an end in itself. Mercury represents the fundamental pivot point that will set us free, as it is impossible to master something that you don't understand. Your Mercury Model has afforded me the opportunity to own and work with my 'mental team' and for that I am truly grateful."

Will Tyers, North America

"It takes some adjustment to realise that what I thought was a weakness is actually strength. Some re-jigging of concepts is called for. And knowing the details of each person's style can be of enormous value when working on a one-to-one level. With the Mercury Model I can know in advance about a client's learning style, even before I meet them, and can prepare accordingly. It would be especially useful for a teacher to determine the common ground they share with a student whose progress they're less than happy with."

Zohar Hartley, UK

About the Author

Helyn was born and raised in New England, USA, and gained a BA and then a Masters degree in physical and nuclear chemistry. She went into research in nuclear medicine and radio pharmaceuticals in Boston, Massachusetts. It was early in this career that Helyn began to develop her interest in expressions of the New Physics, such as energy medicine, and in astrology with its ancient mythologies and the subtle energies linking body, mind and spirit.

As her studies and life experience led Helyn toward the awareness that the healing of all relationship issues must start with improved communication, whether on the personal or an international level, she discovered a secret of success – that your message is most effective when your presentation is geared to the learning requirements of the listener. Her research led her to create, develop and test a new tool, which she calls the Mercury Model, for accurately assessing and describing an individual's natural cognitive and learning style.

Since 1997 hundreds of people have been introduced to the Mercury Model through Helyn's personal development workshops. Active, participatory and fun, designed to reach all learning styles, they often feature her dramatizing each mind – in costume. Her professional development workshops have surprised and delighted numerous business delegates; the corporate sector provided the acid test of the Mercury Model for reliable and accurate learning style assessment.

Helyn gives presentations to business networking organisations, educational teams and conferences, and writes articles for the press and academia. Her book *Learning Without Tears*, published in 2008 by Watkins, London, was positively received as an important guidebook for parents about the terrain of their children's minds, including suggestions for dealing with family tensions resulting from natural differences in mental dynamics. Her practice, Astro Innovation, offers consultations, training, courses and workshops to individuals, families and corporate teams on both sides of the Atlantic.

Helyn and her English husband divide their time between living in the beauty of the Lake District in Cumbria and the beauty of New Hampshire's Lakes Region, USA.

To all those who already know,
and those just about to discover,
why they couldn't ever climb trees.

FISH CAN'T CLIMB TREES

Capitalize on **your** brain's unique wiring
to improve the way you learn and communicate

Discover the Mercury Model™

Helyn Connerr

WATKINS

Sharing Wisdom Since
1893

This edition first published in the UK and USA 2016 by
Watkins, an imprint of Watkins Media Limited
19 Cecil Court, London WC2N 4EZ

enquiries@watkinspublishing.com

Design and typography copyright © Watkins Media Limited 2016
Text copyright © Helyn Connerr 2016
Illustrations copyright © Helyn Connerr 2016

1 3 5 7 9 10 8 6 4 2

Designed and typeset by Clare Thorpe

Printed and bound in Finland

A CIP record for this book is available from the British Library

ISBN: 978-1-78028-923-6

www.watkinspublishing.com

Contents

Acknowledgements

A very special thanks to Dr Chris Lane and his inspirational work using the Mercury Model with adolescents. You have proved beyond doubt that those young people were not 'un-teachable' after all; it just looked that way to those who applied the condemning label, those who did not know about individual learning requirements.

With appreciation to all of you who have written to tell me about using the Mercury Model and *Learning Without Tears* in your personal lives and in your businesses. Thank you for all your stories, studies, tips and quotes.

Thanks to Anastasja Katzinova's Word Magick, because that is exactly what she does.

To Sarah Waterhouse, Graphic Engineer, for the 12 character illustrations, beautifully drawn, inked and coloured; also to Cumbria Business Growth Hub & Rural Growth Network for partially supporting the artwork's production.

To Joanne Bullock for the final illustration, The Big Picture.

To Alan (aka Orca), I thoroughly enjoy repeating my thanks for all things technical, grammatical and comestible.

Deb, Adrienne, Tom & Terrie, Norma and Mary Rose, to Anne, Maureen, Annie and Rachel, and others, you know who you are, who would never let me off the hook, helping me to push forward with TDB.

To the members of the Watkins team who put their best efforts into making *Fish Can't Climb Trees* the finest book it could be, with special thanks to Deborah Hercun, Sandy Draper, Clare Thorpe, Dawn Bates, Vicky Hartley, Jillian Levick and Michael Mann.

With great appreciation and love to Nicholas, for his support at every step along the way and for stabilizing yet another limb I went out to explore.

Foreword

Very soon after qualifying as a teacher at Bristol University over 40 years ago, I discovered that my particular skill was in working with young people for whom the conventional state school structure was an anathema.

I went on to work in a wide range of educational establishments, as a teacher and eventually a Principal, all with a variety of labels including 'special education units', 'maladjusted schools', 'approved schools' to name a few.

What all of them had in common was that many of the young people I worked with were educational failures and social misfits who, for whatever reason, had been left behind by the system.

My own intuitive methods of relating to and trying to engage these troubled, often disruptive young people in the wonders and opportunities of education led me to a discovery that mirrored what I had always suspected. It wasn't the content that was the issue, but the manner in which the curriculum was being taught.

It is often the case that students described as 'un-teachable' are in actual fact unreachable via their teacher's method of presenting and explaining the information.

A student who is not engaged is not learning, and a student who isn't learning or moving forward is sadly the most likely to be punished or excluded for bad behaviour rather than receiving the help he or she so urgently needs.

After all, without them in the class, the teacher can get on with teaching the rest of the group without trouble or disruption.

But what about the individuals who have been excluded?

They are now on a downward spiral that more often than not promises to stultify any future potential that they may have possessed. If they are not lifted out of the cycle it will continue with them, their children and their children's children. This inevitably becomes a serious social and national problem, yet it is so easily avoided with just a little insight.

I first met Helyn Connerr in 1983 and was lucky enough to play a small part in the development of her groundbreaking system, the Mercury Model. I used the early Learning Style Profiles to aid me in working with a very disturbed group of young people in a Special Education Unit attached to a mixed comprehensive school. It was a remarkable experience both in terms of how easy the Profiles were to use, and how immediate the impact of using them was demonstrated by each student's success in the classroom.

The clear and precise Learning Strategies that Helyn identified enabled me to guide and advise my teaching colleagues. They in turn found that the basic truths of the Mercury Model were unquestionable.

The result? A reduction in disruptive incidents in the classroom. A harmonious learning environment with each individual engaged in the material being taught. The steady integration of so-called problem children out of the shadows and into mainstream education. The realization of gifts and talents in individuals previously misunderstood and overlooked by the system.

I can truthfully say I consider the Mercury Model to be the greatest development for education in the last 200 years.

There are many adults now living a useful and happy life who have benefited directly from my use of Helyn Connerr's revolutionary system. How different might the world be now without those people contributing to society, believing in themselves and using their talents to help others?

The Mercury Model has proved itself beyond doubt with some of the most disengaged and demanding young people I have ever taught, giving them confidence, self-awareness and the ability to perceive where their unique talents lie and are applicable to real world tasks and situations.

Whether you are a parent, teacher, student or one of the many adults who have been to a greater or lesser extent failed by the mainstream education system, all the tools you need to change your perception of learning, communication, yourself and your family are within this book.

Find the way in which a person learns and you will tap into a wellspring of that individual's unique gifts. Use it with your children, pupils or students and you will uncover an unquenchable hunger for learning and recognition.

Apply it to your family and, where possible, heal rifts, create harmony and start rediscovering your loved ones in a way that makes space for their distinct ways of communicating, processing information and understanding the world.

Apply it to yourself and discover, sometimes for the first time, your true talents and learn to nurture and develop them.

It is never too late to use the Mercury Model to revolutionize your life and the lives of those around you. The changes it creates are truly magical. Enjoy it.

Chris Lane, PhD, M.N.G.S., M.R.S.
Ambleside, Cumbria
April 2015

Introduction

'Everybody is a genius. But if you judge a fish by its ability to climb a tree, it will live its whole life believing that it is stupid.'

ALBERT EINSTEIN

Have you ever tried to follow along with someone's explanation and found yourself completely unable to grasp it – as if it were a foreign language? Do you wonder why certain things stick in your memory and others don't? Perhaps someone writing in the margins of a book brings you out in a cold sweat ... or maybe a friend asking you to decide where you want to go for dinner next week feels as odd as a question about what you want for your birthday in 20 years' time.

You see, we are all wired differently. Even if we are related, our minds function in line with what I call our 'personal master operating programmes' which may be as different from each other's as a fish is from an elephant.

In my first book, *Learning Without Tears*, I presented what I call the 'Mercury Model' and how it can be used to help parents understand children's learning styles, not only to help the children learn new information in the most efficient way for their own unique minds, but also to improve understanding and communication at all levels between the child and the adult.

In *Fish Can't Climb Trees*, I show you how to use the Mercury Model as an adult, to achieve better relationships, a heightened understanding of others and, most importantly, a greater awareness of your own unique learning style, how it has shaped your life and could be applied to creating a better future.

The Mercury Model provides quick, easy identification and an accurate detailed description of how each mind ticks – naturally and uniquely. It pinpoints mental strengths and blind spots, explains why we opt to take in only certain kinds of information, our particular style of uptake and how long information might stay with us. It identifies common ground between quite different operating programmes and describes the stresses that can develop where unrelated dynamics meet, as well as how to resolve them.

For many of us, the conventional educational view of 'one size fits all' has left us convinced that our natural way of thinking and learning is 'wrong' or has no productive value in our society. We may take unsuitable jobs, appropriate for a polar bear even though we may be a parrot, or convince ourselves we'll never be able to do certain things after the humiliation of being criticized for failed attempts to learn in ways that are entirely wrong for us.

Fish Can't Climb Trees contains a tool with astounding benefits within personal, familial, professional and social relationships, in business, education, politics, etc. The fact is whenever minds are engaged, on any topic, in any setting, at any age, regardless of gender or nationality, each person's mode of handling information stands as a filter to their mental uptake and delivery, to how they learn and how they speak.

It was only when I asked readers of *Learning Without Tears* to send me stories of their real-life experiences of using the Mercury Model that I realized I had not considered those who, for one reason or another, didn't have concerned parents. It also became clear that just as many adults were using the book to discover their own learning style as to find that of the child in their life. I began to hear about 'disaffected' teens and the correlations between disruptive behaviour in the classroom and unmet learning requirements. There are some profound success stories here.

We might have anticipated that this sort of information would have come from psychological or educational theory, but it has not. It is still not available from those sources. Any breakthrough about personal uniqueness in thinking and learning would have to come from an unexpected direction. Drawn from decades of studying the mysteries of the universe through a variety of lenses, from hard science to soft science, and using the principle of mental synthesis discussed in this book, I have linked elements of mythological archetypes and the ancient wisdom of astrology, to produce the Mercury Model. The identification of individual cognitive function and learning dynamics is based upon the astronomical position of the planet Mercury at birth. Personal learning styles can be identified in moments using the Learning Style Tables, which you'll find in Part II on page 235, for births from 1925 to 2025.

The bottom line is that it works. Stories and reports from people who have used the Mercury Model in their own lives, in their relationships, in their families and businesses, in education and training, are scattered throughout this book. Try it yourself. Look up the Learning Profile of your child, your parent, your good friend, your partner and yourself.

Relationships magically transform the instant someone discovers and truly acknowledges that we each handle information in our own way. In that moment of realization and acceptance there is understanding. The tight bands of criticism and judgement are released, old hurts are soothed; respect and empowerment can become mutual. Both people are off the hook, with permission to really look at how their individual minds tick and to celebrate both their differences and their similarities.

Can you imagine the benefit to all our relationships if communication is clear and supportive, based on mutual understanding and respect for natural differences? Imagining one step further, what if people commonly knew about the creative use of tension, which quite naturally develops where there is difference? Can you imagine the advantage gained by people of all ages who recognize their natural mental skills and develop them into effective tools to be enjoyed confidently and successfully for their whole lives – within the family, at school, in the workplace and in the larger community? These are achievable goals. This book provides you with what you need to make it a reality. Stir in your own intention and watch it happen.

You will soon discover that one in four of us is a visual learner, for whom absorption of new information is greatly assisted by pictures, graphics, illustrations of all sorts, and especially by colour. For these minds, words alone just don't do it – neither does black and white. For the rest of us, colour pictures are still fun or lively or pretty or simply entertaining. To view the full-colour versions of all the illustrations in *Fish Can't Climb Trees*, please visit:

www.MercuryModel.com

You are also invited to learn more, post, participate, discuss, use the forum, or whatever might evolve over time, at:

www.facebook.com/MercuryModel

PART I

Individual Learning Styles –
We Are All Wired Differently

Section 1

Learning Styles: Master Operating Programmes – How Our Minds Tick

Let us peer into the private domain of a mind, glimpse the territory, identify the lay of the land and detect what's happening there. Is a gala event under way, a serious business meeting or a dramatic presentation? Do you detect analysis in process; is an experiment in midstream? Are there bright flashes of enthusiasm or overall calm? And if there are other people, an entire scout troop, a professional ball team or boardroom full of them, let's repeat the process for each one. What emerges will be an impression of a vast diversity of mental experience. The differences can be staggering. You will never again hold the common misconception that a mind is a mind and, regardless of age, they all function in pretty much the same way. They do not. Period.

Although all humans do possess a brain, a nervous system and several sensory organs, these physical components link together and function under the guidance of uniquely distinct master operating programmes. Consequently, within those little grey cells between our ears, we have entirely personal mental experiences – experiences of new information, of our existing thoughts and of our impulse to share those thoughts with others. Child, adolescent or adult, we each handle information in our own way. We must – information is not the same thing to each of us. For some it zigzags while for others it's round or parallel or tangible or insubstantial. Some of us are graced by information; others are burdened by it.

Whether we are three or ninety-three, we each have our own natural reaction to new material. Some build strong barriers to keep it out, while others open their arms widely to welcome any and all that is available. Whether we are learning to read, to tie our shoelaces, to master computer skills or understand the implications of fracking, each of us has a natural approach. Fish can't climb trees, but it's a monkey's favourite activity.

And, we all do best what comes naturally.

Along the complex path of dealing with new information, every step is personal. Our individual relationship with information guides each one of us through all the stages of learning from

* initially noticing or missing it,
* to embracing or defending against it,
* to deciding whether to learn it or to reject it,
* to taking it in,
* to sharing it with someone else or containing it,
* to recalling it over the long term or forgetting it instantly.

The unique programme that governs and interconnects all aspects of how we handle information is called our 'learning style'. Everyone has one, regardless of age, gender, intellectual capacity, health, personality or national origin. A learning style is part of a person's nature – it's personal and it's natural. A learning style is neither an option nor a preference. It is not a matter of upbringing or heredity; it is beyond environment, beyond nurture. At birth our unique operating programme is already whole.

A learning style has to do with the dynamics of thought and this book is about your mind and how it ticks, other people's minds and how they tick, and how our minds connect with each other. A learning style is not about ego structure or personality. Some people's mental activities are reflected in their behaviour. But, as this is not true for everyone, we shall set aside all behavioural elements. We will not be looking at how your child, your partner or your boss acts, plays, drives or dresses, or at what they like or dislike. Learning styles are not related to values, social impulses or ambitions. Our learning styles do not assess intelligence, IQ or intellectual capability. Thinking and learning are hidden, inner processes, not visible by observation. The mind is its own place.

Our individually configured minds handle information differently. It is just that simple. You may have noticed that some of us take hold of huge amounts of data and weave it like threads into something brand new, a fabric never seen before, and not resembling the component strands at all. Others are naturally skilled at initiating brand new thought, moving forward, always forward. Some minds share information very quickly, no sooner has it gone in that it comes out again, while others secrete it away, keeping it safely within, only to be shared when the time is right.

AND IN A FAMILY?

It may surprise you to know that even among siblings, or within a close-knit family, there can be, and usually are, astounding variations in learning styles. The inner mental landscapes can differ enormously – from a lush green meadow for one to a deep underwater cave for another. Family members often go about dealing with information each in their own way. Beyond genetic inheritance, despite similarity in family training, this individuality is normal and natural.

So, if you have ever wondered what in the world makes your children's minds tick, believe me, you're not alone! Something that appears to genuinely excite one seems to bore the socks off another. And, with all we hear about family characteristics, how can children's minds differ so enormously from their parents'?

But, there they are, mentally as different from each other as night is from day. You can look in on them doing their lessons, one quietly sitting at a desk working away, another on the telephone discussing the assignment with a school friend, a third jigging around the room, headphones on, book in hand. You might be convinced that at least two of them are not learning or studying anything at all.

AND OUTSIDE THE HOME – AT SCHOOL, IN THE WORKPLACE, IN THE COMMUNITY?

We might well ask what 'learning' is all about. Beyond the biochemistry, is the experience of learning the same for each of us? Does it feel the same? Is one mind doing the same thing as another? And what about teaching? Does anyone actually teach something to another, or does one person optimistically present information to another and hope it will be taken in? Who is in charge of learning, the speaker or the listener, the teacher or the student, the trainer or the employee, the parent or the child? Learning is a mysterious process. A bit like the law of gravity – we can see that it works but we don't know how.

The very word 'learning' propels most adults back into school, the sheltered or confining domain of a formal educational setting. And many shudder at the memory. Although our school years do provide a highly concentrated learning experience, learning in a broader sense neither begins nor ends in the classroom. It is part of everyday life.

Learning can happen at every age and in every setting. It is not restricted to groups of children in classrooms but can extend to solitary outdoor adventures as an older person. Learning even goes on at breakfast whether in the childhood home, in a university dining hall or in a nursing home. Your learning style directs your selection of a greeting card for a friend of any age, shaping how you want to convey your message of 'Thanks', 'I miss you', 'I am sorry' or 'Happy Birthday'. Your learning style is right there with you when sharing personal life experiences with a good friend, the mode, the style and even the content. Instructions of all sorts are filtered through your personal learning style – the procedures at your new job, the techniques of a new sport or reading the hands or numbers on a clock. Your learning style finds out about computers and smartphones, tweeting, messaging and mail merge software. It tries to comprehend what the mechanic said is wrong with your car.

And it will soon discover how individual minds work – that as much as they may wish to, fish actually can't climb trees – because it certainly sits with you now, while you're reading this book.

Every tiny bit of communication during your day (talking, shouting, singing, emailing, giving the 'hairy eyeball' or the cold shoulder, saying it with flowers, written notes, phone and text messages, silence, any non-verbal expression, etc.) engages the learning styles of both people – the presenter and the intended recipient. Communication, and therefore the possibility of learning, occurs constantly – in your attic, in the shower, while dressing, cooking, eating, preparing your tax return and riding your bike. Both people's learning styles come forward whenever you, in any role, want to get your message across, no matter what the message is.

Our minds may function quite differently, but that is not to say that any one learning style is better or worse than any other. It is not! All are valuable and each has its own special skills and contributions to make – at home, at school, at work or out in the world. Without awareness of individual learning styles, you might observe differences among your family members and arrive at any number of sorry conclusions about relative worth and value. But consider this. Society needs the analytical scientist as much as the reflective poet. Your family or your group of colleagues might contain these opposite kinds of minds. The mediator, the organizer and the networker carry important roles as well as the philosopher, the pioneer and the detective. It would be a less exciting world if we all thought alike. Easier, perhaps, but less stimulating, less creative and far less interesting.

> " *Effective and joyful learning comes from knowing and respecting our own learning styles.* "

One part of our individual master programme identifies our learning 'needs' or 'requirements'. We all have some critical parameters which must be satisfied if learning is to be effortless. Information in harmony with our learning needs can be taken in smoothly, without glitches, hiccups, stress or tears.

For example, you may be exceptionally sensitive to physical surroundings, literally unable to think in some locations, while someone else may be surprisingly unaffected by the setting, able to read in a tree or negotiate on a plane. Such things are neither talents nor defects; they are simply personal learning requirements. My mind might easily take in information only if it is seen to be useful, and yours might require a lively discussion of ideas before accepting them. Awareness of such needs is the first step toward meeting them. For example, you could decide to avoid engaging in mental work in a location that disadvantages your thinking and provide the same option to the children, adolescents and other adults in your world.

You might be surprised to discover what aids or inhibits another person's learning process. Possibly, you might never have dreamed that a factor could be significant for someone else, if it is not important to you. Most of us never objectify our learning needs. Nonetheless, they can be grouped into the following three broad categories:

1 For easy learning, some minds require that a specific quality exists within the information itself. This is not an exhaustive list but just some examples. Information must be: practical or applied or pure, logical, intuitive, useful, valuable, traditional, innovative, true, conceptual, functional, powerful, significant, legal, sacred, exciting, fun, poetic, moving, global, detailed, political, smutty or grammatically correct.

2 Mode of delivery is frequently an important learning requirement. You could be speaking to a person for whom any of the following features might either assist or hinder learning: interaction, involvement, repetition, activity,

drama, discussion, colour, time to consider, excitement, a fast pace, a slow pace, fun, action, emotion, the big picture, the tiny details, show-and-tell demonstration, visuals, written instructions or experimentation.

3   Physical and emotional surroundings are critically important to some learners, who take in information most easily if the setting is: comfortable, familiar, physically and/or emotionally safe, colourful, fun, quiet, noisy, out in nature or in a room with the door closed. Some of us have learning needs around solitary versus group activities, or where action and movement are not just possible but encouraged.

Children and young people who are fully aware of their own learning requirements from early on can easily accept a mind's individual nature. They can ask for their needs to be met later on in life, with confidence rather than shame. And they easily understand and accommodate natural difference.

" *Effective communication can occur when we also take account of the other person's learning requirements.* "

When your message is presented in a way that matches another's learning needs, there is a good fit and information uptake can occur smoothly, with neither person becoming snagged on rough edges.

For example, an adolescent's mind might be one of the very fast ones, breathing in information in a flash, needing no processing time at all, restless to get on to the next idea. If your words are presented quickly, almost on the run, matching pace with the other mind, then your message will have a better likelihood of hitting the mark.

Unfortunately, the reverse is also true. Learning can be seriously disadvantaged when a mind's unique needs are not recognized or, much worse, when they are perceived as weakness. Let's look again at the young person with the very fast-paced mind. Consider this scenario: the parent's natural mental style responds well to a slow and steady approach, perhaps requiring a few repetitions to really get a message. Moreover, the parent, being unaware of individual mental differences, thinks all minds are fundamentally alike. Does not bode well, does it? Lacking the tools to understand the absolutely natural top-speed, flat-out pace of the teenager's mind, the parent could view it as dangerously ungrounded, and even seek medical intervention to rectify the problem. Unfortunately, this is not uncommon.

> **Example**: Young Eddie's parents were enchanted with his astounding curiosity – when he was a baby. His attention was drawn by everything from a passing bumblebee to a new sound in his own tummy. It all interested him and he responded to it. His parents proudly described him as 'quick'.
>
> This was great until Eddie's school reports said he didn't concentrate well. Suddenly concerned by the very quality that had previously pleased them, his parents sought further advice, obtained a diagnosis of Attention Deficit Disorder (ADD) and faced the dilemma of drug therapy.

In all areas of life, in the living room, the boardroom or the classroom, people whose learning requirements are not met can come away feeling very badly about themselves. What might have been joyful exchanges otherwise becomes drudgery for both the speaker and the listener, for the teacher and the student, the trainer and the employee. Tension results. Self-confidence and self-esteem can be so easily and unnecessarily damaged. The natural flame of enthusiasm may be extinguished. Mistrust could develop. The situation can escalate into disruptive behaviour and 'exclusion' all too often follows. Harmony is right out the window. Nobody wins.

And years after leaving school, college or university many adults still experience the shame of having felt thick, slow or stupid. Worse yet, they might think it's true. All this because nobody recognized their individual, natural learning needs.

> " *Each of us takes in information most easily (and joyfully) if it is presented to us in a way that's compatible with our own master operating programme. Otherwise we have to struggle to get the message. There are ways to say things that will make it easy to hear and ways that will make it virtually impossible to pick up.* "

If information were tailored to make it easy for me to learn, I would take it in and feel good about the process of learning and myself. On the other hand, information could be tailored to benefit someone else and I would not easily take it in. I would struggle and feel dumb, and the speaker might see me that way also. Or a message could be shaped and delivered to reach me more than my brother and I would learn it and he would not. He's not dense, but he needs a message formatted differently.

For the sake of getting an idea across, a speaker who is aware of natural learning styles can always modify and tailor a presentation to suit others' learning requirements. If we have the knowledge to do so, adults willingly change languages while travelling in foreign countries in order to interact with others. How much more important to adjust the mode of delivery and actually communicate with those we care about rather than missing them totally and just talking to ourselves.

It is likely that a variety of unique learning styles is represented in your circle of associates. A uniform way of presenting information simply will not benefit them all. A person whose mental landscape figuratively resembles the lush green meadow will most easily take in information presented to harmonize with that landscape. But, the delivery of the same message would have to be tailored differently if intended for a person whose mental landscape is more like the deep ocean cave. These two individuals will not both receive your message easily, if it is presented in only one way. One of them might understand what you are saying, but chances are the other will not. Fish can't climb trees. Or, as another example, if one person is a real stickler for detail, and actually learns by dissecting and questioning everything you say, and another needs to get the 'big picture' by taking a wide view first, then their minds will respond to quite different approaches on your part.

> **Example**: Lorraine likes spontaneity. She is a new team member who takes in information most easily if it is lively and upbeat. Richard, her colleague, has a 10-year history with the company and prefers to consider things in some depth. Their manager has sidestepped any difficulty at team meetings by sending out an agenda in advance. Richard has a chance to preview the meeting and prepare his questions before it starts, whereas Lorraine opts to read the agenda five minutes before the meeting and lets it happen as it will.

At every stage of life, we all need permission to grow along the lines of our most natural and therefore greatest mental strengths. Your students, employees, colleagues and friends might have mental qualities and ways of handling information that are quite unlike your own, and the larger community stands to benefit from their unique development. We all do best what comes naturally. A fish would have difficulty not only climbing a tree, but learning to jump rope, and I am just as glad my family didn't expect me to learn underwater breathing.

For so many of us, well-meaning friends, teachers or family members, knowing what helped them to learn, tried to convince us, usually with great success, that their method of information handling and uptake was better than ours. There is the pivotal moment, right there. At that point we could become detached from our own natural mental style and attempt to mimic or imitate a mode that works quite well for someone else. We could separate ourselves from our strengths. It might be years later, if ever, that someone leads us back to our own way of handling information and our unique mental ways.

For example, let's say one of your early schoolteachers learned most easily through discussion. His mind had always been like that. Even as a small child he had discussed notions about shoe-tying and clock-reading with his dog. This method worked for him, despite the dog's lack of verbal response. He got what he needed – the opportunity to form his thoughts into concepts and ideas and to express them. (Some discussion-style learners use computers as the chosen recipient of their fledgling thoughts while others use humans.) At any rate, your teacher grew to adulthood certain that learning is best accomplished through discussion. He had teaching cracked; he knew how to do it. The teacher simply involves the pupil in a discussion. Right? No, not for all students. If you are a natural 'hands-on' 'I have to try it out to get it' type of learner, then the discussion method does not play to your strength. It will take you ages to get the message into your head if you abandon your own need for active involvement with the material in favour of your teacher's need for discussion. He did not hijack your learning process deliberately, but you may have been disconnected from easy joyful learning ever since.

Now let's fast forward a few decades to you as an adult, facing a steep learning curve with today's rapidly advancing technologies. A trainer is there showing you pictures of the inner workings of a big electronic device, a trainer who really has teaching cracked because he knows that people learn most easily when they are shown diagrams and graphs. No, this does not play to your mental strength either. Go for what you need and get your hands on that machine! Try it out. See what it does and what its capabilities are. If you are a hands-on learner, claim what you need. Do it! Try it! Get your hands dirty. Sniff it, taste it. Reconnect with your own natural style of thinking and learning. But, whatever you do, don't make the assumption that everyone else is like you mentally. They may not need to digest the dictionary to learn linguistics. But you might.

We have all heard these comments. Now, they should make us very suspicious.

- 'No, not like that! Do it my way, it works for me. It will work for you too.'
- 'It's how the human mind works.'
- 'It's traditional. It's the way it's done.'
- 'If you do not learn this material the way I am teaching it, you will fail at school.'
- 'We wrote this test to find out if you have learned the material. If you fail it, you are dumb, slow, stupid, retarded, have ADD, dyslexia, learning difficulties, are disruptive in the classroom, non-cooperative, daydreaming out the window, could concentrate better, are not academic material and moreover, will never amount to anything.'

Whew, all this to avoid looking at individual mental difference.

Section 2

The 12 Fundamental Learning Styles

I have presented this information on learning styles as 'Profiles' of 12 distinct archetypal characters, each with its own well-defined essence, pace, style, interests and ways of doing things. Each has a name and an illustration which shows its mode of handling information.

Each Profile is a clear first-person report, by the mind itself, of how it ticks, how it learns, how it remembers (or does not), its openness to new information, its natural strengths and potential blind spots. Many tell us how they appear to and get along with other minds. Some identify specific conditions which assist or inhibit learning. Each Profile includes hints, tips and strategies for encouraging effective learning and improved interactions. All include quotations from real people with the learning style, some of them well known, as another way to look through that mind's point of view. And each Profile is accompanied by stories which, like the quotes, I have gathered over the years from, or about, real people who live with that mind.

> " Reading through these Profiles will demonstrate the huge differences among people's minds. "

Two of the 12 are very formal, very structured, but one takes a traditional view and the other opts for the uniquely personal. Some tell you their story easily; one is reluctant to be seen. Those of you who are visual learners will instantly identify these mental character differences in their illustrations. They all speak to the reader in their own voices, at their own pace, from their own logic, not mine. The author is just the messenger. You will like some of these characters better than others, just like real life. You will want some of them to speed up, some to slow down and some to stop repeating themselves. Each one is brutally honest and totally sincere about itself.

Mental traits and dynamics are neither masculine nor feminine. Either a male or a female can have any of the 12 learning styles presented here. All people can elect to use their natural mental skills in any way they please, including, for example, the apparently opposite pursuits of reflective poetry or research science.

" *Learning styles are not about behaviour or personality and they are not discernible by observing people. If they were, there would be no need for this book.* "

A learning style, a master operating programme, deals with mental dynamics and may bear no relationship to other facets of a person's make-up – feelings, ego, values, social impulses, ambitions, etc. A learning style does not comment on mental or emotional intelligence or capacity. It is a style, a mode, a manner.

Any behavioural terms used in the Profiles describe the activities of the characters. They are ways in which the mind itself might behave and are not intended to correspond to an individual person's performance. You may or may not observe these characters shining forth in your own or in other people's activities, as they represent purely inner mental functions.

" *For those readers who chafe against the idea that our minds can be compartmentalized into 12 groups, please know that I agree with you, wholeheartedly, and have a look at Section 5 on page 214, for more information.* "

This is the perfect time to quickly and easily identify learning styles for yourself, your partner, parents, children, boss, employees, friends, etc. Just turn to the Learning Style Tables in Part II on page 235 and follow the instructions for using them. In moments you will know primary learning styles for all the important people in your life. Then enjoy reading their Profiles, as each of the minds tells you about itself.

The 12 individual minds do not report to you on the common ground they may share with each other. They talk about themselves, not about areas of similarity or difference. And they never mention building bridges, resolving tension or looking through each other's points of view. So I did – in Sections 3 and 4 on pages 179 and 198 respectively.

SCOUT, THE TRAILBLAZER

I am quick on the uptake, active, direct, energetic, positive, lively and bright. I can be unflaggingly forceful and competitive. And to everyone else, I am either stimulating or exhausting.

Those who are not Scouts might be surprised, excited, puzzled or perhaps outraged by some of my qualities. You might anticipate that a Scout child or adolescent will outgrow what you now observe: the flippant enthusiasms or mega-mental confidence. Well, they won't; 20, 40, 80 years from now, they, like me, will still be Trailblazers.

I am first off the starting line when it comes to new information. I literally run at it, like a gladiator, charging with my sword drawn; I always have and always will. I like the idea of knowing something before anyone else does. I am first to get my hand in the air, first to speak – first to get my foot in my mouth. However, I like having the last word too. I am dynamic, eager, assertive, robust and tireless.

Others call me a 'Mental Warrior'. I persistently move forward thriving on challenges as I go. I rarely, if ever, look back over my shoulder. I am not boring.

I am naturally creative, originating new ideas and initiating new lines of thought which you will not have heard before or from anyone else. I like to veer suddenly along uncharted mental pathways, inventing as I go. I am good at this – starting is one of my strengths. So when a fresh new approach is needed, ask me. You may not have to ask. I may be right there making suggestions. Others may think they are good at brainstorming, well, guess what? That's my word – I invented it first!

> "*I am brave, bold and courageous about exploration. I am fearless about the unknown. Some may say I am reckless – exciting, enterprising, but reckless. I am wired to respond to red.*"

I am the Trailblazer; I do not ask for permission or for help in making a decision. I am tremendously independent. I do not refer to other minds; I just go for it. I learn by reference to myself. I am at the centre of the universe – at least my own universe. I am identified with my own thoughts – they are closely related to who I am, to my ego. I take my own ideas very seriously and am attached to my own point of view. To question one of my ideas is to question me, and I usually experience this as a personal challenge. I observe that other sorts of minds do not respond like this; it's classically Scout.

But, now that I have introduced the topic, let's speak of Other sorts of minds. Some of my natural ways seem to make me unpopular with them. Others say that I tend to begin most sentences with 'I' and that this habit is an expression of my link between mind and ego. I am not totally sure what they mean by that, but how else would Scout begin a sentence? You? We?

Although Others might read this as a serious 'me first' attitude in young Scouts, it is not helpful for a child to be criticized or told he or she is selfish or self-centred. It is not helpful for an adolescent Scout to spend his or her young life either in isolation or with a bloody nose or a black eye. Adult Scouts, despite the apparent bravado of those who continue to overuse the 'I' word, are also more vulnerable than you might think to the consequences of being 'taken down a peg or two'. We Scouts have many wonderful qualities and it would be unfortunate for others to thoughtlessly, and perhaps unintentionally, extinguish the flame of our mental courage. Reigniting it is often more difficult than you might anticipate. We might just snap shut and conceal our flame. As an alternative, it may be useful for Scouts, possibly as a defence strategy, to learn about Other minds and how they tick.

> **A game for children**: For some period of time, all family members engage in 'I' sentences and talk primarily about themselves. This game offers Little Scout the opportunity to be on the receiving end of all those 'I's', while the rest of the family has a chance to try it out for themselves. This is not intended to ridicule or to be a Scout-bashing session, but to be a loving experience of similarity and difference in family thinking and learning styles. It could help Scout recognize and come to respect the value of other family minds and to realize how his constant 'I' statements make others feel.

As Scout, my natural impulse is to start things, to take initiative, to speak out, to introduce myself, my topic and my thoughts. I bravely take responsibility for my own ideas and fearlessly tell others about them. If someone disagrees, that's sometimes OK because I quite like an argument and I don't mind being controversial. In fact sometimes I like to stir things up. It is exciting! Thriving on challenge and risk, I often leap impulsively where angels fear to tread. I am naturally competitive.

Here is what I used to think, before I moved on to altogether new ideas:

A mind is a mind, is a mind and we are all pretty much the same. So when I compared Others to myself, I saw:

- They learn more slowly = stupid.
- They do not step forward with their own ideas = they are also cowards.
- They don't fight their corner but negotiate or let the other guy win = wimps.
- They engage in subtlety as if it mattered = softies.
- They don't grasp their own ideas and run with them = quitters.
- They never think up anything new = boring.
- They waste time thinking about other people = misguided.

OK, OK, it took me a while (how embarrassing) to accept that minds are very different from each other in almost every way. So, my tendency to defend my own point of view, without compromise, and to regard every question as a personal challenge may actually have a down side. This was a new thought for me. My previous thinking does demonstrate the high regard in which I hold my own qualities, which is appropriate, but it also might deny the value of everyone else's natural mental strengths and capabilities. Sometimes being 150 per cent true to myself in this regard may interfere with both learning and getting along with people. Hum.

Even young Scouts already have the natural impulse to energetically (forcefully?) share their thoughts with everyone else. To adults, especially those in authority, such as classroom teachers, headmasters and grandparents, the expression of this impulse appears to be out of line. The trick is to realize, without damage to our courageous but delicate temperaments, that impulsively acting on all our natural inclinations does not always bring about the desired results. It can be a steep learning curve for us to accept even the possibility of holding back, of selecting the tone and the time to speak. Treading this path in an effort to improve relationships may require a great deal of patience, practice and self-understanding. But, the Trailblazer impulse can mature to engage courageously and productively with powerful forces like the boss, the board of directors, the drill sergeant or the government.

Some difficult pitfalls may be avoided if we Scouts learn to engage with the challenge of modifying our expressive behaviour while remaining connected to our natural mental strengths. This blend will allow our creativity to flow constructively as a great gift to everyone, as well as to ourselves. The art form is 'conscious socialization' – learning to live in community with others, family members, friends, colleagues, etc., while still retaining one's finest qualities and talents.

Although we Trailblazers can be challenging and confrontational, we are not stubborn. Unless the fight is just too interesting or too much fun, we are usually ready to move on. There are so many other conquests out there!

> *" At any age, Scouts learn best if we apply ourselves in short bursts separated by periods of activity. Thinking is stimulated by movement – our brains slow down with immobility. "*

A marathon session with a schoolbook, an instruction manual or the script of a play accomplishes little in the way of learning but will certainly create a volcano of restlessness. Try a period of mental focus, then a walk or a workout, and then back to the topic at hand. Any activity that gets the blood moving seems to help mental concentration: swimming, skating, stretching, bike rides, chopping wood. (If you are lucky, household chores might be effective.) I like to take in information on the move.

" *'Think while doing' is my motto.* "

As a Trailblazer I am very quick on the uptake. I just breathe in information without needing to process, integrate or digest it at all. I can inhale fully developed ideas in the blink of an eye. But then, while I wait for everyone else to catch up, restlessness takes over and boredom sets in. So, off I dash in pursuit of the next electrifying new idea.

I am not very interested in follow-through, completing, reviewing, revising or repeating. I am not interested in practicality, punctuation, logic or your opinion. I rush forward inexhaustibly and rarely look back.

My energy works in quantum blasts, like fireworks that brilliantly illuminate a dark sky and then quickly fade. It's natural for an idea to stimulate my enthusiasm for a while and then die away. Completing a project, sticking with it to the end, dotting all those i's and crossing all the t's, goes against my grain. Taking care of the details is not my favourite activity. It is not easy for me to accept that life does not seem to allow any of us the luxury of using only our authentic strengths all the time. Many projects do require completion, and many ideas need to be followed through. It takes extra energy and willpower for me to do this. I want to move on to new ideas, not stick with the old, boring ones. But, by striking out, speeding like a rally driver, my forward momentum can often carry me straight on past the point of success.

Using tricks helps me stick with a project, topic or report until it's completed. A useful strategy is to find ways to make the old project seem new and thus to enlist the enthusiasm that naturally occurs at the beginning. I can break a large project into smaller components so that I can view and experience each part as a new project. For example, rather than trying to learn all about my new phone in one sitting, I just figured out how to turn it on and make a call. Then after my morning workout, I looked at texting and how the camera works.

Tricks for Scout: How many new titles can you discover for the same (old) assignment? How many different directions of approach arrive at the same (old) point? How many different facets of the same (old) task can be explored as if it were a new activity? Can doing the same (old) project in a different study or workspace make it seem totally new?

We Trailblazers notice and might still wonder about Other minds taking longer to catch on to new information. Even now, many people do not realize that we all think and learn differently and that no particular learning style is better or worse than another. It would be useful in the long term if we Scouts help to update the widely held misconception that 'quicker' translates into 'smarter', that those who catch on faster are better than those who require more time. Unlike minds that pause to reflect and check out all the angles, or to digest or feel the information, we Scouts leap impulsively upon a new idea with enthusiasm and boldness. To some this may look heedless; to us almost everyone else seems painfully slow. It would help if all of us saw that minds are not inferior just because they tick more slowly, nor superior because they work more quickly, but that we have different processes going on.

Example: A 14-year-old Trailblazer adopted the policy of telling his very busy mother something once, and only once. He would not repeat it. But, he would judge and condemn his mother's quite different learning style, if she just happened to forget something weeks and sometimes months later. 'Mum, I told you my sports schedule at the beginning of term. Why should I have to tell you again? I have a game today! Are you stupid or what?'

WHAT HELPS SCOUT, THE TRAILBLAZER, TO LEARN?

- Recognize that I will have the most mental energy at the beginning of a project and that finishing is likely to take more effort. If you see creative new ways that I can use to 'restart' a stuck project, in order to actually finish it, I'll try to listen.

- Activity aids my learning. I am mentally restless and like to physically move while thinking. This is difficult in a group situation as my moving around clearly disturbs those who need stability and calm. Help find creative solutions.
- I work best in short sessions with activity in between.
- Information recorded onto tapes, MP3 players, etc., allows me to listen during a variety of activities.
- Activity-based learning can positively stimulate my mind: field trips, dramatization, modelling, role-play. I cannot just sit at a desk or in a confined space – I'll explode.
- Energizing music may help to dispel my restlessness and boredom.
- Try to be enthusiastic when presenting information to me. Emphasize an idea's newness.
- Learning by rote is a sure route to impatience and boredom, so avoid this strategy.
- Present information in a way that makes it personal to me.
- Make learning fun and original – I like to be first with new ideas.
- Let me take the lead as frequently as possible; it allows my mind to have a free rein.
- Ask questions about things that I have done. Encourage me to tell you about what excites me.
- Use flash cards or other fast methods of learning, making connections or testing my knowledge.
- Shock me, surprise me – use jokes or punch lines.
- Keep it short!

QUOTES FROM SCOUT, THE TRAILBLAZER

'I think that the quickest way to gather information is the best.'

'I had a great new idea 10 minutes ago and I've given it a great deal of thought.'

'Look I've told you once. I'm not telling you again.'

'I think while I'm driving.'

'I have great enthusiasm, especially at the beginning.'

'I find I can move on with new initiatives at work. Others find it hard.'

'I do like to poke people a couple of times to get them to say what they really mean.'

'When I was writing a newspaper article about youth unemployment and I wanted some statistics on numbers of young people excluded from the classroom, or from school altogether, and the grounds for exclusion, I just picked up the phone and called the Department of Education and asked the question. I got my answers right away.'

'I did not arrive at my understanding of the fundamental laws of the universe through my rational mind.'

ALBERT EINSTEIN (SCOUT)
b. 14 MARCH 1879

SCOUT, THE TRAILBLAZER: STORIES AND STUDIES
Polly's adventures

'One Sunday morning when no one was taking much notice of her, my then six-year-old granddaughter decided to take herself into town to go shopping.

'It was a familiar route, as she walked most of it every day on her way to school, so for that part of the expedition she was quite happy and confident.

'As the route began to change from the routine school walk into needing to get into the town itself, though not unknown to her, she started to need some reassurance. She had helped herself to a shopping voucher in her mother's purse with the intention of buying some sandals and armed with the said piece of paper she approached a lady for directions to the relevant store.

'Fortunately the woman in question realized the child was too young to be shopping on her own. She took Polly to the store and after placing her in the care of the shoe department (where incidentally the sandals were duly purchased) she contacted the police.

'After a chase around the store, because by now she knew she was in trouble, my very annoyed grandchild was taken home under police escort. A severe ticking off ensued and the sandals were returned by my daughter and granddaughter the same day.

'Fast-forwarding through a few volatile years, Polly stood at a crossroads. Fortunately her mother recognized this and, with positive action, advocated for her daughter in the schools where Polly had become 'marginalized'. The other children and teacher ignored her, in the classroom, on the playground and around the village. Nobody would take any notice of her; she was alone, isolated and excluded.

'The four other little girls in the class would have nothing to do with Polly and wouldn't play with her. She was made to sit on a table with all the boys. Her mother went to the teacher asking that the boys and girls be divided up, but nothing was done.

'On occasions there would be some trouble, a disagreement perhaps, and invariably Polly was labelled as the troublemaker. She was always seen to be at the core of the trouble.

'She was having huge difficulty reading. Again, her mother went to school to discuss this with the teacher, saying that Polly was mildly dyslexic and asking for additional help. Again, nothing was done. The school was incapable or unwilling to help her.

'The school used a practice called "saturated teaching" – the process of repeatedly forcing facts at a child with the idea that eventually the facts would be taken up. It was no good for Polly, as she would just switch off.

'My little granddaughter looked forward to the Christmas show. She was brilliant at self-expressing; she loved dancing and all. But, she was not allowed to have a role like that. There was a dance routine and all the other girls were in it – Polly was not allowed. Her part was just to walk on and walk off in a costume. She was miserable.

'Her mother went to look at other schools and decided to move both her children. Polly has flown since she has been there. She is accepted and liked and is blossoming. On a school outing a teacher thought Polly was a little quiet and approached her to see if something was wrong. It was and the situation was quickly dealt with. What was important was that the teacher noticed and took action.

'She is being helped and is now reading much better. They found her some different books, with a larger typeface that is supposed to help dyslexic children, who cannot cope with standard print. They do lots of outside activities there and lots of play, which works well for her.

'In her previous school, she was sick all the time; she didn't want to go. There was trouble every day. She was deeply unhappy. Now, she is doing well. Polly is a happy little girl – she skips down the street toward school with a friend.'

Hannah brings harmony to her law practice

'The Mercury Model helps to explain how different people learn, which helps me to adapt my style when communicating with colleagues, clients, friends and loved ones. Rather than persistently voicing full-on Scout, my communication skills are more effective and my interpersonal relationships more harmonious. The results speak for themselves.'

Anne earns double trouble

'My youngest son is Scout, The Trailblazer. Knowing about the Mercury Model, I advocated for him in the classroom right through his schooling, fought for him every inch of the way. And for my reward, I now work closely with another Scout.

'I recruited a Trailblazer as a team member in my network marketing business. What a handful he is. It is fortunate that I know this mind well. When I am talking to him, he fights, looks away and then walks off. Mentally, he is just not there anymore. It makes me think he is not interested. I know he wants to interrupt me but he has learned to override the impulse. I understand he learns very quickly and gives quick, short, soundbites of information without any detail. I know he thinks he's in charge. When I need to get something across to him, my strategy is to be very direct and focus on only one thing.

'He is doing well in the business and has begun to recruit others into his own team. This puts him in a position to teach the new people. I have had to let him know they are not thick or stupid, just because they learn more slowly than he does. Hopefully he will catch on to the fact that people think and learn differently and speed of uptake is not an indication of greater intelligence, but of individual learning style.'

Cherie relaxes the bands of strict discipline

'I no longer make my son Alex, The Trailblazer stay at his desk right through his assignment. Now I let him move around, do handstands and backflips between things.

'His teacher also saw that asking him to just sit still badly affected his learning and she now lets Alex stand up in class.'

STEADY, THE VAULT

I do not race at new ideas. I take my time; I chew things over to be sure we will sustain each other happily over the long term. I am not easily pushed, cajoled or led. And, please note: if you try to hurry me along, I tend to slow down.

Affectionately known as Steady, The Vault, I approach new information slowly and with reserve. I do not rush. I do not jump to conclusions or to anything else. I ponder and deliberate.

If your intention is to teach or train me, at any stage of my life, your task will be easier if you recognize that I decide what to learn and what not to learn. For some minds, learning is not a matter of choice, but it is for me. It has to be. Any new information coming my way will be subjected to qualifying tests. If it does not pass, I will not take it in – no matter how much you might want me to, no matter how much you threaten, plead, shout or demand.

Sometimes you might think I have taken in certain information, when in fact I have not. I may be still in the process of deciding whether or not it's for me, or I may be just using it for a while, trying it out. Time will tell. If it looks as though I have forgotten something, then I never actually learned it. You will come to realize that I do not forget.

Now, about my qualifying tests: I quite naturally measure all new ideas against my own values, and in this way thoroughly test the new information before even considering learning it. Regardless of age, I am concerned with the appeal and charm of new information. Does it have worth? Does it delight me? Is it beautiful? Does it please all my senses? Does it taste good, smell good, look good, feel good, sound good? Will knowing it increase my attractiveness, security or stability? I may ponder financial or artistic benefit. Will it enhance my beloved Earth? Is it practical, worthwhile and valuable? Will it endure over the long term? Only when criteria of this sort have been met – and that can happen either instantly or slowly – will I elect to take in, actually learn, the information.

This is the key to my great tenacity and 'groundedness'. As I test the value of new information by my attraction to it, any idea deemed valuable enough to be learned is deeply integrated and will be retained and preserved over time. I simply cannot change my way of thinking like an article of clothing, as many others can. You probably thought minds like me were just being stubborn and wilful. Well, perhaps it does appear that way.

In truth, it is a very good thing that I carefully consider new information before taking it in. I learn by consuming ideas, just as the body ingests food. I chew things over – and swallow! Ideas become part of the body's fabric, incorporated at the mental equivalent of physical cells. As Steady, I will not be changing my mind soon. The decision to learn something is a commitment that can last a lifetime. That's why I am called The Vault. I contain all the thoughts, ideas, data and information that I consider valuable. But, if I failed to stop, look and listen before accepting every new concept that comes down the road I would become a vault full of useless and unappealing drivel.

As part of this scrutiny, I even reach behind and beneath the new information to evaluate where it comes from, weighing the appeal, the reliability and the solidity of its source. The information's origin has to pass the value tests as well. Books have to be in clean and good condition. A top-quality hardcover or first edition might be best. Believe it or not, I find it almost impossible to learn from anyone who lacks style or who does not dress according to my personal sense of quality. Sorry, but I am not fabricating this. It's real for me. You might as well forget about making suggestions if you are wearing your grubby or tatty old clothes, and need a haircut. Trainers, teachers and team leaders should beware, and pay attention to their appearance.

> **Example**: A middle-aged Steady who decided to pursue his life-long dream of studying art was filled with great enthusiasm at the start of the Adult Education programme. Although he especially loved the sculpture course, he seemed to hit a roadblock with oil painting. While discussing this with the other students, he surprised everyone with the strength of his statement that he could not possibly learn anything from a tutor who didn't even dress properly. The man thought his reaction would be evident, obvious and shared by everyone else.

And further to how we appear to each other, I have always been Steady, The Vault, and it comes totally naturally to me. I do realize that others interact with information quite differently. But, I just do what I do without self-conscious awareness of it, as you probably do too. Occasionally, I wonder how I might appear through a different mind's point of view. Do you ever do that? Unless you too are Steady, The Vault, you might view my steadfast commitment to ideas as obstinate, inflexible, intractable or even 'bull-headed'. You might think I am stubborn. You may find it disturbing to patiently wait for my decision on something simple and then to observe my slowing down even further if I feel pushed. Do I need to point out that criticism will fall on totally deaf ears?

> **Be aware**: If you have a Steady, The Vault, parent, you might admire the relatively more free-thinking, more upbeat, fun-loving mental styles of other people's parents. You might wonder why yours has to be a 'stick in the mud' sort of person who rejects nearly all new ideas out of hand. It's probably fairly predictable by now that this will happen. You certainly notice other people's easy acceptance of exciting new suggestions, their enjoyment in considering new ideas and exploring the world's far flung horizons or even just a little bit of technology.

Those who know a young or adolescent Steady can make the obvious comparisons. Our strength lies along the lines of steadfast commitment; yours may reside in a totally different direction, possibly levity, frivolity and fun. Unless we all decide that the world will spin more smoothly if we are all exactly the same (in which case only one of us is necessary) then our best hope is mutual respect for individual difference in how we think, learn and communicate.

For the sake of getting along with others, I need to make sure that my steadfast commitments are always based on my true values and not on a habit of being steadfast and committed. If I become accustomed to the activity of keeping on keeping on, without the qualifying tests and deliberations, then I go down the road of plain ordinary garden-variety heels dug in stubbornness, which negates others' different natural strengths and precludes 'right relationship'.

When a piece of information or an idea has met my tests of quality, attractiveness, etc., and I have decided to learn it, I do so most naturally and most easily through a hands-on approach. I learn by getting involved with the material. We Vaults can be delighted by all the beautiful things that Earth has produced – wooden objects, driftwood, precious metals, beach stones, gemstones, geodes and crystals and flowers. We appreciate fine art, fine food and wine.

> " It's natural for us to involve our senses in the learning process – taste it, practise it, look at it, sniff it, try it on, act it out."

We are practical thinkers who take easily to common sense. To us an idea has merit if it can be applied to real life in a useful and down to earth way. Actually, it constantly surprises us to discover, and it may be difficult for us to accept, that other minds can value ideas just because they feel right, or are interesting, or are new, while totally disregarding the importance of practicality. But, they seem to!

Because we each have a unique and individual style of learning, thinking and communicating, it's necessary that we interact differently with information. It really does make the world go around. Society needs all kinds of thinkers, with each expressing different mental strengths. This is as true of Steady as it is of the other kinds of minds. And just think about it – those who easily embrace new ideas by the bucketful discard them just as quickly, changing their minds with every passing breeze. By necessity, we all grow up to make quite different contributions to the larger group. If we all thought alike, the world would be a far less interesting home.

So let's look at some of the special qualities of my make-up. I am very stable with great powers of concentration enabling me to ignore outside disturbances and stick to the matter at hand. I am Steady! Others appear to be much more easily distracted. I consider things carefully. I am unhurried and refrain from leaping to conclusions or onto bandwagons. Whether I am telling you about my day's experiences or preparing a report, I will tend to cover the groundwork thoroughly. I speak deliberately and with intention. I do not leave big gaps in my stories.

My natural appreciation of beauty and design may express itself as mental gracefulness and artistry. Learning is physical – senses are instruments of learning, with touch possibly better developed than hearing. But if you ask me to describe how something feels or tastes or smells, you will discover my ability to capture these sensory experiences in words. Others may not, but I can recall how things taste. A Steady, if interested in cooking, will know which flavours blend well together. If interested in gardens, interior design, clothing, furniture or buildings, a Steady may express natural talent with colour, space, fabric and line. If interested in money itself rather than in what it can provide, a Steady might find particular appeal in projects with long-term growth and sustainability, possibly banking, insurance or investments.

Of course, I do not forget easily. The proverbial elephant would be challenged by the reach of my memory which holds ideas over the long term, carrying them, preserving them and sustaining them – no matter what. The Steadys of the world provide cultural stability in thought, ensuring that what's beautiful and valuable is not lost. Wherever would you be without us? Who else would have the patience, interest or capacity to shape the living earth, to design and sustain elegant gardens, which please the senses with harmonious colours and fragrances? Who would see to the continuity of long-term financial investments or countryside and agricultural policies and practices? Who would be interested over the long run in preserving the arts, architecture, and the wellbeing of the Earth?

WHAT HELPS STEADY, THE VAULT, TO LEARN?

- To relax and take my time. I am bringing new ideas all the way down to earth and into myself and my body when I learn, not just into my head.

- Learning is best when my mind is allowed to proceed at an unpressured pace. I may have to ask for the space to learn according to my own timeframe.
- To become aware that I test the appeal of new information.
- To realize that I decide what I will or will not learn. The 'teacher' has not 'failed' if I choose not to take in something that has been offered.
- To see the practical benefits of any information. Relate ideas to usefulness, comfort, durability and beauty. I often reject abstractions that are unrelated to everyday life.
- I dig into topics as if I were digging the garden; I get my hands dirty. Provide me with a variety of hands-on activities so that learning can be through experience and direct involvement.
- Show me how I might apply new ideas or thoughts to a real-life situation.
- Link new information to what I already know.
- Give demonstrations, and then let me try it myself.
- Allow me time for careful consideration of ideas, and pause before asking me questions. The length of 'wait time' will depend upon the individual Steady and the topic.
- Present information concretely with tactile sensory aids – construction materials, blocks, real money or its symbols, beads, Lego, measuring tapes, rulers, paints, clay, etc.

QUOTES FROM STEADY, THE VAULT

'I can learn anything as long as I'm interested in it.'

'I sometimes persevere with something long after I know I should leave it alone.'

'I like this school – the teachers have style.'

'I don't forget things.' (A five-year-old.)

'I can never face a new idea cleanly, without the filter of the baggage of what I already know.'

'I only read fact books. I can't see the point of reading fiction.'

'I do not like short-term things. I like things that are solid.'

'Forgive your enemies, but never forget their names.'

J F KENNEDY (STEADY)

b. 29 MAY 1917

STEADY, THE VAULT: STORIES AND STUDIES
A county councillor expresses committed values
'In a County Council meeting one member criticized a long-term colleague, remarking that he had yet again treated the Council to "the same old songs about accountability and sustainability which Mr A had been singing for years". Ignoring the not-so-veiled insult, Mr A expressed his delight to have had his steadfast commitment acknowledged. "Sir, at least I am consistent."'

Denise attains her goal
'It took me nine years to fulfil my stated career aspiration and qualify as an accountant, but when I finally decided to bite the bullet and put all my energies into doing it, and because I had the support of a new manager who believed I could, I finished my studies within one year. I took every available training course and revision. I can so relate to not being pushed, but all the while having a feeling in the back of my mind that "eventually" it would happen.

'It took me a long time to move office – the thought of it horrified me! It made me stressed and I felt like things were happening too quickly, even though I actually discussed the move for nearly a year!

'But now I am here and have all my things around me – I am very settled – I love it – but I still need to make the space "feel nice" – I need homely things in here (I had to go and buy some flowers yesterday to brighten it up) – it's not just an office – it's somewhere I will be spending a lot of time and it has to be comfortable.'

Jean is a steady camper

'Many years ago I got into summer camps with Rainbow Circle. As my first camp was for two weeks, I wanted to be sure I would be as comfortable as possible in the middle of a field in an English summer, far from shops etc. So I made lists – practical stuff like tent, cooking utensils, washing-up bowl and that sort. Bedding, clothes, wet weather gear including wellies.

'My second task was how to get all this to camp. I had done a lot of camping and had observed what a tip other people's tents usually seemed to be – clothes, bedding, food items, etc., all mixed up together. I wanted none of that.

'I bought three large plastic boxes with lids which hinged in half: *1* Clothes and towels, *2* Cooking utensils, kettle, cutlery, plates, mugs, chopping board, clothes line and pegs, *3* Food – tinned and dry stuff like coffee, tea, biscuits, porridge. Fresh veg and so on was in an old supermarket basket, which sat outside on some stones. Bedding was just rolled up ready to put in the car. This proved to be an easy task, with no loose bits . . .

'Camp was in the Forest of Dean a drive of just over 200 miles, so when I arrived late in the day I was glad of my tidy arrangement.

'I got my tent up, which had a little sleeping area – the rest of the space I divided with boxes to one side, a small camp table and stool at the other.

'Outside I had my washbowl and veg rack and in front a ring of stones ready for a firepit to cook on.

'Before I knew it dark descended. As I woke next morning I was pleased with my new home; it answered all my needs and looked tidy and comfortable.

'Many comments were made about my set-up. But I still have these boxes with my camping gear ready to go off to Midsummer Camp this June. I have been using them for over 25 years, during which time I have been called "The Great Provider" by the children that come to camp, as I always seem to have whatever little thing they want from a plaster to a staple gun or a hammer.'

A young man discovers Steady through his school exams

'I think I'm starting to notice Steady more, things such as general knowledge, something that everyone knows but I don't because I didn't think it was relevant. I also forget things on my course, but I think that maybe I'm not forgetting, I'm just deciding not to learn it. This is generally true for quite boring subjects such as systems analysis. Around the time of the exam I did a lot of revision, repeating exam questions over and over and a lot of it seemed to stick nearer the time. I felt a lot more confident with it as the exam came closer. Maybe Steady thought I needed to learn it now, because my exam was approaching.'

Dr Chris Lane's report on Sarah, an adolescent at the Special Education Unit

Observations: Sarah is a more intelligent girl than she appeared to be upon our first meeting. It was not totally clear if some of the qualities she expressed were attributable to her learning style, Steady, The Vault, or if they were ploys to gain the attention she so desperately craved. Her intractability was evident, but it seemed to be more wilful than a natural quality. Her mind approached things slowly and with reserve; she pondered and deliberated. She constantly said she did not understand or could not do something. She considered herself to be stupid or even 'thick'. Is this aware self-assessment from an otherwise immature girl who lacks self-confidence? Is it a bid for some of the attention directed to a young sister?

Her responses were more appropriate to someone aged eight or nine, rather than twelve. Naughty, especially in the company of her friend, with whom she seemed to be joined at the hip. They were always in trouble with the same teachers. (All the dysfunctional children were friends and influenced each other badly. Some of the teachers seemed to exacerbate the girls' problems.) She would do inappropriate things for the attention she constantly wanted, but reacted poorly when shouted at or disciplined. Her problems were always someone else's fault.

Actions: Although there was insufficient time to make significant progress, I did develop some classroom strategies, which I passed on to her other teachers and which apparently produced good results:

- To see how she might apply new ideas or thoughts to a real-life situation.
- To link new information to what she already knew.
- To give demonstrations but then let her try for herself.
- To provide a variety of hands-on activities so that learning could be through experience and direct involvement.
- To give lots of praise.
- To be patient with Hannah and not push her natural pace.

DR C. LANE

Dr Chris Lane's report on Charlie, an adolescent at the Special Education Unit

Observations: Charlie earned over 50 complaints and a reputation for being 'cheeky' to teachers. He was repeatedly excluded from the classroom due to disruptive behaviour. He was consistently in trouble with teachers, who said he was awkward and very stubborn in the classroom. He seemed to have difficulty taking in information. His first reaction to verbal instructions or to anything new, like a worksheet, was, 'No, I do not understand' or 'I cannot do this'. They said Charlie was very quick to not engage with what was being explained. Sometimes he would just switch off and go to sleep. He appeared to be embarrassed about reading aloud in class; if pressured, he became aggressive and abusive.

In an informal situation, Charlie was quite sociable, but closed down in a formal one. He said about himself that he couldn't hear and that he was boring (yet also happy, interesting and successful). His home life was fine and his family held him in high regard. They were unable to understand why he had problems at school.

There appeared to be a deep division between school and the rest of his life.

Actions: I liked Charlie and saw him as a boy with lots of potential. He needed to move through things at his own pace, which is slow and methodical. If he is pushed to speed up, he might either grind to a halt altogether or become angry. I found that sitting and talking to Charlie always solved the problem. I identified a core issue as his lack of confidence in his ability to read. Provided with sufficient time and reduced pressure, he really turned around.

Initially, if I left him with something to read, he would read it. But if we were looking for comprehension and a report on what he had read, he couldn't do it, but became abusive and aggressive. Charlie reported that if he read too much he couldn't understand it. (Overload?) We came to a mutual agreement: it was that Charlie should learn enough to get through life.

He moved from saying, 'No, I cannot read' to reading newspapers daily, but also discussing content of topics which appealed to him. He came to not only see but also experience comprehension as a practical reality, not just a theory. He took on-board the instructions for an assignment that was *important to him*, went out into the community to research aspects of historical interest to him and wrote reports of very acceptable quality. When not pressured, Charlie did very well at some computer assignments. He admitted, 'Sometimes it is just convenient to have others think you are thick.'

DR C. LANE

BUZZ, THE CURIOUS

I am inquisitive – about absolutely everything, from bison to butterflies. One WHY question follows another and another and another.

If we are going to be spending time together, at work, in school or in our family, as chums, partners, colleagues, or in any other capacity, you might as well get accustomed to being asked 'WHY?' This is one of my lifelong patterns – it does not go away with the terrible twos, or threes or childhood at all. I enquire. I talk. I ask. I talk. I really am interested in both my questions and your answers, but for just about as long as it takes to get the ideas into words. Then I am off on another tangent, off to other fascinating inquiries.

I am Buzz, The Curious, and I am full of interests, full of ideas, and I love to dart and flit among them. Ideas are complete in and of themselves. I don't need to do anything with them. I don't need to actualize, analyse or retain them in memory. Having the idea and certainly sharing it with someone else is enough. Ideas are tangible and can be bounced around like ping-pong balls. The more balls in the air at a time the better, and the absolute minimum is two. I earn high marks on levity, agility and adaptability!

I am a generalist. Just as a garden butterfly naturally touches lightly on every flower, stalk and stem, I dash across the surface of a wide spectrum of information. My job is not to plumb the depth of a topic, any more than the butterfly's job is to reach down into the roots of your plants. No, I gather what I want from the shallows and move on. I move information around. I like to know a little about a lot.

> " To learn, I have to fit a new idea into a concept.
> I only need to grasp the sense or logic of it. "

In the overall scheme of things, I am a little slower than the sort of mind that just breathes in information as a spontaneous blast. And, I am considerably faster than those that need to filter new information through the feelings or take it into the physical cells. So I seem very fast on the uptake to some minds and a little slow to others. Clearly, speed is important when interacting with people, but it does not reflect upon intelligence or intellectual capacity. Fast and bouncy are some of my natural features.

As a conceptual type of mind, I can take in new information from either the written or the spoken word. I can come away from a classroom, a boardroom or a presentation with the message intact. I can read a book once and have it. Different minds may need to go over new material a few times, but not me! Others might need time to ponder or feel their way through new information, or try it out for themselves. Not me. I read it, I hear it, I have it. This does not mean that I will remember it.

" *Buzz-type children, adolescents and adults thrive on new information. We evaluate its merit by its newness and its interest factor – not usefulness, intuitive truth or human component. If we have not heard it before, we want to – right now.* "

One of my mental strengths is the ability to take in an enormous mass of information, stir it around and make it into something brand new. I specialize in conceptual synthesis and I am good at it. I look at a body of data through my own lens and then reshape it. I paraphrase. I enlist my natural mental flexibility and adaptability to put ideas, lyrics, jokes, views and suppositions into my own words, with my own slant, giving it a totally unique imprint.

I have fun and like fun. I learn best if the learning process is fun. I understand that other minds may need repetition to learn. Some require silence, nature, movement or a beautiful environment. Some minds even require a sense of emotional safety and security in order to learn. But we Buzzes need fun, levity, logic and freedom to fly. Did I say it's fun to invent new words?

And while on the topic of fun, I am very funny. I have my own take and twist on humour. I love to laugh and to make others laugh. This is one of my gifts to you. Sometimes other minds don't get the joke. Not everyone can follow me through my conceptual maze and realize that the last sentence was in fact the punchline. But it was.

I like words and games that involve words and letters: crosswords, puns, Scrabble, blocks. I am stimulated by noticeboards, books (better to be reading two at once!), libraries, comics, newspapers, telephones, both the old tools for sending out messages (paper, pencils and pens) and all the newest gadgets of communication technology – especially owls.

Let's talk about memory. Do you think the butterfly remembers the lily it lingered on yesterday or even the tulip it touched earlier today?

Not very likely. When I move on to the next task, I move fully. When I finish a project (reading a book, viewing a DVD, having a conversation) I am apt to jettison any information associated with that activity (the author's name, the starring actor, the time or location of the meeting). Data that is not being used on an ongoing basis is forgotten as quickly as this morning's news. I am then ready to approach the 'New', which is much more fun than holding on to the 'Old'.

Fortunately, information that is in active use is retained, and an adult Buzz is very well suited to what is called 'project work'. Here's an example: let's look at a journalist assigned to a story. First he gathers a mountain of new information and then he moves it around into a logical and cohesive pattern. The article is composed, written and submitted, with luck by the copy deadline. Unless a follow-on story is planned, our reporter instantly forgets all about that assignment, becoming mentally uncluttered and ready to move on to his next activity. Sometimes projects last for years and years, with the necessary information staying right there where it's needed. But as soon as it ends, out goes the unnecessary mental clutter.

> " I have to tell you that my memory is something of a mixed blessing. And it meets with a variety of different responses from others. "

On the positive side – and I am very glad to say there is a positive side – I do not become encumbered with old baggage, ideas that were bright and lively ages ago, but are now dry and dusty. Storage of the Old is not part of my experience. (Did I say that already?) Remember, the archetype here is The Curious, and it fits Buzz at any age. We do not become mentally obsessive. We do not even want to think about the same things today as we did yesterday. We are fresh and clear and ready for whatever new thoughts are coming our way. We live and breathe the mercurial qualities of agility, levity, buoyancy and flexibility. We give a natural lift to any conversation. We are clever and funny and fun to talk to. We have interesting new ideas. At any age Buzz is youthful. However, if you are blessed with very good long-term memory, I would appreciate your viewing my 'short term memory' as a different but positive quality.

I know I can be challenging to minds that are very different from me. I can even infuriate other people. Believe me; it is not always easy, for either of us. Punctuality does not seem to be part of my vocabulary. Plans and promises are forgotten, resulting in cold or ruined meals, missed deadlines and unused tickets to musical or athletic events.

> " *Do remember that I am not being disrespectful if I forget what you say. In fact, I am not doing anything to you; I am simply being myself and doing what comes naturally.*"

Sometimes, I just buzz off when a new idea catches my fancy. You have the choice of accepting this and letting it be, recognizing my positive/creative/charming side, as different as it may be from your own, or of rejecting it and being hurt. You simply cannot change The Curious into The Rock.

However, for the sake of my relationships, I try to introduce strategies to make life run more smoothly, for all of us. To be effective and last a lifetime, these tactics have to be fun, not drudgery. I put post-it-notes in my briefcase and backpack. I leave surprise messages on the bathroom mirror. I programme alarm notices on my phone. I tuck memos into my schoolbooks, drawers and coat pockets. I have created an annual/weekly/daily diary system. Some of my friends and family members have started levying novel and amusing 'penalties' when I forget dates and promises. I have even used the time-tested string around the finger. I had to get creative with this, had to make it a game.

To others I can appear to be forgetful, flighty, insubstantial, air-headed, motor-mouthed, indecisive, frivolous, superficial, ambivalent, wishy-washy, unstable and changeable, to list just a few appropriate words. But, without Buzz, life would become so totally serious, heavy, sombre, sober, grim and grave that, well, it just wouldn't be as much fun.

You may have read about the increasingly popular condition called ADD (Attention Deficit Disorder) or ADHD (attention deficit hyperactivity disorder). You may have been concerned that your child or adolescent suffers with this condition and you might even have been considering medicating him to make him more 'normal'. Mental restlessness is entirely normal for Buzz-minds. It is part of our nature. We love variety, diversity and anything new. We thrive on leaping from one topic to another. Please think carefully about this before medicating.

WHAT HELPS BUZZ, THE CURIOUS, TO LEARN?

- Recognize my short-term memory is a strength, not a failing. I should not need to apologize for it! I have much more flexibility and adaptability than most people with good long-term memory. Encourage me to enjoy these qualities, while developing strategies to bring focus.
- Writing things down or saying them aloud helps me to learn.
- Telling others about things I have learned helps me to solidify the ideas.
- Offer me opportunities for discussion and storytelling.
- Appreciate, value and indulge my curiosity.
- Ask questions, especially those that arouse my curiosity.
- Help me to find answers to my own questions.
- Make learning fun for me. It might even show you that learning for its own sake can be a joy.
- Provide me with lots of books, audio books, taped lectures,

journals, radio programmes, magazines, newspapers, videos, DVDs, CDs and Internet access.

- Tell me stories, jokes and anecdotes.
- Encourage me to seek out common themes and connections among different ideas.
- Suggest I apply my mind to a task in short bursts. It's a curious mind, and can chafe against concentrating on a single topic for a long time. I want to learn a little about everything.
- Show me how to write lists, diaries and notes to myself as strategies to help me keep track of things and live in harmony with others.
- Recommend that I prepare for a test or presentation shortly before the event, not way in advance. Information that is fresh in my mind is fresh in my mind.

QUOTES FROM BUZZ, THE CURIOUS

'The funnier something is the easier it is to remember.'

'There has to be a reason for this.'

'I wonder why . . . ?'

'Tell me that again.'

'Did you know that . . . ?'

'Have you heard the one about . . . ?'

'Why is a banana called a banana?'

'You wonder if I related to the Profile for my learning style? Well, yesterday when I read it, I read it seriously and considered it. It easily slipped right in, and now it seems to have slipped right out again.'

'I've just watched two films on TV at the same time. Why? Because neither of them was interesting enough on its own. I just watched one until I saw where it was going and then flipped over to the other for a while.'

'Oh, sorry, would you repeat that. My focus went elsewhere.'

'She told me that information but I didn't write it down – I have forgotten it.'

'I thought I would paint the black iron rail around my porch, but I went in and read the newspaper for an hour or two, and now it's too late.'

'I wanted to be some kind of captain of industry. Then I wanted to be in advertising, and then I wanted to be a newspaper reporter. Actually, that's what I did become ... but I wasn't great as a reporter. I started writing stories in my spare time.'

KEN FOLLETT (IN A 2008 INTERVIEW WITH OPRAH WINFREY) (BUZZ)
b. 5 JUNE 1949

'There are no limits to your being, only those you ascribe to yourself.

There are no limits to your understanding, only those that are due to trying to understand with the mind.

There is no limit to your light, except the dark shadows of the ego cast upon the sky which we call the self.

Shake your soul! Awaken it from slumber! The time has come to awaken to your divine being.'

PIR VILAYAT INAYAT KHAN (BUZZ)
b. 19 JUNE 1916

BUZZ, THE CURIOUS: STORIES AND STUDIES
Tracy's father is Buzz, The Curious
He phones her and asks one question after another. After a lifetime of being offended by this, she finally sees that he is just being curious, not grilling her as she had thought. She understands him now. Tracy says the Mercury Model is life altering – it helps her understand people.

Linda's mind bounces
'Did I tell you that Tom has become a wellness coach? He's a nice young man – I never would have thought he would want to talk to people

about their health, their weight, how they look and how they come across to others, but he does want to do that and has started learning the ropes. And Tom needed a haircut, so he went to a lady who has set up her business in the new cattle auction mart. She has just a tiny room, but all the farmers will find it convenient to have their hair cut there, as they are there anyway. And I had been thinking about my next 90-day goals for my business, what I could do that's a completely new development, moving in a totally new direction and I thought about the fact that vets do talks for farmers about animal nutrition, and I could do talks to farmers about their own nutrition, and I could call it: "Why the Farmer and his Wife got Fat while the Sows got Lean".'

Dr Chris Lane's report on Kevin, an adolescent at the Special Education Unit

Observations: Initially, the highly agile, exceptionally inquisitive and unusually fast-paced mind generally attributed to Buzz, The Curious did not show itself at all. One would observe a considerably overweight boy who could, at best, barely stay awake in the classroom. Both his size and his falling asleep provided his classmates with ample ammunition to ridicule, bully and tease Kevin mercilessly whenever the teacher stepped out of the classroom. These verbal assaults deeply upset him.

Actions: The home situation was primarily responsible for the sleepiness in class and was addressed directly, with some success. On the learning front, Kevin began writing absolutely amazing stories when he began using a computer in class. I saw some very sophisticated writing, although the spelling was awful. My feeling was that this boy's IQ was in the region of 130.

In order to bring some structure into his life we introduced a system of lists and notes to remind him of school appointments. I gave him an alarm clock to use both at home and at school. He spent a great deal of time thinking up the next pieces of the stories he was writing. I encouraged him to use the alarm to remind him to write down a little more of the story. On sci-fi themes, these stories were highly descriptive, full of humour and very well-observed detail. Kevin was on the road to getting his life into a better place. He now works as a journalist in a local newspaper.

DR C. LANE

Joan has her own room

'One complete wall of my room is made of bookshelves which hold my 200 to 300 books, all non-fiction. And there is a TV in the middle of the shelf unit. The headboard of my bed is made up of desk units, one on each side, with boards run between them to make a long shelf. It's covered with more books. Over in the corner is a desk, where I set up my accounts, business and household files and more books. To calm my mind in preparation for sleep, I read for a little while, and then play a game, probably Scrabble, on my iPad. The TV would be on, with a timer so that it will shut itself off after I drift into sleep.'

Sheila speaks Buzz

'Did you know that I have many qualifications? I have ONC and HNC in Business Studies, Level 3 Hairdressing, Complementary Therapies which includes massage, aromatherapy, Indian head massage and reflexology, and I did that in a year. I am a qualified Reiki master and crystal healer. I have just done a weekend and qualified in angelic Reiki. I started a Combined Honours degree but had to give it up for family reasons. I can also spray tan and do gel nails. It looks like I am flighty but each was an attempt to create a life for myself and these were tools to help me. And I learned more than just those skills. As I am an eternal student learning is not a problem . . . just don't ask me what aromatherapy oils help what ailment, as I can't remember until I look it up and then it floods back.

'I currently work on a children's ward. My fun side comes out with the children and my ability to lighten the atmosphere when appropriate is beneficial. I always have at least two jobs and my second job is working casually on adult wards.

'But I like the light-heartedness . . . it doesn't feel like me if I'm not. Please don't think I don't care or am not committed as you view my behaviour, as that could not be further from the truth. I probably have too much passion, but you don't always see that as it is spread between all my projects. This is probably a good thing as if it was focused on one thing it would be too intense.'

Bev sees Buzz in the mirror

'I have a laptop PC and iPhone and an iPad for work, I have a laptop PC and an iPhone and an iPad for personal use (why, when I can legally use all of the work ones for personal stuff?) – I have a Filofax because I am obsessed with writing and I love to see things written down because it feels right. I have a calendar that I write stuff on – then I transfer all the info on the paper calendar to the iPhone calendar (which copies it to the iPad calendar). Why? Because I am obsessed with missing birthdays and play dates and work appointments (I am in sales, can you imagine?) and then HORROR – I have just missed my godson's birthday! Why? Because I am so embroiled in something new that I have forgotten to check the multiple electronic and paper copy calendars.

'I work in software sales, and have God knows how many conference calls a day to attend – I do make most as I am training myself and have alarms associated with work stuff. I can find conference calls a strain because if it's a boring subject, I wonder on to other interesting things in my office (I don't even know I'm doing it until someone asks me a question), luckily with my "Buzz" ability to multitask some part of my brain will be listening and nine times out of ten I will pick up on the question. If it gets really boring,

I can't help myself, I will have to crack a funny – I have a reputation for it – generally if it's going to be a dry subject I'm asked to attend to liven it up.

'The multitasking thing came in handy: I remember when I was in my late twenties, early thirties working for a software company in London running from one meeting to the next. Running up Oxford Street to get to another meeting – having a very serious negotiation with a customer on the mobile (one of the early mobiles – small brick) – broke the heel on my shoe – ran into Selfridges – carried on the negotiation with the customer – looked for – chose – tried on – bought new shoes all while talking an angry customer down – customer was placated – I had new shoes and was up and running to my next meeting. No idea how I did it but that was the "Buzz" for me then.

'That desire to keep it light wherever I am in the world and whatever I am doing has saved me over the years from some pretty dark times. And, I want to kiss who ever invented spell checker – it has saved this girl's professional career many a time.'

Paula usually keeps us laughing

'Remind me or I will forget . . . Everything is always new and fresh – just walking around the corner is an adventure . . . I wrote notes before phoning you, or sure as anything, I would have forgotten something ... My daughter tells me I have the attention span of a gnat.'

SPONGE, THE SENSITIVE

By the time I was a teenager I was sick and tired of hearing people say, 'Oh, why do you have to be so sensitive?' Well, here's the simple truth: I just am, and always have been. Despite my occasional hearty presentation of robust behaviour, in truth I am impressionable and tender.

It would be really helpful and supportive for my family, friends, teachers/trainers, bosses, employees and colleagues to understand and work with my sensitivity, to see it and accept it as a natural part of my mental dynamics.

I do not have the option, as some other minds do, to take a giant step back from new information or to pause and decide whether or not to take it in. No, I soak it up like a kitchen sponge close to a puddle. Nor am I able to distance myself from information by keeping it in my head, in the safe realms of intellectual concepts and flashes of insight. No, afraid not. I drink in messages from the environment and filter them through my personal feelings, making them my own without further processing. For me there is always emotion associated with the activity of learning. This is part of my nature and I am not going to outgrow it. Even as an adult I can still flood with tears simply watching TV commercials. Information coming from the outside gives rise to feelings on the inside. That is just the way it is.

I react to information deeply and personally. As I learn, I relate the new material to myself and to those close to me. I sometimes put myself into the plot of what I am hearing or the book I am reading and feel the impact of being in the middle of that situation. Or, I might mentally reframe a news story to include my family members, and then struggle through an emotional response to having people I love involved in the episode. Reading stories and watching DVDs or TV programmes are emotional events, full of joy or sadness, enthusiasm or despondency. This just happens. It is my natural mode of handling information and is unrelated to choice or control, age or gender.

While on the topic of family, many of my ideas and attitudes come from childhood – home and family have been very important to my thinking. The images I absorbed there are foundational. Throughout my life, I have often referenced the exploits and life experiences of my family members in conversation.

> **"** *I evaluate the merit of an idea by how it feels;*
> *knowing good ones from bad, interesting ones from*
> *boring, right from wrong, exciting from dangerous*
> *by my personal emotional reaction.* **"**

A good idea is one that feels right. This interwoven blend of mind and feelings is totally natural to me. Like most others, I was surprised to find that all minds are not alike. I was stunned to realize that others judge an idea's value on grounds of logic or practicality. I consider it too cold and detached to separate feeling from thought, but you may notice that I can be swayed by an appeal to my emotions, sometimes against the dictates of 'common sense'.

When you ask what I think, I often respond with how I feel. It can puzzle other people that I come forward with a great deal of emotion when they intended to ask for factual information. A linking of head and heart is natural for me but perhaps not for others.

We say a picture is worth a thousand words. This is especially true for me, as I very definitely link ideas with visuals. If you show me a picture, I will get the sense of it instantly. But if you offer me the thousand words, I first create in my mind's eye a visual version of what you said and then I take in that picture. I require an extra step, the translation from words to visuals, in order to learn. And I remember ideas in visual form; perhaps I have what's called a 'photographic memory'. Words simply do not produce the necessary direct emotional resonance, but pictures do.

Because my mind requires the additional step of converting language to pictures, I do not take in either the written or the spoken word as easily as some other types of minds do. I never have benefited from the stock in trade of traditional education – 'chalk and talk'. My particular requirements for learning have often gone sadly unrecognized, as have appropriate methods of testing and evaluating me. I do learn easily from visuals of all sorts. Pictures directly engage my feelings, while words do not.

Tip: To enhance learning, provide Sponge, The Sensitive with a wide assortment of graphics, photos, DVDs, charts, illustrations, models, sculpture, abstract and realistic diagrams and drawings.

A quiet and safe learning environment is essential, and it is obvious, if you just stop and think about what I am coping with while absorbing new material. My mind works by linking ideas with the feelings they call forth. Strong emotion, loud noises, raised voices and even very bright colours can overpower the gentle process of my learning. If the surroundings feel 'unsafe', a sense of fear or worry can dominate the delicate inner emotional message generated by an ordinary session about history, maths or music. The lesson will not have a chance – the material will just not be learned.

As an example, I will share a story about a school inspector with a Sponge-type mind. She is a strong, powerful woman whose behaviour conveys supreme confidence, totally masking her mental sensitivity. She reports that when her family moved from a small town to a sizeable city during her childhood, she was so frightened in school that she didn't learn anything at all for a year and a half. Nobody understood.

> **Tip to parents**: Although it may not be easy to arrange, try to have someone greet your children personally at the door of a new classroom, sports centre or meeting place, introduce them to the other children and allow a little time for them to settle in before beginning the activities.

The school inspector's tip given above is just as applicable to social situations and to the workplace as to the school setting. With age and experience, I have developed some skill at masking my mental sensitivity, but it is still there and can still be an issue. This may surprise you. It does not take much to overwhelm my delicate mental sensitivity. But if emotional safety and security is provided or insisted upon in learning environments, at school, in the workplace, during family or social situations, then I will flourish, and so will others like me.

At the same time, I can really stir things up. Like nobody else, I can get an entire family, a classroom or an office going with just a few words, especially if I am bored or there isn't 'enough going on'. I can experience an emotional threat when someone questions one of my ideas, another feature of the strong bond between my mind and feelings. But, if I react to the perceived threat, it can thoroughly confuse communication, agitate the other person and ultimately generate a whirlwind.

I quite naturally dream up new ideas – one after the other. I thrive on beginnings; I am very good at starting new things. But I am not skilled at completing. When an idea loses its emotional appeal, goes cold and no longer interests me, my first inclination is to turn toward something more stimulating. Although this comes naturally to me, it's useful to know a few tricks to help me finish projects, at home, in school or out in the world.

> **Tip:** If it feels like your big project has gone cold, isolate a single component and establish a renewed emotional connection to just that section. Drum up a bit of appreciation or perhaps rejoice in the project's beauty! Do this a few times and before too long, the project is completed.

Are you wondering if there are any compensating benefits to all this sensitivity? Resoundingly, yes! Every type of mind has its own strengths and contributions to offer.

My unique mental strengths stem from, and actually grow out of, the activity of translating between words and pictures. I have developed considerable skill at reinterpreting verbal and written language into visual forms, a skill with a wide variety of professional applications. For example, my mental strengths can be focused on logo design, concise graphical representations, leaflet and brochure design, packaging and other examples of high-impact advertising where a specific message is conveyed at a glance. If you need a simple picture that can speak volumes, ask Sponge, The Sensitive.

Enjoying all sorts of design activities, I use my imagination to craft powerful emotional messages from both musical and visual imagery. My skits, songs, plays, videos, photos and blogs pack an emotional wallop. My greeting cards, invitations, posters, announcements and letters convey meaningful messages with strong emotion.

" Throughout my life, I have picked up feelings or 'vibrations' around me. "

Many things do not need to be spelled out – I don't need to be told when you are unhappy or when something is wrong. I often come away from a conversation with considerably more information than anyone intended to provide. Over time I have developed an ability to absorb an entire picture from just a few sketchy words, an advantage in both personal and professional situations. I just feel it – and usually it is correct. However, when I speak, I have to remember that others need a more complete explanation. I need to use more words in order for others to get my drift. I can see that most of us present information in the mode that best satisfies our own learning requirements, thinking it will be just right for others too. I had to learn to fill out my stories and presentations to meet the needs of other types of learners.

From the deep inner place where thinking links with feeling, I originate ideas which are concerned with emotional issues or have an emotional impact. I am sensitive to other people's feelings and consequently can make a real contribution to activities in which the human factor is important. I have applied my mental skills to taking care of others, making people feel happy, safe and comfortable, either at home or away, by creating the ambience, colour schemes and interior design features of clubs, hotels, hospitals, planes, trains and restaurants, in addition to private living spaces. My natural sympathy has led me toward human resources. Adopting the role of a counsellor, I can easily talk to children, adolescents and adults about themselves.

Of course the link between my mind and feelings could have driven me in the opposite direction. Nobody would know better than Sponge, The Sensitive, how to scare moviegoers to death, or how to write horror stories. But then I would scare myself with my own images too.

WHAT HELPS SPONGE, THE SENSITIVE, TO LEARN?

- Appreciate that I need to feel comfortable and safe in a learning environment in order to do my best mental work – in the living room, the classroom, the boardroom, wherever.
- Help me to create a positive, supportive learning or work space with an eye to colour, music and pictures.
- Encourage me to embrace the emotional component of my learning process and make a friend of it. I might as well recognize this as a strength because it is not going away.
- Seek out illustrations or DVDs about whatever topic is at hand.
- Use visuals of all sorts, gestures, word pictures or dramatization, to present information.
- Suggest I take notes in graphical forms, charts, diagrams, mind maps and use them to help commit information to memory.
- Recommend that I take time and space to reflect upon activities, meetings and presentations.
- Engage your own emotions when presenting information to me and ask me to do so in return.
- Use colour to present and record information: flipchart work, PowerPoint, handouts, newsletters, etc.
- Explain, demonstrate and use visualization techniques.
- Encourage the use of symbols, metaphors, stories and examples.
- Present information in a way that is relevant to human needs and feelings. Talk about it; ask for my feedback and opinions.

QUOTES FROM SPONGE, THE SENSITIVE
'My job is getting the feel for a client's business and then designing

a logo or visual that captures the idea of what they are trying to do. After I have visited a business I always know a lot more than they have told me. I just absorb it.'

'How does it feel to be an eyeball?'

'When I was sent away to boarding school it broke my heart, but I then just got on with it and had no hard feelings toward anyone.'

'I hear the words and I see the pictures.'

'My mind seems to flow over the surface of life, consuming by absorbing. I take it all in.'

'Information is the fuel that feeds my emotion.'

'I think the British people need someone in public life to give affection, to make them feel important, to support them … '

PRINCESS DIANA (SPONGE)
b. 1 JULY 1961

SPONGE, THE SENSITIVE: STORIES AND STUDIES
A teenager took personal responsibility

Arleyne really did not like school and longed for the day when she could leave. Considered by her teachers to be less than the sharpest tack in the box, no effort was made to move her education forward. A short and sweet story: Arleyne attended a Mercury Model workshop with her mother and grandmother, and got it instantly. Everything offered to her in the classroom was provided in a way that disadvantaged her learning. She realized she was not thick, slow or inferior; she just processed information by filtering it through her emotions. The super-charged classroom atmosphere, so stimulating to some of her classmates, caused her to close down. During her final year, she took responsibility onto her own shoulders, turned a sow's ear into a silk purse, and is now doing well and loving university.

Dennis gained perspective at work

The Mercury Model helped him to step back and identify his own patterns and his team-mates' patterns and to get perspective. All of them want to understand what is going on, but only he is content to live in chaos for extended periods, just absorbing new information and looking for the next idea.

Ruth and her daughter now enjoy mutual respect

'My teenage daughter, Sponge, The Sensitive, was struggling at school and I had become frustrated with her desire to watch so much television. After reading her Profile, in *Learning Without Tears*, a whole new level of education opened up to us. I know everyone learns in their own way, but the subtle differences had never been so clearly explained before. I have an Air learning style and my daughter has a Water style (covered in more detail in Section 3 on page 179); she likes to immerse herself into the action of learning, such as films, stories or plays. Not my style. She is totally in the picture, feeling everything that happens and learning in the process. Not my way either. Now she selects what she wants to watch to help with her schoolwork. No more frustration for either of us. She has also learned a valuable life skill: scary films really scare her. Now she understands why, and doesn't worry what others think, she just tells them Scooby Doo is enough for her and the peer pressure is laughed away.'

Ana expresses the strongly visual aspect of her mind

'When meeting people, especially in a group, I am taking in so much about them I don't remember their names and often have to ask again. But I intuitively feel I know more about them than I could explain, and I don't forget it.

'Over 60 years ago, when I was five, my mother took me to school on the first day. The teacher was waiting at the front door and walked toward us, smiling. She was wearing a green and white striped skirt, a white blouse and a green corduroy jacket and she had black hair pulled into the nape of her neck and very pale skin. I knew I liked her and trusted her immediately, and I was very happy at that school.

'Everything I think of comes to me in pictures so my thoughts and memories are like videos. If I can't "see" something, I can't remember it. If I'm feeling flat I'll find some images to look at, photos, the sky, a landscape, flowers, anything with colour to lift my spirits.

'Feeling is everything, I can think of nothing in my life I couldn't have a feeling about, from a close relationship to a packet of firelighters. I can take pleasure in everything from its shape and form, its touch and the look of it. Some things I wouldn't buy if they aren't pleasing, even though they may be proven to do a good job. It just wouldn't feel right to have something ugly.'

Adrienne emphasizes the importance of flow

'Words are very important to me. I understand and take in thoughts and ideas when the words used to express them create or allow a flow of conscious thoughts. Ideas either flow or they do not. This is true with spoken words, my own or someone else's, or written words. If something is not quite right, the flow stops, like a river running into a dam, not just an obstacle which it can go around and keep flowing, but a full stop that backs everything up. When that happens, then I cannot go on until it's resolved. I lose track of a conversation or a talk, from the point where the incorrect or inappropriate word has created the flood barrier onwards. When the word used was not quite the correct word more often than not my train of thought is derailed. Resolution would then require identification of the right word, or a better word.

'Just a while ago, I was talking to you about a transparent coloured sheet, and I thought of the word "acetate" but I knew it was not quite right. The flow of my ideas stopped, until you suggested the word "transparency". That was a better word and I could then continue expressing my thoughts freely.

'It's easier to deal with when I am writing, as I can go back and find a better word or change the punctuation, but with speaking, it's often too late. The wrong word is already out there.

'When someone else is speaking or interjecting in a conversation and they use the "wrong word" this often has the same effect. The flow of my understanding stops and I lose track of what is said next whilst trying to allow the flow to start again.'

Ronnie reflects on his mental sensitivity

'I really identify with the visual learning – I could never learn by concepts and words alone – I see pictures and when I tell a story, I am watching a video tape in my mind so that my whole body is vibrating with the emotions of the story so my audience can both hear and feel the story I am telling.

'A problem with being the Sponge is that you can never be sure if the feelings you are picking up are yours or someone else's. This was a real problem when I started doing therapy and I had to learn not to take others' feelings home with me. To feel empathy means to feel someone's inner feeling but then to release them and not carry them around with you.

'You are right about education too. I could not read in elementary school, not because of learning problems, but because I felt unsafe at home and then again unsafe at school. All I needed was a teacher who was warm and encouraging and then I was fine most of the time.

'I can no longer watch any movies or even read many books that have too much sadness or emotional pain in them. But my sensitivity allows me to feel love and joy at full force.'

Linda's daughter takes charge

'Emma loved reading *Learning Without Tears* and attending the Mercury Model workshop we went on together. I would say our relationship was even further strengthened and, for Emma, it made a big difference to how she manages herself and communicates with others. Emma is, Sponge, The Sensitive. She is intelligent, sensitive, thoughtful and considerate and can readily see where others are coming from – and, while this is a strength it can also be a source of weakness. Emma appears very steady, but can get hurt easily and she would sometimes find at secondary school that she would be seen as the "fixer" for everyone. People would come to her for advice and this would often lead to her being put upon. Her friends, who were coming to Emma for help, would not see her as a "fun girl" to invite to their parties.

'From the workshop, it became apparent that Emma is a "container" – information she receives is held onto for a while. This is directly opposed to a "sharer", like me, who immediately shares information with others. Although she is very chatty and will share her feelings, giving the appearance of a sharer, Emma will only tell me bits! With the insight into her learning style, she has been able to learn to protect herself and not put herself in a position where she can get damaged. She gets less hurt and is able to use her strengths to her advantage. Emma is now studying Applied Psychology at university.'

Norma sees solutions

Norma is a Sponge with an incessant flow of ideas. If anyone in her general vicinity expresses something that might possibly be a problem, Norma is right there offering a solution. If she could start a business to get paid for this she could call it 'Ideas Abound'.

People hear her observations and wonder why they didn't think of it themselves. When asked if she thought of others as a bit slow because they hadn't thought of the solution, given that it's so obvious to her, she said, 'Yes, I used to.' Knowing now that we all have different skills, she is more subtle about being a fountain of ideas. When asked how these ideas happen, she said she just sees it. People tell her a problem and she just sees the solution. It's visual.

REX, THE DIGNIFIED

I might consider learning, and I might even try out new ideas, but I absolutely will not invite them into the kingdom of my mind unless I know they will be worthy subjects.

Certainly not! My mind is a special place. Plain old ordinary thoughts are simply not welcome here. Ideas have to be of the highest quality to gain entry. And the perimeter wall is carefully guarded and diligently defended. Each and every new piece of information presented at the gate is examined for worthiness and value. Each one is considered and tested individually. Oh, jubilation if a thought satisfactorily passes the test – it's in! And there it will remain, indefinitely, a respected resident of the kingdom with all the associated high level rights and privileges.

So, what is the test all about? What criteria must be met? Which ideas will be accepted and which will be banished forever? And do I really have individual choice and total authority about what to learn, what to take in? Well, yes, I do and my selection is related to the role that ideas and thoughts play within the kingdom of my mind.

The crux of the matter is this: my thoughts are closely related to my identity. The information I hold contributes to my sense of selfhood. I am what I think. Any idea that I take in goes right to my heart, to my core. So, I will single out only those ideas on which I am willing to stake my identity. They must confirm who I already sense myself to be. I have to be proud of them.

> "*When I speak as Rex, I speak from the heart. When I proclaim my ideas, I proclaim myself.*"

Information that has gained entry is well and truly ensconced within the walls. But you might wonder how I handle simple daily information, which not even I would bother to remember, let alone use as building blocks of identity. Well, it depends on the particular Rex individual. Some of us are surprisingly rigorous about this while others develop the skill of just 'using' material without learning it. Essentially, it camps out for a while on the grassy area outside the perimeter wall and performs some temporary service for the kingdom. Rather like a travelling minstrel, it entertains without belonging, and soon departs. If I forget something, it's due to my never having learned it in the first place. The material never truly became 'my own'. Otherwise, it goes without saying, my memory is phenomenal!

Selecting ideas need not be either a lengthy or a conscious process. I do not ponder the question: to learn or not to learn. I do not concern myself with the future benefit or liability attached to taking in particular ideas, nor with the ensuing consequences to my identity. These things are not reasoned out. It's not a logical process and I am unlikely to be aware of it objectively. My mental process is intuitive. I just know if something is for me or not. If a particular idea gets a thumbs down, I will reject it, stop it right at the gates – outcast!

Possibly you will have observed my doing this. For example, you may have made a pronouncement of your own (perhaps to me as child Rex about bedtime, bath time, or wash your hands it's lunchtime, or perhaps to me as adolescent Rex about coming home by 9:30 p.m.) and I failed to respond. It may have seemed that I didn't hear what you said or that I was not listening. But, just as likely, your words were repelled at the outer ring of my mental defences. They didn't harmonize with my self-image.

However, if I recognize and welcome incoming information, I simply inhale it, I breathe it in – quick as a firefly flash. I can do this without any additional mental processing. I do not need to try it out with a real-time hands-on application in order to learn something. I do not need to discover its logic by getting the idea behind it. I do not need visuals as many other minds might. None of this! I am fast, direct and positive. Once I decide to allow access to my mental domain, the idea is in.

Did I mention that the perimeter wall, including the gate, serves as a defence in both directions? Worthy ideas, having walked the red carpet, are expected to become loyal subjects and stay inside. No little trips abroad or wandering off. Of course not, what would become of my identity? I am not whimsical about my ideas; I am committed to them. I am passionate about the subjects residing in my custody. I will neither toss them out nor allow them to leave. They are there for the long-term. This is not a take-it-or-leave-it situation.

My mind is persistent, determined, tenacious, resolute and obstinate. I can apply myself to a task and keep on keeping on, through thick and thin, like a dog with a bone, against powerful opposition. On occasions when my will is pitted against yours, you might use other, less flattering words like stubborn, headstrong or unyielding. But now you know what's beneath it. To change my mind is to change my identity. It will not happen easily or willingly. It will certainly not be precipitated by force or bribery. My convictions are the subjects of my kingdom, whom I will protect and defend against assault from the outside world. They comprise my strength, my stamina and my constancy.

My courage is said to be legendary. Sometimes I am unaware of it, neither objectifying my bravery nor seeing it as anything special. When committed, especially to battling any form of unfairness or injustice in the world, I do not falter in the face of adversity.

> " *Fearlessly standing alone with an unpopular opinion, I can hold fast to my principles, refusing to compromise my integrity.* "

I am willing and well-suited to serve in challenging roles as spokesperson for causes which strike my heart – from groups lobbying for environmental protection and human rights to those dedicated to defending a nation's interests. I can advocate vigorously – for alternative medicine, for the highest-quality TV programming especially when the children are watching or for equal rights of access for the disabled. My dedication sees things through and provides society with stability and continuity. Rex, The Dignified, can be a mixed blessing in a political leader who on the one hand sticks to his guns no matter what, and on the other has a hard time even hearing alternative suggestions. There are notable examples on the world stage, now and in history.

This report is about the invisible inner realm of mind and my natural way of handling information. It does not comment on behaviour, a very different component of overall human make-up. Behaviour, which is evident, observable and can be modified according to a person's intentions, can mask my strength. For example, some Rex-minded people quite naturally present themselves with a soft, gentle or even retreating mode of behaviour, despite their concealed mental power, while others outwardly express all the energy, conviction and authority of my Dignified mind-set. Don't be fooled.

> *"My natural mode of communicating has pizzazz, colour, spirit and, often, high volume."*

Because conviction comes from the heart, I speak with authority, whether delivering with a velvet glove or a sledgehammer. I can even be bossy. The addition of a little costuming and acting can make my presentation even bigger than life itself. I can be very entertaining and put on a great show. But, I can also carry it a bit over the top and adopt centre stage in the drama of life, failing to note the rest of the cast. That was particularly and embarrassingly true when I was young, inexperienced and practising at my role.

If you occasionally feel the need to 'take Rex down a peg or two', please remember that, despite the apparent bravado, I am sensitive, in the extreme, to humiliation. It may be easy for you to overshoot the mark, thinking my apparently robust strength could withstand it. A shamed Rex can be a very long time recovering composure. This is especially, but certainly not exclusively, true of the young ones.

WHAT HELPS REX, THE DIGNIFIED, TO LEARN?

- Help me to see that I make choices about taking in the information that is offered to me. I may not always realize this.
- Don't take it personally if I do not learn what you are teaching. I decide what to learn and what to leave; my decision is not always a reflection of your methods or the quality of your presentation. Yet, quality information is pivotally important to me.
- Help me recognize the link between doing well/poorly and making a decision to learn/not learn the material. If I do poorly, it may be from lack of interest, rather than lack of ability.

- Once something is learned it is never forgotten. If it seems that I have forgotten something, it may simply be that I did not decide to learn it. It's helpful for me to be aware of the difference.
- Accept I learn and test more easily when no one is pressuring me.
- Experiment with dramatization, modelling, role-play and storytelling. Encourage me to participate and contribute.
- I learn best when I am allowed and prompted to make a creative, personal contribution to an idea or project.
- Let me take centre stage once in a while to express what's on my mind.
- Make the information personal but be careful to respect my dignity.
- Present ideas with enthusiasm and passion. Dramatize your points with gestures.
- Suggest I move around while learning. Physical and mental activities are linked for me.
- I expect to be received with respect and attention. Realize that what I say is important to me.

QUOTES FROM REX, THE DIGNIFIED

'I always thought that if I spoke from the heart then people would understand me.'

'You know, one of my colleagues actually disagreed with part of my report! I took it as a matter of personal disloyalty.'

'I remember people who are interesting, who talk with energy about what excites them.'

'Everything I teach has to come from my heart and experiences. I have to believe in something to teach it. If I don't understand or believe in an idea, I will not try and preach it to others.'

'I can remember being bottom of the class in geometry, because I hated it, and top in English. This really confused my teacher. Is he dumb or smart?

They were very black and white.'

'Glory is fleeting, but obscurity is forever.'

NAPOLEON BONAPARTE (REX)
b. 15 AUGUST 1769

REX, THE DIGNIFIED: STORIES AND STUDIES
Deb's memory reflects her Rex learning style

'I was required to take a course on the workings of the brain and how certain medication worked to help ease depression, anxiety and the like. I immediately shut down because this was scientific and I didn't – couldn't – do science. The professor was great and she said of course I could do it. I wouldn't be in the programme if I were incapable of doing the work.

'With the positive encouragement I was able to pass the course (and do well, I might add!) but it was "learned" because I had to learn it . . . I let it in long enough to fulfil the requirements of the classwork but it is not a part of me and I don't remember any of it except the encouragement I received!'

A grandmother questions the child's hearing

'Reading my Rex granddaughter's Profile, it seemed as if you'd witnessed her growing up over the last six years. As you said, she has her own way of learning and although extremely bright, she can sometimes make me think she needs a hearing test.'

On relevance and respect

'My work situation has become the very essence of how I see myself and all that I believe in.

'Working in a retail environment promoting complementary healthcare I have gained respect and trust by reputation, something I value greatly.

'It has also provided me with the opportunity to acquire

knowledge which I then enjoy sharing. At school I struggled with many subjects because they didn't seem relevant but now I'm able to consume information in workshops and training days. A much-preferred method of learning for me – it is "relevant".

'As a child I often "piped up" with statements and ideas and would frequently be cast as a Miss Know-it-all. Sometimes this would be in the form of humiliation, which, to this day, I have difficulty dealing with. As a consequence I'm reluctant to contribute in a forum for fear of not being taken seriously and am wary of how I come across to people who may have belittled me in the past.

'However, I have often beaten the drum for unfairness; various political/social or legal injustices where minority voices are ignored has my indignant condemnation and I have marched in protest where appropriate to support a voice against issues being dealt a raw deal.

'On a lighter note, ballet dancing from the age of eight allowed me to shine and be recognized as a success in my world. '

Dr Chris Lane's report on Robert, an adolescent at the Special Education Unit

Observations: Robert was a very intelligent 16-year-old boy who actively pursued education. However, in the classroom, he frequently became aggressive toward the school in general and some teachers in particular, asserting that school was boring and teachers were not good enough at their jobs, they were not teaching properly. Robert's attitude worked against him; he was seen as arrogant, bossy, fixed and loud by students and teachers alike. They called him stubborn or 'stick in the mud' which puzzled Robert, who was proud of his staying power and consistency.

Robert was not excluded from the classroom but, as his questioning and confrontational attitude disrupted the class, he and the head of Upper School decided together that Robert should seek my help in the Special Education Unit.

Actions: Robert was not with me for very long; he didn't need to be. The result was rapid but dramatic. Most of our time together was spent talking through Robert's view of himself, a process that allowed recognition and acknowledgement of his unique individuality. Two important strategies emerged and when implemented, our work together was completed.

First, he was given a copy of his Mercury Model Learning Style Profile, which he took away to study. In so doing he connected with the information and integrated it, recognizing himself and his options. His previous classroom behaviour came into perspective as he understood, as Rex, The Dignified, how important 'quality information' was to him, and why.

Second, Robert was provided with an audience and permission to perform. He was assigned the task of preparing a lesson for and presenting it to the younger students attending the Special Education Unit. He developed a complex and exciting piece of work, exploring some dynamics of our solar system.

This experience changed everything. Robert had the opportunity to speak from his heart, and he received recognition. On reflection he thought doing the exercise was not hard, but he saw teaching from the other side. Realizing how incredibly difficult it would be to keep that high level performance up, hour after hour and day after day, he became more sympathetic toward teachers.

According to his House Tutor, Robert's behaviour in the classroom changed. He knew what had happened to/for him. He saw which parts of himself were undermining him and became less confrontational. He will most likely continue to challenge people to do better. Seeing him later and asking how things were going, he would say 'Good, sir, and thanks for everything.' He had come at long last to recognize who he was and why he thought and acted as he did.

DR C. LANE

DETAILS, THE ANALYST

As I tell you about myself, I intend to be thorough, complete, and provide you with all the, err, ah, details – as nobody else can do, really, or even wants to.

I shall present myself as fully and honestly as possible. Details does try to get things right.

Agile, flexible and adaptable, I love the new, and readily throw myself open to new information of all sorts. I collect considerable amounts of it, from junk mail to academic papers. But I actually learn by separating large pieces of information into tiny bite-size bits. I dissect. I analyse. I tear ideas apart, limb from limb. I have to do this in order to learn. Understanding comes with the activity of breaking down and breaking apart. I thrive on discovering the details and to do so I ask questions; this is what gets me into trouble. Other minds, not quite sure about my need to dig out the details, misunderstand the questioning. I am not being intentionally difficult with the never-ending 'WHYs', I am just mining for more detail in order to understand and integrate the new.

It has come to my attention that people sometimes feel interrogated when I ask questions. Does it really appear that I suspect they don't know what they are doing? Truthfully, I am really just interested in discovering how that machine works or the duties and responsibilities of an accountant. I have learned to apologize, in advance, explaining that it's me, not them. I try to explain that's how I work, I learn by asking detailed questions. Some believe me, some don't.

> *" Inside, I experience an ongoing critique of everything that comes to my attention, along with an ongoing narrative, usually to myself, but sometimes out loud as well."*

It goes something like this: 'Oh, look at that! My neighbour has missed pulling that weed, right there behind the hawthorn hedge. I wonder why my little brother just sank below the surface of the bath water. If I find exactly the right greeting card, 'Across The Miles, On Your Birthday, For a Dear Daughter-in-Law', she'll love it. I better find out how my doll's arm attaches to her shoulder'. Believe me, if I could turn it off, I would. Do you think I like being called 'picky', which is almost as bad as 'probing'? You will realize, now that I have told you, that my questions demonstrate far more than just idle curiosity: it's an active process.

Beyond just collecting it, we Details are hands-on learners who need to become involved with all incoming information. Talking about it simply is not enough. We have to pick it up, turn it over, feel its weight, sniff it and taste it. We have to get our hands dirty, try it out and see if it works. An idea that does not work is not worth taking on. If it cannot be applied to real life, in a practical, tangible and useful way, it is simply not worth its salt. We are not theorists. Abstraction does not cut the mustard – unless it will have a practical application further down the road.

When teaching or training us, please try to devise a practical demonstration or an activity that will provide the direct involvement we require. If information remains just a spark of an idea, or stops its descent at the level of intellect, or even comes down to the emotional realm but fails to be integrated at a cellular level, then we do not learn it.

For example, a youngster with a different kind of mind might take in information about fractions as a beautiful idea, on the conceptual level. But to learn the same lesson, we Details need application rather than theory. I personally would benefit from using a measuring cup (calibrated in both fluid ounces and millilitres, if you don't mind) and a recipe which needs to be cut by a third for a smaller group event (which will be held in the school lunchroom, the day after tomorrow at 2:15 p.m., with six people attending).

And, speaking of time, I really have to get things right, whatever it is: report, article, letter, diary entry. Please don't try to rush me. If you push and, against my better judgement, I agree to write, scan and email the press release right away, because you want me to do so, I will feel very badly about both myself and you when I find the wording was not quite right, not what I had intended. Compared to many other minds, my process of grounding information into practicality takes real time. I do not work well under pressure. I cannot rush the process.

Example: The eldest of Annette's four sons is Details, The Analyst – she absolutely is not. As a young mother, who was very interested in her child's early education, she thought learning should be fun. After all, he was a little boy. She tried teaching him through a wide variety of games, and was particularly drawn to using flash cards. She can laugh about it now, knowing not only how his mind ticks, but that it does. It was not funny at the time. His responses to her best, but totally misguided, efforts put her off trying to 'educate' any of the other boys.

Annette, who is Buzz, The Curious, might need learning to be fun, but it's the last thing on a Details mind. Learning is something you knuckle down to. And flash cards, or other devices designed to speed up Details' pace of analysis, serve to befuddle his neural connections not encourage them. His need to digest new ideas in his own time was overpowered. His mother had tried, but it would have been hard to miss the mark of his learning needs by a broader margin.

Here are some of the possibly annoying but nonetheless real facets of Details, The Analyst:

- That which has been dissected might not be made whole again. Putting the pieces back together is not the interesting part. The act of breaking things down into the little components is important. For example, if the vacuum cleaner or the carburettor has been subjected to 'analysis' it may need a specialist for reassembly.
- If the answer to my urgent question is not going to be used in a real and tangible way, I will not retain it. In fact any information which is not part of an ongoing 'project', is likely to be cast aside.
- Others say I can become a wee bit picky or critical. I am only trying to make things perfect. Hey, someone has to do it. Please make it a point to remember that I am far more critical of myself than I ever am of others. I don't need your criticism as well.
- That's it. Everything else is perfect.

My learning process has created predicaments for me at every age. First, I am interested in just about everything. Then, my mode of processing a mountain of interesting things, separating and analysing, takes dedicated time. And additionally, I learn hands-on by getting involved with the information. Obviously a backlog is going to develop, with a considerable amount of unprocessed and semi-processed material lying around waiting to rise to the top of the pile.

> " *Despite being extremely analytical,
> I am not well organized.* "

I compartmentalize; I stash things away in folders, files, plastic bags, and then cannot find them; storage locations require yet more lists. I can create a lovely, well-researched and analysed document on my computer and file it away sensibly, for 'safekeeping'. You know what I am going to say, yes, you're right, I can't find it later.

I seem to always be surrounded with masses of information which I honestly want to read, intend to learn and digest, but have not yet finished the job. These things take time. You may see stacks of papers, books, birthday cards, technical reports, magazine articles, comic books (a collection of vacuum cleaner bits or dolls' arms) covering all available surfaces – especially the desk, the floor around it and the kitchen table. Those heaps are at varying stages of mental processing. If you tidy them away, I will not be able to find anything; your helpfulness might set my analysis back by months. Let me do the tidying myself. This is true.

I really do love new information and, as I have said, I open up widely to any and all of it. Then when I have finished breaking it down into tiny bits, I move the pieces around, reshape, re-colour and make something brand new from the component parts. This is called 'mental synthesis' and we Details people are very good at it. This is our special brand of creativity on the mental plane. Let me offer an example: if one activity involves being blindfolded while performing certain tasks, while another involves preparing drinks and nibbles for friends and yet another calls for collecting bait for a fishing trip, a Details individual might suggest some fascinating examples of synthetic genius by blending these, as if they were component parts, thus inventing a most disgusting but original Friday evening activity.

Other types of minds retain information over the long term, as if they were glued to it. I don't do that, unless I am using the information on pretty much a daily basis. As you already know, I tend to take in mountains of it. Given that my capacity is not infinite, I have to reserve storage space for the most used and most important information and let go of the rest. Sometimes I let go of more than other people think I should, and forget, err, the details of a tax return filed a few years back, or the star in a movie from the 1970s. I mean, really! Who cares? I have forgotten much more important things, but not the VERY important ones which don't leave me as quickly. Ideas in ongoing use, or those of particular significance, are right there where I left them the night before. I do not lose track of the fundamentals of my career, for example – until I change jobs or retire.

So, you ask, what am I good at?

As Details, my way of acting upon information is to 'process' it. Did I use that word already? Let me explain it in practical terms, with a solid physical analogy. Physical bodies process food in the digestive tract. That means chunks of food are initially broken down into basic groupings like proteins, carbs, fats, and then each group is further divided, for example proteins are split into their component amino acids, and amino acids further fragmented into smaller molecules. The tearing asunder continues as the partially processed material passes through. At specific points, particular bits are absorbed through the intestinal walls into the body – they are assimilated! (Analogous to a properly dissected and analysed piece of information being learned!) And finally, when nothing of further benefit to the body can be extracted, the remainder is eliminated. I do not take in all information to which I am exposed; even Details flatly rejects some things.

" Here is a thought you might appreciate.
The activity of 'processing' occurs on every level
of human experience, from the physical through
the emotional (not all emotional experiences are
absorbed) and the intellectual (not all ideas are
taken in) to the spiritual (the energetic reality
which surrounds people often goes unnoticed).
Conscious processing is personal development."

My Details skill set includes the ability to 'pre-digest' complex areas of thought to make them more readily accessible and understandable to other sorts of minds, those with different skills and capabilities.

For example, so that medical students could have a direct experience of lab research, without the time-consuming, unforeseen difficulties generally encountered in lab work, a Details job involves pre-digesting experiments, 'de-bugging' them by encountering and working through the problems, in order to facilitate the students' research projects.

In the field of education, a professor whose mind works on the outer edge of knowledge, would pre-process his ideas, bringing them down closer toward practicality, and plan his presentation before exposing students to the new areas of thought.

I engage quite naturally in pre-planning, in anticipating what will be required and making sure it will be available. I used to think all minds had this capability; it made me judgemental. Here are some practical examples:

- Stage-managing the circus – don't forget the little gismo that tensions the safety net under the trapeze act.
- Packing the first aid kit before the mountain climb – remember the moleskin, someone might develop blisters.
- Organizing the conference a week on Tuesday and realizing it will

require 40 handouts, printed, collated and stapled together. Is there enough printer ink to complete the job? Staples? Did anyone order the lunch?

- Strategizing the day's route to town for maximum efficiency: first the bank, then the post office, collect the dry cleaning on the way to the garden centre. Never go out for just one thing.

As Details, my natural skills dovetail perfectly with many activities, both professionally and socially. My capabilities travel well, and are valued in the classroom and the boardroom, on the shop floor and in the shop. We just need to watch the tendency to become too picky, too critical and too judgemental.

Details engages very well with anything about wellbeing – physical, emotional, mental, spiritual levels of being, and the interplay and alignment of them. It examines how intervention on any one of those levels affects all the others. Details and nursing is a marriage made in heaven: the practical details of patient care – when is the medicine given, how many tablets of which strength, for how many days, what are the side effects? It embraces dietetics and nutrition, veterinary work and all forms of healing.

Science – especially applied. Any field that looks at how the component parts fit together: engines and engineering, automotives, architecture, research, etc.

My ongoing critique is somewhat selective; I notice, but not everything. I observe what's important to me. For example, I may not appreciate that the windows are too dirty to see through, until I become aware, and decide to focus. Then I will pay attention to try to get it right (perfect) no matter how long it takes (practice). Or, the car can be in use as a mobile recycling bin, while activities concerning my work will be scrutinized to perfection.

It must be me who selects what to focus on and what to ignore. If it's worth doing (that means Details has seen it, noticed it, focused on it) then it's worth doing right (that means practising until it's perfect) which can apply to any down-to-earth practical activity: tailoring, sewing, painting, cleaning, weeding and gardening, ironing, playing music, learning a language, water skiing, eating properly and so on.

Others tell me I have a natural humility. I wonder if that is what I experience as a natural insecurity. How can a mind possibly cope with so much detail? How can I attempt to get all the important things right, or even to contain them all within me? Sometimes I can reach a point of overload. I can become overwhelmed and feel the chaos approaching when there is too much detail to get my arms around.

At that stage I can undermine myself with either of two natural strategies:

I can let the little things draw me away from the big things. Oh, I'll just complete this list of tasks and then get down to writing a book, painting a picture, publicizing my business. Oh, I'll just put a load of laundry in before I . . . Defrost the freezer . . . Check the emails . . . Whew where did the day go; I have accomplished nothing. The big things never happen as I drown in a sea of details.

Or, I can try to escape the chaos, escapism grocery shopping – everything needed for each meal in the next month, three days, etc. I need to quiet down, maybe a TV show, glass of wine, a Sudoku, etc.

Or, rather than undermining myself, I can resolve the situation with acceptance of the large, the diffuse, the universal, the big picture, the place where all the detail coalesces into the whole. Or I can look at the funny side.

WHAT HELPS DETAILS, THE ANALYST, TO LEARN?

- Help me to recognize my short-term memory as a strength rather than a weakness, while guiding me toward coping strategies (lists, notes, diaries) that work on a practical level to keep really important information at the forefront of my mind.

- Suggest I recopy untidy class or meeting notes into my own format with my own sense of organization. It will help with revision further down the road.
- Point out my mental flexibility and adaptability so I can observe and appreciate these qualities.
- Be sure to allow me time and space to digest and assimilate new information and to carefully consider new ideas. For Details, processing information is much like digesting food. Neither activity can be pushed or hurried. Forget about flash cards!
- Give me time to process information before asking a question about it. I want to give a quality response and will do so, but only after new information has been adequately integrated. I do not respond well to pressure. Learning this as a child will encourage me to more easily ask others for this most necessary space later.
- Help me to recognize the onset of information overload and to avoid it. You could suggest, kindly, and without an edge of criticism, that I go outside for a walk, clear my head in nature and then resume my mental activity.
- I respond well to practical demonstrations, but then need to try it for myself. Provide hands-on activities so that I can learn through experience.
- Suggest practical applications for new ideas.
- Help me to break down large topics into smaller chunks, like dismantling a jigsaw puzzle.

QUOTES FROM DETAILS, THE ANALYST

'Anyone who reads through this information quickly will not appreciate it for what it is and what it has to offer.'

'Of course I didn't read the instructions, I just tried it out.'

'Well, you could have an instant, off-the-cuff reply now; but, if you wait until tomorrow, you can have a quality response.'

'My mind is in total disarray. Someone tidied my office and moved all the piles of paper around.'

'This stretch of road has a somewhat shinier surface than the last one. I wonder if it is new or has a different chemical composition.'

'We do not recommend suicide as a way of life.'

ALFRED HITCHCOCK (DETAILS)
b. 13 AUGUST 1899

'The body is the end terminal for difficulties. If our difficulties are handled on the mental and emotional levels they need never manifest on the physical level.'

ISABEL M. HICKEY, *ASTROLOGY, A COSMIC SCIENCE* (DETAILS)
b. 19 AUGUST 1903

DETAILS, THE ANALYST: STORIES AND STUDIES
The girls' weekend away
'Five ladies visited a friend who lived on the Isle of Man – my first trip there. It was all new, and I needed to find out about everything. We went out driving and apparently I had been asking one question after another for several hours, when in unison, they all burst out laughing. They were weeping. "So, what's so funny?", I asked. One who could just about regain control of herself asked if I really, really wanted to know what was under the mounded-up hedges along the roadsides. Was it built rock walls or just mounded-up earth?'

Comments from Corrin
'Humour is good for Details. At least it makes things easier to take in and relate to. I laughed right out loud at a few things while reading about Details, occasionally a bit ruefully . . .

'I can definitely relate to other people's moving my stuff around messing with my mind. I think I build mental maps of where things are and where they are in relation to each other. Anyone moving things around destroys that map and it's not good.

'I love the new, and can forget lots of things if they don't seem relevant long term or I haven't integrated them properly, which can lead to repetitive questioning and other people perceiving you as being a bit stupid.

'It also strikes me that Details, The Analyst, is being creative in the rearrangement of things to create new things or ways of seeing things. If this kind of creativity isn't honoured or allowed then frustration can set in big time.'

Christine's early schooling

'I was a quiet, well-behaved child but managed to call attention to myself for the way I learned (or didn't learn, depending on one's perspective!). In my first year of school, I was failing miserably. It seems that I could never finish a test and so failed every one. My mother had a hard time understanding this as she had always thought that I was a bright child. It turns out that these tests were composed of tasks to be completed: draw five apples, four houses, three trees. Being Details I did just that: my apples had to be perfect – each one had a stem and little leaves; I grew up in New York City and we lived in a five-storey apartment building – so each of my houses was an apartment building! Each floor had two apartments and each apartment had two front windows (the living room, you know) and each window had shades and curtains! Since they were made of brick I would have drawn them to show that as well. I probably never got to drawing three trees but if I had they would have had roots and bark and many branches and leaves!

'My mother's solution to this was to sit me in the dining room and time-test me with an egg timer to answer the test questions in the fastest way possible. Clearly this was not as satisfying for me but I did graduate into the second year. Over the years she made sure that I was signed up for any and all speed reading classes and the like. It was extremely stressful. Eventually, I would return to my "evil (but natural) ways!"

'My husband's mind works much differently than mine. He can remember a vast amount of detailed information and finds it unbelievable that I cannot remember the plot of a movie or if I've even seen the movie, even though we watched it together.'

Another parent advocating for her daughter in the school

'Our eldest daughter, Details, is a very talented writer but finds writing by hand quickly and neatly really tricky. A perfectionist in almost everything, using a pen is no exception and so each letter must be perfectly formed before moving on to the next. Over the years I've battled with teachers for demanding that she "produce more" – a politically correct way of saying they think she's lazy – and championed her quality over their quantity. So for her senior school we chose one that advocates the use of laptops and reading her Profile and what can help, reassured me that we'd made the right choice. Now in the first term of school, she's flourishing: free to get her ideas down on the page while the computer takes the strain of forming the letters neatly, she's visibly more relaxed and truly excited about what she can create on the page.'

Dr Chris Lane's report on Arthur, an adolescent at the Special Education Unit

Observations: Arthur was a sad, thin, undernourished little boy, but one who was socially and emotionally well balanced. He struggled academically and had a serious lack of self-confidence with his schoolwork. Arthur gave the impression of not listening to instructions; it was said that he was unable to absorb information successfully. Teachers reported that they would explain assignments and Arthur would not listen. He found it very difficult to concentrate and his mind would wander. When the others began working, he would get annoyed, shout and act up, but he didn't understand why he was being told off.

Arthur would become frustrated, apparently with his own lack of understanding, and this led to angry outbursts. I observed that Arthur really wanted to do things right – for himself and for his family. True to form for people with this learning style, he worried and became enormously self-critical when he did not get things right.

His worry about his schoolwork led in turn to a greater sensitivity to his areas of weakness. Particular problems: handwriting, maths, French, German, English, literature, possibly anything with an emotional component, although he liked science.

Actions: Arthur's poor handwriting could have resulted from an attempt to write down every detail of the lesson, for future reference and revision. To deal with the issue, I suggested Arthur should recopy his classroom notes. This met with good and positive results, particularly in that he actually learned the material through being actively involved with it in this way.

Arthur's struggle in school is understandable when his learning dynamics are identified through the Mercury Model. His mind takes in information very well by using a practical, down-to-earth, hands-on approach but it does not do well with either written or oral instructions. He learns effectively by applying new information to something real and tangible. Far from being unusual, this is true for 25 per cent of the world's population.

I arranged for Arthur to have a computer and he quickly began writing very good stories, beautifully put together with excellent structure and grammar. These were well presented using an attractive selection of fonts. Arthur had previously only used a computer to play games and didn't know about its creative uses.

I suggested Arthur build conversation into one of his stories and turn it into a play and we talked about the form it would take. His play was really excellent. It was well formed with a beginning, middle and end. He got another student involved and they performed it for a half dozen other students. Although Arthur was nervous before it, he felt fantastic afterwards. This was a breakthrough! It was a clear task, with simple rules and it was practical.

Arthur's learning style could become very focused on one facet of verbal instructions. Trying to work it out on a practical level, the next 20 facets would start to build up and produce 'information overload'. Personal pace, far-ranging curiosity, perfectionism, trying to digest a mountain of detail, all conspire to make Details, The Analyst, look like a bad boy when he is not.

In his 'end evaluation' Arthur said he enjoyed the Special Education Unit. The work was fun and he wished he could stay on longer.

DR C. LANE

PROCON, THE DIPLOMAT

Always ready for an exchange of ideas, I thoroughly enjoy conversation, dialogue and debate. I establish relationships with all kinds of information – with the spoken or written word, with other people's ideas, and with a variety of my own points of view.

Let me tell you about myself. As ProCon, The Diplomat, I like the idea of harmony and will go to considerable lengths to achieve or preserve it. I dislike any expression of unpleasantness, finding no need for a raised voice or a harsh word. A message is certainly not clarified by shouting – communication is never improved by crudeness or coarseness. Since I prefer to be polite, I embrace the rules of good behaviour. The very last thing I would intend is to hurt someone else. On the contrary, I go out of my way to put others at ease, to introduce them and include them in conversations. I am a natural Diplomat; etiquette makes my world go around.

I learn by approaching new information along at least two tracks and at least a few times. I see the validity of opposite points of view and understand a central idea by looking at it from both sides. Some say I swing like a gate – back and forth, back and forth, relating to a concept from alternating vantage points. I look at one side and then the other, and I am apt to consult other people, asking for their opinion about a topic, as it provides a new and possibly different outlook. And then I will go back and forth again from my view to the other person's view and back around again, always looking for the balance between them. Yes, and no and, well, maybe – what do you think? This is all part of my natural mental process and it is valid for me. I am truly sorry if my 'indecisiveness' exasperates other types of minds.

> " *To really learn a new idea, I need to frame*
> *the information into a concept – to take*
> *the hint of an idea and firm it up with some*
> *good rational structure.* "

I have to grasp the logical sense of it. I respond to clear-headed reasoning, a sound principle, a detached presentation of fact. Don't bother showing me pictures, just talk to me. An emotional appeal is not a productive approach; I do not need to filter ideas through my emotions to see if they feel right. Nor do I need to test for practicality or for long-term validity. Those qualities are unimportant. Information just has to be interesting, sensible and coherent – my mind evaluates intellectually. I learn easily from books, magazines, letters and any other print media. I learn from lectures, radio programmes, conversations and any other form of oral presentation.

As a pupil I was well suited to the chalk and talk teaching methods of a traditional classroom setting. I understand that many teachers are also ProCon, The Diplomat. Having both enjoyed and succeeded with their school's methods, they pursued education as a career – apparently we self-perpetuate in this field. But, as a gentle reminder to ProCon teachers: all students are not like us and do not learn easily from discussion and debate. The tried-and-true Socratic method does not benefit the other 11 styles of thinking and learning. Some minds neither require nor value logic!

> **Suggested learning strategy**: When teaching a ProCon child to tell the time, try presenting the logical structure of 60 minutes comprising one hour and 24 hours comprising one day. It will make sense to him and will carry more impact than either the visuals of looking at a clock's hands, or the practical approach of physically moving the hands around.

Whether children, adolescents or adults, we ProCons learn most easily through discussion, but not just because it provides a forum for experiencing multiple viewpoints. We actually can discover what we know or think while telling it to someone else. The learning event can happen during a chat. Here's how it works. To speak we must identify the correct words and link them together in an appropriately composed sentence. But first we need to have something to say. · Until an idea is verbalized, it possibly has not been conceptualized either, and therefore has not been recognized, acknowledged or understood. All these subtle mental dynamics can happen in an instant, prompted by our impulse to talk to each other, to share points of view. How important conversation is to learning! We have all heard people say: 'To really learn something you have to teach it to someone else.' It is likely that a fellow ProCon said that initially.

" If there is no one else around, I can hold a conversation between components of myself,

going back and forth on the topic at hand.
Sometimes I use a computer in the role of 'the other',
as it can hold one point of view while I consider
my comeback. I like computer-assisted learning."

Communication benefits me, and I enjoy it in verbal or written, traditional or electronic form. I often prefer to work in a team, do projects with colleagues, study with a buddy, or connect via social media. And although you may have noticed my attraction to all the newest devices which join people together, you may not have realized that the draw is not necessarily to the technology but to the global link with other minds and access to new ideas and points of view.

I also like words. I like their sound and their appearance on the page or the screen. I dislike tatty books because they do not show proper respect for the ideas they contain. I prefer pristine new volumes, comics and even newspapers; I am frequently unable to relate to a book someone else has read. I establish relationships with both the information itself and with its sources – the words, the book, even its critics and publisher. I read the author's bio on the jacket before buying a book; knowing something about the author actually enhances my ability to relate to the content. Proper introductions are important. I want and need personal relationships with all those from whom I learn – teachers, team leaders, trainers, journalists, bosses, politicians, sports coaches, etc.

Concepts are tangible objects, and I bat them around like tennis balls, weaving them into intricate patterns. Any idea is worth considering. I see no reason to establish limits along lines of truth, practicality, feasibility or permanence. An opinion I state emphatically today may change in the future. Statements are true when I make them. I mean what I say – when I say it. But, things change. Good ideas are those that are sensible, reasonable, rational and wise. I take a balanced and impartial approach.

" My ability to argue both sides of an issue lets me develop excellent skills for debating, politics or law. Ideas of fairness and justice are fundamental to my thinking. This started in childhood and continues through my life."

My best comes forward within the context of a mature exchange of ideas, the back and forth of speaking and listening, considering, negotiating, finding the balanced position. I believe in equality when sharing points of view. It is a mutually respectful way to interact. I would rather communicate with those who are prepared to justify their ideas in terms of fairness, regardless of roles, regardless of age. It is unreasonable for one person to just assume a position of authority based upon age, job description or family status. An adult may say to a child: 'I am the parent. You are the child. You will do it because I say so.' But, this is not an acceptable exchange between family members, between foreman and worker on the shop floor, or between Directors and the CEO in the boardroom. Concepts of fairness and mutual respect are always important, and particularly important when speaking to adolescents. Mental harmony, or at least the impression of harmony, is pivotally important. Keep up the appearances.

I like starting new things – ideas, theories, essays, conversations, petitions, etc. I am good at it and I am original. My natural mental strength is beginning; finishing is not as easy. Sometimes I seem to go from one interesting thought or project to another without completing anything. As frustrating as it may be, life does not seem to allow me to do only what I do well. I expect this is true for you too. To get along with others, we ProCons do need to complete what we begin. Here is a new idea that may be worth some thought.

Strategy: When the initial buzz of enthusiasm for your new mental activity begins to fade, try considering the project from an alternative point of view, one that actually makes it seem brand new. For example, isolate a single facet of the overall task, reframe it and apply yourself to just that small component, as if it were an exciting new brief. Carry on doing that; in time the job will be finished! This trick is frequently successful.

Sometimes I seem to consider and reconsider endlessly. I may hesitate before committing myself to almost anything – what to wear today, which book to read next, if I want a second helping. I hear myself using phrases such as 'but, then . . .' or 'and on the other hand . . .', as I sit on the fence looking back and forth. You may find my indecision frustrating and wishy-washy. So do I, but there is little I can do about it and still be true to myself. I really do view an issue through equal and opposite lenses, so landing firmly with a decision on one side rather than the other is like joining the opposition. It seems like a judgement against half of myself. At those moments I cannot win.

Even in small ways such as, 'Do you want the green one or the yellow one?' you might glimpse my terrible struggle. And I might turn to you and ask what you think. (Do notice, however, that I am not asking for advice, just for your opinion. And I am apt to ignore it further down the road when/if a decision is ultimately reached.)

Or I may defer to you and say, 'Oh, I don't care – whichever one you want.' You may discover years later that I did want the yellow one but wanted to please you by selecting the one I thought you wanted me to have. Back and forth, my point of view, your point of view, what I think is your point of view, and the even more subtle lens, what your point of view would be if I were you. Which decision or reply will benefit the relationship by leading to conceptual harmony or its impression? Which is logical? Where is the balance? These are all honest dynamics for ProCon, The Diplomat.

WHAT HELPS PROCON, THE DIPLOMAT, TO LEARN?

- Offer opportunities for discussion and debate, especially one-to-one.
- Ask questions. Listen to my answers and respond.
- Engage me in conversation. Encourage me to talk, for example, about a book I have read, or what my day was like. Share your thoughts with me.
- Suggest I ask myself questions and find the answers by holding conversations in my head.
- Provide balanced feedback on my work and encourage me to request the same from others.
- Assist me in making my study or work area harmonious and pleasing in every way.
- Explore the many ways in which a computer can help me learn. For example, a computer may provide the one-to-one interaction I need. I may appreciate how beautiful my work can look when word-processed and with the addition of colour.
- Recognize that I will have more energy at the beginning of a project and that finishing is likely to take more effort. Help me find ways of 'restarting' in order to finish.
- Suggest I work with colleagues, friends or schoolmates on projects or assignments.
- Encourage me to say aloud things I have to remember.
- Provide high-quality books, audio books, recorded lectures, radio programmes, journals, magazines and newspapers.
- Tell stories and anecdotes.

QUOTES FROM PROCON, THE DIPOMAT

'Can I just roll this past you so you can tell me what you think?'

'That's not fair!'

'I think that it might rain today. On the other hand, there aren't many clouds and they're very high up.'

'What are your thoughts about ... ?'

'I like to get a sense of the person behind the book, so I go along to "Meet the Author" evenings.'

'As a teacher I have trouble with grading and evaluating. I can see why the student said or wrote what they did and cannot call it wrong.'

'When I don't know how to do something I phone someone and ask.'

'I just couldn't concentrate. The scraping noise of all those chairs on the wooden floor was awful.'

'I love argument. I love debate. I don't expect anyone just to sit there and agree with me – that's not their job.'

MARGARET THATCHER (PROCON)
b. 13 OCTOBER 1925

PROCON, THE DIPLOMAT: STORIES AND STUDIES
Dee resolves the conflict
'I used to struggle with my indecision – backward and forward from one decision to another. Now I go to a third position, above them both, above the struggle, and I see that it does not matter which I choose. Either choice will lead in a direction. One is just as good as the other.'

Carol pursues the middle ground
'From the point of view of an adult ProCon, I find that I can empathize with myself as a child. I can see that as a child my mind liked the idea of harmony. As you say, I actually did go to considerable lengths to achieve or preserve it. The trait has perpetuated as an adult. I intensely did not and do not like disharmony, and so still go to great lengths to maintain harmony when threatened with adversity.'

Michelle has her own take on ProCon, if you don't mind
'It's true. Once I think I have made a decision, I run my question past

someone I trust, asking for help; and when I hear another's opinion that does help me clarify my own, I would rather die of politeness than say I'd rather work this out myself.

'Once I have thought of the solution, I am uninterested in exploring it further. Hmm. Meaning I like to ruminate, which is another way of saying looking at things from multiple sides.'

Charley is not altogether sure he relates to the Profile

'Like a true ProCon, I asked my wife to read it and tell me what she thinks. And like a true ProCon I have discussed it with her from several aspects.

'I certainly embrace the idea of harmony in interpersonal relations. In my work I have gone to considerable lengths to try to bring opposing parties with conflicting ideas into agreement and co-operation. I believe I can see more than one side of most arguments. I rarely shout.

'The chalk and talk teaching method worked well for me as a student, and as you know I used it extensively in my teaching. However, I did use a lot of 35mm slides in later years. I would hope that the combination of methods might have reached a broader spectrum of students.

'Words – and the correct use of words are very important to me. As an administrator being interviewed by the press I have been accused of "choosing his words carefully". I do believe that the process of learning a concept or formulating an idea depends on expressing it in words. And the more precise the expression, the more fundamentally sound the concept or idea is likely to be. I used to tell my students that the best path to the brain was through the right arm – in other words, write it down (until someone told me she was left handed).

'I listen to other people's opinions, but I can usually decide and choose what I think is best.'

Lucy has come to know and love being ProCon

'I'm not sure why I have a difficult time putting my thoughts into words. Maybe it's because I am a ProCon and want to say the right thing that is helpful or meaningful to you. So many points in this chapter describe me and my learning style well.

'Until my later years I was always insecure about my thoughts and decision making. I could always see more than one side of a discussion point and thus was hesitant to express my thoughts. In large groups I let those that have strong opinions express theirs and I listen to all sides. I often have no need to chime in because others will express my thoughts for me, on both sides of the debate. Yes, small groups or one on one have always been better for me. In this situation I have to talk and I know someone is listening. In large groups I always feel insignificant since other's opinions are usually so strong. I get strength from one on one discussions because when I verbalize my thoughts I take ownership of them and learn from them too.

'In my career as an architect, I've found that my strength is listening to people and asking the questions to get them to really define what they are wanting in their home. I also know that there is no one answer to a design solution. So I take many things into consideration and can narrow down the options. Sometimes I will show a number of options for the design solutions, if I know they are all valid. Clients will ask me what my style is but I will say that my job is to determine what their style is and reach a pleasing solution for all the requirements.

'I love being a ProCon. Yes I own it now. I know that even in social relations, people admire me for being level-headed and listening and understanding all sorts of people and getting along with everyone and for seeing the differences in people and accepting them. I do like to please people, but I've learned to have opinions when they are important and I know when to give and when to hold my ground.'

SHERLOCK, THE DETECTIVE

I try to hide my extreme sensitivity. You will observe my defensiveness more than you will see what's going on inside.

The Sherlock mind – a reluctant self-disclosure:

Here's how I work. As Sherlock I focus on new information with X-ray vision, seeing right to the core of the issue: the person, the lyrics, the news story, the painting, the game plan or whatever it is. Although I may not conceptualize the logic or interpret the meaning of what I perceive, I always take in a lot more than you tell me or intend to tell me. I accurately evaluate 'truth' through a laser-like process that includes instinct and gut feelings.

This goes on deep within me. Learning is not simply a mental activity; information is absorbed from all around, and at every level from the obvious to the subtle. My natural way of learning is through perceiving, sensing and feeling, not through intellectualizing. I am aware of and am affected by other people's emotional states. I am exceptionally sensitive and am disturbed by loud noises or bright lights. When I feel fragile, I use cunning ploys for self-protection. One of my favourite defensive strategies is to frighten any 'opponent' away with clever tactics, like blustering ferocity, bone-shaking intimidation, total boredom or crippling humour. I have watched little birds try to look big and dangerous by puffing themselves up to the full extent of their feathers to frighten away an adversary. I can do that, so convincingly, that sometimes I do not realize I am doing it. Another protective strategy is tactical retreat into my inner depths. Interestingly, as a result of practising the art of concealing my sensitivity, I have created a rich inner life with which nobody can interfere. They don't know I am in here enjoying myself.

I become so securely and comfortably nestled into my deep inner space that I am reluctant to venture out. They tell me I am secretive, but I disagree. I do not withhold information from others; at least I do not set out to.

> " I am an open book. Of course, the pages may be redacted, but still an open book. "

It might be that others don't accept the importance and privacy of my depth, my inner home. They constantly try to follow me in there or drag me up to the surface. They interrogate me with unimportant questions: 'What do you want for lunch?' or 'Did you have a good night's sleep?' A snap or a snarl usually sends them packing. Why should I take the trouble to come all the way up to the surface just to say 'good morning'? I know these things are natural to me. They always have been.

I live in a vast sea of information and am besieged by it at all times. I must discriminate between the drivel and the precious, choose what to learn and what to dismiss. I carefully select only those ideas that I am willing to live with for a very long time, no matter what others think I should have in my head.

Before I decide to learn new information, I need to commit to it and that means subjecting it to rigorous testing – intuitively. The source must be authentic, truthful and sincere, and the definitions of those terms are mine, not anyone else's. I experience the validity of those definitions at my core. It's not an intellectualization. It really has nothing to do with anyone else or what information they want me to take in.

To become eligible, new information must in some way increase my power or the power of my personal database. The ideas themselves need to incorporate power. I shall tell you what I mean by that word.

To fathom power, I look to nature and observe the power in the cycle of renewal, the wheel of life and death, the rhythm of creation and destruction, the changing of the seasons. Here are the bare bones of this cycle: everything that begins, or is born, grows from the potential of a seedling, through the bud stage, to its full manifestation in the flower. That is the half-cycle of creation. Then the disintegrative or destructive process takes over, moving from flower to fruit, and finally returning to the seed, once again ripe with potential. From potential to manifestation to potential, and on and on – power. Circling around, with the creative balanced by the destructive – the white and the black together complete the cycle. As Sherlock I must be attentive to this balance and not overly emphasize either half cycle above the other.

Nothing in nature interferes with this cycle; nothing can step in to prevent autumn from becoming winter or the full moon from waning. Nothing on earth is more powerful. As Sherlock, I instinctively ponder these things, and the power of these things.

I observe power residing in forces that are sometimes invisible, but can be either subtle or flagrant, and which can embody either the entirety of the cycle or only one half of it, mastery and dominion, for example: love, money, sex, nutrition, knowledge, radiation, the press, police, guns, jokes, the tax man, music, art, fuel, advertising, etc.

I observe the rise and fall of movements: artistic, political, religious; the rise and fall of theories: economics, finance, education; the rise and fall of social norms: birth rates, beards, clothing styles, automotive styles, house and furniture designs, musical and dramatic forms. What do people like, what captivates them, what controls them? Power, empowerment, disempowerment.

> "*I only let information in when I have both absorbed and accepted it. Then it becomes lodged in the deep recesses of my instinct.*"

I capture a new idea, merging and fusing with it. I wrap around it like thick cream around a strawberry, becoming one with it. This might explain why I do not change my mind easily. An idea would not have gained entry without my instinctual approval rating of excellent. Asking me to change an idea is like asking me to go against myself. From someone else's point of view this might appear to be simple stubbornness and maybe it is. But it's also within my nature. I know how to hold on. I know about commitment and persistence. I do not quit.

I knew a great deal about the power of words from a very early age. I was skilled at wrapping my parents around my little finger. They thought it was cute, maybe it was, but it was also an early expression of my talent for manipulation, the covert use of power, going around behind them, rather than approaching them head on. It was an easy way to get what I wanted without exposing my vulnerability.

Example: My two-year-old tantrums in the supermarket were never soothed quickly or easily, especially with the same old threat or a bribe they'd tried before. This is just as true for the adolescent and adult equivalents of my childhood tantrums. Don't waste your energy trying to trick or cajole Sherlock. We will not be deceived. You will only lose our respect and drive us more deeply into the caverns of our inner life.

My laser-like perception is always full on; it has never had an 'off switch'. I always know the inner depth of things and this trait can be a mixed blessing. The question becomes what to do with all that insider information. Most people do not welcome hearing their closest secrets talked about in public, especially by young children. Apparently I told a group of my mother's friends who had a crush on whom – when I was about five years old.

How was I to know that other minds didn't have the same level of penetrating insight? I assumed we all did. But, we do not. I discovered the hard way to be careful with the use of my insights and to develop sensitivity in the way I talk to others. Depending upon my phrasing and delivery, people can be either wounded, exposed, or violated by what I say, or else liberated, uplifted or mended. It was a startling discovery to realize that my mouth could annihilate or heal with the power of words, that I always have a choice – a black or white choice – to damage a person or to cure them. But, I cannot shut down the insights. This is how I am.

Sherlock youngsters will benefit from some guidance here. Those who reach adolescence or adulthood, as I did, without mastering the space between perception and communication, are not pleasant to be around. I did take it to heart when I heard someone refer to me as a 'nasty piece of work'. That really got my attention.

> " *I do not engage with ordinary lateral thinking. I have always taken unconventional twists and turns as my instinct flows around in the sea of information.* "

Others say this is evident in my quirky sense of humour, which sometimes veers toward the bathroom, bedroom or barnyard. My tendency to link totally unexpected elements can express itself in extraordinary diagnostic or problem-solving abilities, as a unique solution flashes onto the screen of my inner eye. I like puzzles, mysteries, enigmas, secrets and riddles.

Solutions come to me unbidden, and, again, I can undo myself by not taking sufficient care about presenting my insights – what, how and to whom to express.

> **Example:** I knew a young man who couldn't seem to stop himself speaking out at work, he was so sure of the importance and profitability of his brilliant solutions. He refused to accept that his employers had not asked him to find a solution, to identify 'a better way' to run the company, to streamline the shop floor operations, to schedule activities, to procure materials, etc. He was fired from a number of jobs just for trying to help out.

Other people can rely upon the instinctual solutions that flash into a Sherlock mind. It happens when one of us realizes that there is more to the CEO's request than meets the eye, and recommends caution. It happens when your Sherlock psychotherapist knows what triggered your problem and how to help resolve it; when your Sherlock architect understands your unspoken wishes for your new home; or when your Sherlock best friend phones you just when you need it most.

Once I am interested by something, I become fascinated (perhaps obsessive) and dig ceaselessly until an answer is revealed. As I leave no stone unturned I am an excellent researcher in any area on which I choose to focus, from art and architecture to science and technology to humanities, law, psychology, cosmology, forensic or spiritual studies. I take a very long view of human and social development, transformation and racial memory.

But, despite all this talent, as a student, I still experienced difficulty with traditional educational practices. My mind, which absorbs information so easily, did not benefit from the usual lecture style used by many schoolteachers. At a deep level I was already a student of the power of thought, the power of words and even the power of silence. I could always see straight through ploys of manipulation, deception or incompetence. I suppose I could unknowingly be intimidating and I made myself unpopular with teachers. Aside from that, I was always drawn to 'odd' ideas, like having a picnic in a cemetery or keeping a pet spider.

Here is something I learned slowly and over time about myself. This is real self-disclosure. Early on, when I failed to acknowledge and claim my own mental dynamics and assumed other minds functioned much like me, I not only disconnected from my most positive strengths, but I burdened others with unreasonable expectations as well.

For example, by assuming that others shared my penetrating insight, and yet having observed that these others were oblivious to what should have been crystal clear, I concluded that they were slow, thick and mentally inferior. Furthermore, when I assumed others were as sensitive to subtlety as I was myself, then I expected them to be aware of what I was experiencing. Essentially, I expected others to be mind readers, when they were not. This led to considerable difficulties in relationships, at home, at school, at work, everywhere. I realize now that most minds need many more words, considerable detail, and even repetitive explanations of things in order to get the message, while all I need is to do what I do. But, for the sake of relationship, I can choose to participate in verbal and other modes of communication. I draw the line at computers, email, mobile phones and social media.

Other minds may be able to climb trees, but I am a Sherlock fish, and cannot.

WHAT HELPS SHERLOCK, THE DETECTIVE, TO LEARN?

- Suggest I learn to relax. Although I may appear to be mentally tough, unless I feel safe and secure, I cannot learn anything.
- Advise me to use visualization. It can enrich my mind and help my body do things I might otherwise refrain from doing.
- Work with me to create a suitable learning/working environment, one that feels positive and supportive, one that excludes subtle distractions and discord, and may include colours, music and visuals.
- Gently let me know about my resistance to taking in some ideas and my compulsive capturing of others. It helps me to sense myself doing these things in order to realize that I can decide to learn anything I want to learn. Such is my will.
- Help me to sense how I might benefit from learning particular information.
- My solutions to problems will be original and different, as I am unusually good at non-traditional, sideways thinking. Help me to value this.
- Point out the funny side and give me the freedom to do the same.
- Rational logic is not my mental strength. Instead I tend to take in information by osmosis. Encourage me to get the feeling sense of what I am trying to learn, to get a picture of the topic and absorb it.
- Realize that proof of my having learned something is in my gut, not in my head.
- Allow me time and space to reflect.
- Engage your own emotions when presenting information to me.
- Present information in visual form, using gestures, videos, DVDs, drama, displays, pictures, etc.

- Use colour to present and record information.
- Present information as mysteries, puzzles and problems for me to solve.
- Most of all, practise not taking it personally if I will not learn what you want me to learn. I decide what I will or will not take in according to my personal parameters. This is natural, not obstructive.

QUOTES FROM SHERLOCK, THE DETECTIVE

'I don't understand why you have to communicate all the time.'

'Oh didn't I mention that?'

'I don't seem to remember well, only what's deeply important.'

'I like getting to a deep level very quickly.'

'Horrible things, mobile phones. When I see one on the road, I take aim and try to run over it with my car.'

'For a person like me, it's easy to hide the fact that I am hiding things from people.'

'As a child I needed a vivid internal world – perhaps as a buffer against the outside. I was a vulnerable child and remained so into my teens when I created appropriate defences, which have continued even into adulthood.'

'I was as scrupulously honest as I could be in bringing up my Sherlock daughter. But, as time went on, she saw me as a puzzle, a mystery, and set about unveiling the character strengths and defects lurking within my own depths.'

'It is far better to grasp the Universe as it really is than to persist in delusion, however satisfying and reassuring.'

CARL SAGAN (SHERLOCK)
b. 9 NOVEMBER 1934

'It's kind of fun to do the impossible.'

WALT DISNEY (SHERLOCK)
b. 5 DECEMBER 1901

SHERLOCK, THE DETECTIVE: STORIES AND STUDIES
A wife's observation: Sherlock sees beneath the surface

'We were waiting in a bakery for some sandwiches to be made. It was our first visit to Ingleton and we stood looking through the window at the jumble of old stone buildings across the street. An architect by profession, my husband said, to himself more than to me, "I wouldn't buy that one over there. It's not sound." Typically for me, I asked how he knew that. His response exposed his own mental dynamic – "If one of my clients owned that building, I would produce the evidence to prove that the structure is not sound, but actually I just knew at a glance."'

Annie's Profile has provided insight and perspective

'Being Sherlock is natural, because it's what I've always been, just never knew it, so it's comfortable most of the time. The thing is, you expect most other people to think and reason the same way, and you feel disconcerted when they do not.

'I'm afraid that I have, more than once, become exasperated with my husband when he requires every fact and little detail spelling out. I hope that I am more understanding now that I know this is important for him and how he thinks and makes connections.

'I am also uncomfortably aware that when I do come to a conclusion, I am difficult to shift from that notion, unless someone can provide me with good evidence why I should. I'm not easily swayed or happy to be a follower, even when it seems that a lot of people think that way, but if it makes me stand out (which I do not like), I have learned to appear to go with the flow, for good reasons, whilst in fact keeping my own opinions intact. It's all about getting on with others, so I do not think it is dishonest. The recent Scottish Referendum is a case in point. I thought everyone up there had gone mad, yet so many people voted for independence despite all the realities and reasons that they should not. Not one such person could tell me why they would vote "yes", other than "we're fed up" or "let's give it a go". I was totally perplexed.

'I do use visualization on a number of occasions, and find that it enriches my mind and helps my body do things I might otherwise refrain from doing.

'When I think about it, I often do see through people's outer self to something deeper, which is not supposed to be shared, and just keep quiet about it but keep it filed. It never surprises me when it all comes out "officially" later, but I am always happy to be wrong, and sometimes hope that I am!

'Internal life has always been important, from childhood onwards. A real place of refuge.'

A sister admires her Sherlock-brother's problem-solving abilities

'My eight-year-old brother is Sherlock. After reading his Profile, I visited my mother and reviewed it with her. She confirmed having noticed many of the Sherlock patterns throughout his upbringing. I found it interesting in "What helps Sherlock learn" you mentioned safety and security as being important. It just so happens that my brother has been having instances of incontinence at school. He came up with the solution of wearing containment briefs during class/tests so that he would feel safe and secure and know he could avoid embarrassment. I believe that there will be other means for him to gain a sense of security within himself, but his own intuitive solution works well at the moment.'

FLASH, THE PIONEER

If you are going to spend time with me, you'd better have your mental roller skates on just to keep up. I am fast – a ball of flame rampaging through the workplace, the neighbourhood, the classroom, the boardroom – a conflagration on the loose.

I am Flash, The Pioneer, one of the fastest minds of the 12 types – fast on the approach, fast on the uptake, fast to pass around any new ideas, fast to forget, fast to get on to the next new topic.

I am curious about absolutely everything and there is just no stopping me. As soon as I breathe in a new idea – and that's really all I have to do to learn, just breathe it in – I am ready to move on to something else, something new, or expand upon the idea, adapt it, rejig it, contort it, twist it, re-create it. Then I am ready for a mental move. Any place! Just not here!

I wonder what's over there, what's around the corner, what's down the street? What's it like on the far side of that hill? Oh, gosh, look, there's another hill. I wonder . . . There is so much to learn! It must be infinite! And, I want it all – right now!

As Flash I am a positive, forward-driving mind. I am optimistic and enthusiastic. I am bright and lively and spiky and adventurous. I boldly go where no mind has gone before, explore every far-flung horizon of thought. I dare, I challenge, I goad. I think big thoughts. I want to expand on what's currently available. If one is pretty good, five is ever so much better. It doesn't matter if we are talking about building blocks, horses, or DVDs. More is better, bigger is better, louder is better.

EXPAND! INCREASE! **INFLATE!**

Apparently I exhaust everyone else. They say being with 'Torpedo-mind' (me?) is like having a forest fire bearing down on them. But, for sure, it must at least be exciting.

I am one of the most restless minds of all. Full on all the time, I want constant stimulation. Otherwise I get bored. As The Pioneer, I do not have to filter new information through concepts to learn it. I do not have to compare it to my existing ideas to see how it fits or if it stacks up. I do not have to pass it by my emotions to determine if it feels right. And I certainly do not need to integrate it physically. No, none of this! All I have to do in order to take in new information is sidle up to it and just breathe it in. I inspire it. Then I have it! I get the whole idea instantly. But, while the rest of you do whatever it is you each need to do in order to learn, I get fidgety. I start to twitch. I get fed up. I go truant and race off in search of more life, more mental excitement and more immediate action.

If you ask any Pioneer, adult or child, to chill, sit quietly, fold our hands and look tidy, we close down instantly. We all need motion, both mental and physical, in order to learn. Learning is linked with action. Sitting at a desk for prolonged periods is simply not productive. Flash at any age can benefit from this tip: try it out for yourself.

> **Tip**: Try alternating periods of mental focus with periods of physical activity; any physical activity will do: bending and stretching exercises, short drives, walks, runs, bike rides, a trip to the water cooler, dancing, tai chi practice, etc. For those like me, such activities are not time wasting, but promote better mental focus and concentration.

It may not be easy to implement a rhythm of mental work and physical activity in a group with different learning needs. I recognize this – but it is possible. For example, in business, present the option for a Flash team member to stand up for a while during prolonged meetings, or for the whole team to change seats occasionally or build stretch breaks into the agenda. An adjustable-height desk or workstation could increase mental focus and productivity by allowing for differing physical postures during the workday.

> **Example**: A classroom teacher who cleverly asks a young Flash to run quick errands for her while she recaps lessons for other types of learners keeps him or her moving with occasional chores like distributing materials to the group. Furthermore, the teacher uses the opportunity to help all the children recognize and respect their own and each other's quite different learning requirements. Well done, her.

Let's talk about my way of communicating. Pay attention; this is important. Here is a situation in which a Flash child in your life really needs a bit of your loving guidance. Some direction from you could make a big difference to the potential success of all his or her future interactions and relationships. And for an older Flash, listen up, this discussion might show a wide gulf between your self-image and how others view you.

You might find the Flash-minded person to be candid, frank and downright direct. Others would say we speak up, speak our minds. But, here is what's going on for us behind the scenes: We love Truth. We search for it everywhere. We know Truth on the experiential level as an enormous blast of intuitive perception. Truth is a gigantic, all-inclusive, holistic, multifaceted 'ah ha' moment! And, in light of that sort of experience, we just KNOW when something is right – beyond question. It happens in, well, a flash. Who could possibly argue with it? Who could know better? An insight gained in this way is not analysed, questioned or refuted. It's Truth! And when this truth is spoken, which of course it will be, and quickly, non-Flash-minded people often experience it as BLUNT.

For example, here are some typically Flash statements:

- 'Why does it smell so bad at your house?'
- 'Hey, look over there, that person has scaly (green, bumpy, black, pink, purple-spotted) skin!'
- 'My mother said we don't have two sticks to rub together.'
- 'I hear you're going to lose your job this afternoon.'
- 'Guess what my dad said about your dad?'
- 'You look really fat; are you on steroids or pregnant?'

Tip: Although we cannot control how we take in information, we can surely do something about how we express it. We can all learn to regulate our behaviour. If you want to help a Flash-child smooth out some big potential potholes along the path of life, try working with dramatization and role-play about which kinds of truth are seriously hurtful to others. An adult Flash might want to take this point seriously and, for the sake of both personal and professional relationships, ask for feedback about the effects his or her comments have on others.

Now let's address my memory. Obviously I quickly inhale all information in my general vicinity, without restraint or discrimination. What happens next? Do I carry on inhaling and inhaling until I blow up like a balloon? Or, do I just as rapidly exhale and actually forget everything I learned during my mad dash for the next exciting topic? What, if anything, is retained? Well, interestingly enough, some ideas are retained, if (and only if) I am using them as part of an ongoing process or project – and even then only for the duration of the project. After that time those ideas will be blown out, jettisoned, dismissed, forgotten. It would be good if information for tomorrow's presentation or spelling test were included in the definition of 'ongoing projects' and would be retained overnight. By the day after tomorrow, it might all be gone. This is a natural Flash process; it is not a defect.

" Prepare for tests, reports and presentations just before them. Long-term advanced studying, revising or practising is not useful for Flash."

But, please do not worry unnecessarily about future prospects. Some 'ongoing projects' last a very long time, for the duration of a person's career, for example. An adult may easily retain a grasp on both the fundamental and subtle principles of financial planning, accident and emergency nursing or particle physics right up to the point of retirement or a job change. However, during those successful careers, we Mental Travellers might just as easily forget important family events, such as birthdays and anniversaries. I could forget to return a borrowed book, pay a bill on time or arrive at an agreed restaurant to meet you for lunch. Sorry.

Tip: Write lists, keep a diary, use a reminder service, programme things you need to remember into your phone, set the alarm and make very sure you back it up.

As The Pioneer I am an extraordinary brainstormer. I have fresh new insights and ways of looking at things. I can put ideas together in original ways, while others may miss an innovative twist on an old theme. New ideas have to come from somewhere, why not from me?

I particularly enjoy exploring the far-flung horizons, not only of thought but also of my agility and of possible ways of engaging with thought. I push my limits. It's exciting! It's adventurous! In a flash I can see patterns emerge where others might see only chaos. I spot trends long before solid supportive data is available.

I see the pattern of where things are going, and the likely outcome of continuing on that course; it's like an intuitive perception of a line drawn from here to there. Sometimes I am wrong. Or, possibly an unrecognized variable ever so slightly curves the line, resulting in a changed destination or outcome. Others might say I take risks, and I suppose I do. It is possible that my intuitive identification of the trend is coloured by my natural optimism, my belief that it will all work out in the end, and the outcome or end point was not located where I thought it would be – I missed the mark – in my normal Flash-like way.

But, risk-taking on the mental level propels society forward. It enlivens academics, philosophy, politics, science, business, etc. Although the practical level is not my personal long suit, if you want to know what I can actually do for work, I will spell it out. The identification of trends is fundamental to many professions and I can broadly apply my skills in any of them, in the military and in social activities, from weather forecasting to stock and futures trading. Just think! Every country and city needs to assess future requirements for housing, classrooms, electricians, policemen and food supplies. I can move anywhere and find a job! Wonderful.

I relish symbolism and I see it everywhere. It excites me that a tiny representation can incorporate and convey immense meaning. Businesses are careful about the symbols they use to represent themselves – their logo or brand. I know beyond logic that symbols impassion people. Consider these examples: a heart, a cross, the Star of David, a country's flag, a dove. I am particularly fond of the semiotics of number sequences like on a car's odometer and the movements and flight of certain birds. I notice these things and wonder what they mean. I do not mind if they mean something else to you.

Sorry if you think I go on and on, letting myself leap from one example to another, but it's what I do. Here goes . . . As Flashes, we embrace all things foreign to our homelands, words, clothes, cars, travel, sports, horses and betting on them, mastering our chosen field, studying, teaching, writing and publishing, thought beyond logic (meditation, dreams, intuition, beliefs), rituals, religious studies, philosophy, etc. Did you keep up? Did you follow me there?

Here's another great example of Flash in action: I pay tribute to Caroline Myss, a Flash-minded author who observed and described an overlighting pattern, linking large areas of health, personal power, philosophy, religion and spirituality – the Christian commandments, the Hindu chakras, the Kabbalistic Tree of Life – and she presented the whole system as a practical, down-to-earth tool for improving health and wellbeing, personal development and spiritual growth. What a gift to all of us! Go, Flash!

Please note my creative spark is fragile and can easily be damaged. Even when I am exhausting to be around, do be careful not to extinguish my glow of enthusiasm with a wet blanket of disapproval or a bucket full of the sand of practical assessment. A flame blown out by premature criticism might not easily be rekindled.

" *Look for my brilliant core ideas, even if in the rough.*
Encourage and celebrate the inspiration, in the living

room, the classroom or the boardroom. A good idea can always be refined at a later time."

WHAT HELPS FLASH, THE PIONEER, TO LEARN?

- Present your ideas with enthusiasm and make learning fun for both of us.
- Keep it short and snappy.
- Allow for spontaneity.
- Introduce some foreign words.
- I grasp things very quickly so don't labour the point.
- Use symbols and metaphors – they appeal to me.
- Match the pace of my mind. Ask sudden questions; use flashcards; shock or surprise me with a joke.
- Accept my short-term memory as being a strength. I do not need to apologize for it! I have compensating qualities like much more flexibility and adaptability than those minds with good long-term memory.
- I need to use notes, an appointment book or a diary, electronic or otherwise, to keep track of things.
- Activity aids my learning, as I am mentally restless and like to physically move around while thinking.
- I benefit from short lessons with physical movement in between.
- Learning by rote is a sure route to impatience and boredom.
- Let's record material onto my phone or digital player so I can listen while out and about.
- Provide me with an opportunity to teach what I have just learned to another person.
- Present the expanded picture when introducing a new topic to me.

QUOTES FROM FLASH, THE PIONEER
'I sometimes listen to people and just wish they'd get on with it! I've got the message in the first few sentences and they insist on going over and over.'

'I've got this great new business concept which connects some of the ideas I've been having for a while and will catch the latest trend in Internet shopping. It'll be mega!'

'At the beginning of the course I quickly read through all the handouts. Then I was bored for the rest of the day.'

'Are you taking steroids? Your face is much fatter than before.'

'When I was a very young girl I used to spend ages playing with dolls and telling them stories about things that I wanted to do.'

'I don't want to achieve immortality through my work; I want to achieve immortality through not dying.'

WOODY ALLEN (FLASH)
b. 1 DECEMBER 1935

'There is more stupidity than hydrogen in the universe, and it has a longer shelf life.'

FRANK ZAPPA (FLASH)
b. 21 DECEMBER 1940

'Faith in anything, be it positive or negative, produces results.'

CAROLINE MYSS (FLASH)
b. 2 DECEMBER 1952

FLASH, THE PIONEER: STORIES AND STUDIES
An unfortunate clash of learning styles between teacher and student

'While reading *Learning Without Tears* I instantly recognized Ben's learning style as Flash, The Pioneer. Full of positive enthusiasm and fast off the starting line when it comes to new information, he literally runs at it. With the benefit of hindsight, I see that Ben could have been helped, during his early school years, in a nightmare journey that resulted from a clash of learning styles between teacher and pupil.

'My son was naturally fast at learning and with teachers going over and over facts for the benefit of the rest of the class, he would get frustrated. Quick witted and a bit of a performer (class clown?) he always wanted to move on at a faster pace and when the pace was too slow he would become restless. Unfortunately, he was often made to sit alongside remedial children to keep him "out of the way" of the rest of the class. The constraints caused him to close in on himself. His natural enthusiasm drained away, the result was self-doubt and depression.

'It's a great pity I didn't have access to *Learning Without Tears* when he was growing up. I would have seen the problem immediately. I could have stood up for him and his natural ways of thinking and learning, instead of assuming the teacher knew best. She did not. Now 22, Ben has found himself again. And, he has completed his degree to a high standard.'

This boy's brain just whizzes on to the next thing!

'My son would like to be an astronaut and likes to talk about time travel. This is a typical conversation over Saturday lunch. He has just been talking about his food, and then says, "What I don't get is time speeds up in space. So if you go into space, and leave your friend on Earth, when you come back, will I be a day ahead? Or does that mean I'll have to travel back in time? Or will my friend be able to travel through time?"

'As a mum who didn't take physics at school, this is when I have to say, "I don't know son, but we'll look it up on Google."

'He definitely likes to learn whilst moving, and he always "rocked" when asked to sit still in a circle at nursery school. He now comes for little jogs with me, and doesn't stop talking all the way round.

'And his brain just whizzes on to the next thing but he would probably not be considered a fast-moving brain in school. The idea of sitting down learning all day does not really appeal to him, and he has been described as lazy. He is also not overly confident and has a great new teacher this year, who is working on this.'

Bonney, Flash as a schoolgirl and still Flash as a mature woman

'As a child, I learned very quickly, and got bored with the repetition most teachers employed to reinforce subject matter. When I was in a history class at about age 12, I took in the material right away, and being bored began to fidget, to read fiction books hidden in my large history book, or draw pictures in my notebook, to while away the time. There were two other similar kids in the class, so our wise teacher gave us all a task – to draw and paint pictures, and write about the history of the Earth from its fiery inception to the present time. We researched the planet's history, then drew and wrote throughout the term at the back of the room while the teacher repeated and repeated and repeated the history lesson. We then created a huge diorama that unrolled to give our account of our beloved planet's history. The teacher kept us busy and out of trouble and got the diorama bonus at the end of the school year. We three were high-attaining students, able to multitask, and enjoyed hearing the history lessons while creating our masterpiece.

'I was unable to attend college so my school advisor said since I was a bright kid I should take the commercial course. I could become a secretary or a bookkeeper and get a good job, according to him. I was interested in biology, even got the bio teacher to give me a dispensation to enter his college-bound class, but the school principal would not allow it, even though I had several study halls scheduled throughout the day. Sorry, he said, biology was not part of the commercial course. I really took to shorthand – it was fascinating, just like learning a new language (which essentially, it was). Typing was interesting and important and I enjoyed it also, since I liked challenging myself to improve my proficiency. But bookkeeping was another story. After I got the basics down, it bored me; and it bored me. Over the course of the year, my grade went down from the highest to the lowest, directly correlating with my absolute lack of interest. At the end of the school year, the teacher called me in and said, "I'll give you a passing grade for the year if you promise never to take another bookkeeping class!"

'"It's a deal," I said. "I don't want to take another bookkeeping class ever again."

'On a recent trip, a Rainbow Journey to unite indigenous grandmothers from around the world, I travelled with several wisdom-carriers from various tribes including Hopi, Navajo, Yaqui, Mayan, and the Pacific Islanders. In New Mexico we met with Grandmother Flordemayo, a Curandera Espiritu, or a healer of divine spirit. She is a seer, who has the ability to experience other realms of colour, light and sound. And she connects with the nature spirits on her land. Her spiritual grandmothers guide her. She and I had instant "recognition" of each other, feeling we had met before.

'She owns many acres of land, and is spiritually guided where to plant seeds, and where to place large rocks and dolmen-like boulders to enhance the healing energy of her site. She told of "hearing" that she must have a large boulder to place in a specific location. When she checked out a local quarry, she found the perfect rock (or maybe the rock found her!). It was a representation of the Divine Mother, with an indentation to represent the Divine Feminine. Flordemayo was distressed when she heard the price of the boulder ... much more than she could afford. Also, it would have to be transported to her land. But where would the money come from?

'The phone rang upon her arrival home; it was a donor wanting to donate the exact amount it would take for Flordemayo to buy the boulder, and have it transported to her land. The huge rock does feel as if it has found its proper home. This is a fine example of listening to that still, small voice that lies within each of us, and heeding its guidance.'

EXEC, THE ACHIEVER

For me, thought moves ever forward, ever upward toward the goal. Even as a child I thought along grown-up lines, and eventually I grew into my already mature mind. Careful, respectable, practical, responsible.

I am disciplined and very well organized. There is a place for every idea and every idea should be in its correct place, stored in my personalized mental filing cabinet. Thoughts and ideas with something in common are filed together. New information is subject to the filing system, as it exists at the time of filing. These are the rules.

Let me track for you the very interesting adventure of new information coming toward me. I shall structure my story as if the information were interviewing for a position as creative assistant to the boss, which of course may be realistic. For convenience let's call it him and name him 'Data'.

TO LEARN OR NOT TO LEARN

THE PRESENTATION

Right from the beginning, a piece of information, the applicant for the position, will be viewed in a more positive light if he is attired correctly. Data needs to look right or he will be out of the door, with a rejection slip in hand, without even an interview to show for his trouble. I prefer Data to arrive outfitted in clean, pressed, traditional lines, not rumpled, crumpled or misspelled. Data should have proper form in shape and sentence structure. Ideally, he should not be too avant-garde. Only after my very careful scrutiny might he still be accepted sporting spiky purple hair.

THE RATIONALE

OK, Data gets an interview. But I will be looking for assurance. To be considered, Data will have to serve a useful and practical function. He must work well in real time. He must possess and offer qualities that are applicable to real-life situations. He needs durability, profitability and originality. He must have both feet planted firmly on the ground, or prove beyond question that he can get his feet on the ground in the near future. I simply am not interested in any fly-by-night Data. Theory is fine if it can be made real. Abstraction is highly questionable. And if he is smart, Data will not even consider an emotional appeal.

ACCEPTANCE

Now here is where our little analogy becomes tricky. You see, as Exec, The Achiever, I am a hands-on learner. I do not learn by looking, reading, talking, intuiting or feeling. To really learn any new information, I have to get involved, try it out, test it, apply it in different circumstances, touch it, smell it, use it, measure it. On their way to my mental filing cabinet, ideas are being integrated at a physical, cellular level.

INCORPORATION OF DATA

(For me this means working with organization/structure.) If I am going to take Data on board there needs to be somewhere appropriate to put him – like behind an office desk or out in the corridor or in the storage room. This keeps me organized. As with any well-planned system, similar items will be filed together. Ease of managing this system improves with age. Let me explain:

My early years were challenging. I was not born with a ready-made conceptual framework into which incoming data could readily be slotted. At first there were no partition walls, doors, or even floors. I had to build all the little cubbyholes from scratch. My primary tool was always the tried-and-tested technique of repetition. I forged new mental pathways, like grooves in my grey cells, by going over new material, maybe just twice, maybe several times. Repetition – from the old school – does not work for everyone, but it suits me right down to the ground. I found another useful tool – introducing new incoming data to information already properly filed. Slowly, I linked ideas together. This takes time, sometimes quite a lot of it. Eventually the filing system was completed; I had laboriously built a fully personal and very reliable, well-organized structure. I had storage capacity for new data; I knew where to put it and where to find it – easy deposit, easy retrieval. I grew in confidence as management improved.

CONSIDERING ADDITIONAL NEW DATA

Let me fast forward to a point when I am not quite so young and my personal conceptual framework is coming along nicely, one step at a time. By then anyone trying to teach me anything at all (team leaders, foremen, parents, colleagues, teachers, trainers), having long since let go of the limiting belief that quick is best for everyone, would have recognized how I depend upon my good friend Repetition. But, here comes more New Data and it seems to be very new indeed and quite different from that already on file. I will have to choose from three options; please allow me to talk through them with you:

- If I have an ongoing decision to cling to the traditional, and this New Data is not just new but too unconventional, innovative or weird, then I will simply reject this piece, untested.
- But, if I can find a similarity between New Data and some information already on file, then I could possibly subdivide an existing storage area. For example I might be able to integrate 'email' into a file labelled 'tools for communication', which also contains information about antique fountain pens.
- Or if I want to embrace New Data but cannot subdivide an existing folder, I could always enlist the help of Repetition and construct a new cubbyhole, from bottom to top. This method works for me every time.

MENTAL STRENGTHS AND TALENTS

There are some among us who are traditional thinkers, whose ideas help bind the fabric of society over time, keeping things on an even keel. This is Exec's job description and the world simply could not get along without us.

" *When other minds might be driven toward progressive thought and innovation, we hold to the traditional ways, providing stability and continuity to group life – to the family, the tribe, the community, the company or organization, the nation and the world.* "

Our talents include identifying, developing and upholding the rules and codes. This single trait can be widely applied to many facets of group life. Football games, for example, would be even less disciplined events without the formal game rules. Driving cars without collective consensus or legally imposed traffic regulations would be chaos. Can I turn right at a red light after stopping in this country? On which side of the road do people drive in Bermuda? And think about a country's special recipes and customs. If we, the world's Execs, were not looking after the traditional ideas, countries might lose their rich cultural traditions like a Firemen's Field Day, Pace Egging, July 4th fireworks and 5th November bonfires.

I have a natural interest in the proper use of language. This includes language of all kinds, from music to maps to mathematical formulae. I am responsible for preserving the rules of correct grammar, sentence structure and word usage. I disapprove of personal creativity in spelling. Individuals should not take liberties with rules held in common. I enjoy combing through the dictionary or poring over maps. You might remember this when thinking about my birthday present.

We Achievers tend to know where we are by looking back at where we have come from. We frequently have a particular interest in and therefore ability with anything old – antique furniture, cars, equipment or buildings, archives, museums, genealogy, ancient civilizations and their calendars, artefacts and lifestyles. Many of us have a strong affinity with older people.

History is one of my favourite topics, especially if it can be made current – the history of science, of artistic movements, of religion or spirituality, the history of people. From a very early age, I enjoyed belonging to the history society. My tendency has been to focus on the traditional and to retain traditional values.

If you need someone who would be exceptionally well suited to look after and preserve the customs and traditions of the Royal Household, vernacular architecture, the Morris Dancers, the veteran and vintage car club, it's an Exec. Or if you want someone to collect and archive the world's ethnic/folk music, here I am.

I am comfortable in business, government, boards of education and any system that has structure and runs according to established regulations. I can be called upon to bring an organization out of chaos, to restructure a failing company and turn it around.

I perceive the inherent order in things and accordingly I organize them into suitable frameworks. I have remarkable originality in developing ideas with definite practical application. In maturity these ideas have generated profitable new businesses, while as a youngster, if I were given encouragement and opportunity, I applied my talents to the creation of new games, complete with formal structures, procedures, rule book, etc.

If you were writing a grant proposal to fund a project, you would want an Exec-mind on your team. If your business records were in good order and you were looking for an accountant to ensure your annual return utilized every possible tax advantage, you would be looking for me. I could organize anything from a family gathering to a state visit. And it would be done correctly.

I quite naturally set goals and just put one foot in front of the other until an objective is achieved, whether it involves pulling weeds, completing an assignment, tidying my room or brushing my teeth. Time does not matter. A successful outcome does.

PITFALLS AND STRATEGIES

I will have to admit it. I do tend to be a perfectionist. (Please, remember, however, that I am telling you about mental dynamics, not behaviour. An Exec-mind like me is sometimes concealed within a high-flying, high-risk exterior.) And although it's great to strive toward excellence in all things – spelling, grammar, formatting and so on – it is something else to become inhibited, or even temporarily paralyzed, by my Inner Critic. This can happen to adults, adolescents and children from time to time. It is similar to 'writer's block', the awful experience of sitting, looking at a blank piece of paper or computer screen, unable to make a start. I have been blocked from starting a first draft by my concern that it will not be perfect and, from my point of view, it should be. I have sometimes been reluctant to share my own ideas, at work, at school or at home, for the same reason. I am hesitant to present my thoughts, until they are perfectly arranged and developed. I would rather remain silent than appear stupid. Better to play it safe and present ideas that will meet with approval – surface level ideas, not serious ones.

> **Strategy**: I came to realize that other people do not always expect perfection along these lines, that stepwise progress toward a mental ambition is just fine. I needed that reassurance in order to permit my high-level expectations to relax and my rock-solid blocks to release. It might help you as well.

Many of us make incorrect assumptions: that all minds function along the same lines, that all minds work in pretty much the same way and that way is like me. Here is what happens if I stumble into that particular pitfall: because I require New Data to be presented with thoroughness, then I work diligently to provide comprehensive explanations to others. So, I like to make sure all the bases are covered whether telling a story, writing a report or telling a joke. Consequently, I can come across as pedantic, wordy, bookish and rule bound to those with different learning requirements.

> **Strategy**: A businessman passed this trick on to me. Try this yourself as a practice or make it into a game – with clear rules, please: systematically reduce the number of words required to get a point across, whether in writing or speaking. If you have written five pages, try to distil it to three, and then to two. Or practise summarizing the central idea into a single paragraph. This activity incorporates form, rules and patterns, but with the added goal of identifying the essence of a story or situation. Look into and write haiku poetry.

A child with a quick answer or with his or her hand in the air instantly may be viewed as the 'smartest' child in the classroom, but only by those who have not looked into our very different ways of handling information. The educational paradigm of 'fast is best' disadvantages those with many of the learning styles, and certainly those like me. The young Achievers of the world simply do not function that way. But do not doubt they have their own set of mental skills. The Exec mind requires hands-on learning experiences and repetition to physically integrate the material. Regrettably, these children can sometimes experience exclusion, being labelled as 'slow' learners and unfortunately can leave school with scars as a result. What a shame. These are children for whom learning takes real time, but they are not 'slow learners'. They are careful. Note this important difference.

WHAT HELPS EXEC, THE ACHIEVER, TO LEARN?

- I learn by experience, by doing. Don't worry if a hands-on approach results in dirty hands. It's natural.
- Show me how new information links with existing ideas or prior learning.
- Repetition is my ally, even if it is not yours. Going over things a few times is essential to my learning. And some ideas will be integrated more quickly and easily than others.
- Present information to me in a structured form.
- I will have more energy at the beginning of a new project; finishing is likely to take more effort. Help me find new ways of 're-starting' just a portion of an ongoing project in order to complete it.
- Allow time for me to carefully consider ideas, time to really integrate a new thought, before asking me questions about it.
- Relate all new ideas to practical application. Emphasize the usefulness and concrete nature of new information. Suggest examples and analogies.
- I like to initiate new ideas that have practical applications to daily

life. Encourage me to design facets of my own learning activities – schedule, content, timing, testing, field trips and other activities.

- Give demonstrations. But then I need to try things out for myself.

QUOTES FROM EXEC, THE ACHIEVER

'Let's get all these ideas organized into some sort of framework. I'd like to have some idea of where we're going with this.'

'My son doesn't know anything about the proper structure of poetry. I don't see how a person could really appreciate poetry without understanding the rules.'

'At about age 12, I created a game with strong similarities to the football pools. All the teams had proper names. They were formed into divisions, regions and groupings and played each other according to very formal rules. I kept myself entertained for months playing it.'

'As I read a book, whether fiction or non-fiction, I write notes in the margin.'

'One thing I really hate is attending badly run meetings where there is no control and everything dissolves into general chitchat. Inevitably I stage a take-over bid when this happens.'

'I have never played any of the games on my computer. I just can't see the point.'

'I think the reason I work so hard is because I'm the type who has to understand everything, from the foundation upwards, before they feel they can do or say anything worthwhile.'

'I know where everything is around the house, including everything that's inside my refrigerator. If someone moves things around in the refrigerator, I know what they have had to eat.'

'Justice is merely incidental to law and order.'

J. EDGAR HOOVER (EXEC)
b. 1 JANUARY 1895

EXEC, THE ACHIEVER: STORIES AND STUDIES
The Mercury Model has been an eye-opener to Lynne

The Mercury Model is a great training day as it allows you to understand how you communicate, how others communicate, which then allows the communication between yourself and others to be smoother and more effective.

- With my partner I am now able to understand what he means instead of interpreting what he says in my own style, which causes fewer arguments and misunderstandings.
- I am now able to communicate with my work team in a way that makes them more effective and respond far better, producing greater business success.
- I no longer ask myself questions about what exactly did they mean by that or why don't they understand what I am saying to them.
- Personally, the Mercury Model has given me a greater understanding of myself. I realize why I ask certain questions and I no longer expect others to communicate or respond the same as me, as we all have different styles.

Margaret's day off

'When I have a day off to spend at home, I usually have a number of jobs to do – like changing the bed, dusting, vacuuming the carpets, cutting the grass, doing the borders, etc. I might start on one job, like taking the sheets off the bed, and go onto another job, like dusting the bedroom. Then I might go outside and get the mower out and cut the grass and then go inside and use the vacuum the bedroom. Then I might go back outside and put the mower away. Then I might put clean sheets on the bed and then trim the border along the front path. After that I might dust another room, then another border. Everything gets done.

'I have always liked moving through the day like this. At the end of the day I have accomplished all my jobs, just as I would have if I had started at the beginning and finished each task straight through before moving onto the next one. But that would be boring and I wouldn't have enjoyed any of them.

'I have been criticized for this and used to think I was a "flit". However, the Mercury Model helped me make sense of my style of thinking. My mind likes to start new things. The Mercury Model places me in the Initiators Family, a group that doesn't like to stay with the same thought or activity for very long. Our minds would rather go forward and plough new fields. Moving on to new thoughts, ideas and projects keeps them all alive for me; it allows me to finish them all, rather than getting bored and not accomplishing anything. I don't get bogged down with my own sense of responsibility.

'What a relief it is to now realize that Exec, The Achiever, may have to live according to rules, but they do not have to be someone else's rules. You can form and structure them yourself.'

Carlyn wants to do it right

'I haven't forgotten my promise to contact you with my opinion of the "tone" of your chapter. Although I am still not 100 per cent understanding of what "tone" implies. But I promise I will send you another email in a week with my views. Please feel free to tell me in an email what "tone" means. That way I will be able to refer back to it. There – that might be an example of how an Exec, The Achiever, handles information!'

BOFFIN, THE INNOVATOR

There are some among us who are traditional thinkers, whose
ideas help bind the fabric of society over time, keeping things
on an even keel.

There are others who seem to be charged with the task of
cracking the mould of the traditional, the customary and the
expected in current thought, allowing space for the New, the
Unusual and the Innovative.

So, where does Boffin belong?

Which group will recognize and welcome me?

I was born knowing all about commitment. I could, still can, become
completely captivated by an idea – fixated, no matter what, like a
dog with a bone. They called me the 'wilful child', thinking I would

change over time. You know, grow up. Ha! Well, the 'child' part has changed, but sticking to it comes naturally. I am known for it.

I will tell you about myself. I am Boffin, The Innovator. I do not commit to every idea that comes along. And sometimes, in special circumstances, I even change my mind, as you will see.

Here's how I work:

SELECTION: TO CONSIDER LEARNING IT OR TO DISMISS IT OUT OF HAND?

Since I am like a steel trap, serious pre-selection of what to take in and what to ignore is most important. If I took in everything, as some minds do, I would clog up, quickly getting too full to function. So, you may wonder, are there certain types of ideas that will potentially captivate me? Will the ideas that appeal to me share any common ground? Well, yes and no.

My very favourites comprise the set of all those ideas that nobody else has considered – the completely original ones that spring into or from my own mind, ideas that can become statements of my own individuality.

But, if I take to an idea which someone else had already, chances are it will have to do with friends getting together, belonging to a group with shared ideas, caring about friends and how friends are treated, cliques, how people link together into groups. I could use terms like humanitarian, political, sociological and community.

> "I am a non-conformist and do not like to find myself thinking just like everyone else. I am more of a trendsetter than a follower. If one of my trends happens to catch on and become popular, I may stop thinking that way, and move off in a different direction."

Sometimes I like modern technology, sometimes I do not. The real draw is not necessarily to the technological gadgetry itself but more to the thought process behind the idea that originated it. I can become captivated by an original seed idea, back when it was just a concept, not yet actualized into a clever invention, a video game or a political ideology.

Frequently, the fascinating idea itself, which grabs me by the jugular and won't let go, may be out of step with mainstream thinking in some way or another. It may be either too new or too old for current times. Other minds simply do not think like that right now. Perhaps they did during the heyday of Atlantis or will do during the 22nd century, but certainly not today.

Now here is where my self-disclosure story becomes very personal. New information will have to pass a particular test in order for any Boffin to commit to it and take it in. Yet the qualifying tests are unique to each one of us. I have my own – others use quite different criteria. First, let me tell you even young Boffins, and certainly the adolescents and adults, have constructed a conceptual framework that is both wide and deep. This is exceedingly important to each of us and will not be infiltrated easily. But here is the test: I will compare any new information to the contents of my existing database, the body of my current thoughts. If it fits, on a conceptual level, it's OK to come in. Otherwise, I do not even hear it. I really don't hear it. Perhaps you recognize some of those moments. It may look to you that I am not listening. But, I don't see it that way, because I know that I am totally open-minded, to all sorts of ideas, concepts, thoughts, principles or suggestions. Could it be that you see things differently?

Example: The Boffin Chief Executive Officer of a medium-sized UK company prided himself on his totally open mind and his equally wide-open office door. He invited thoughts, ideas and comments from his staff. The staff said he did not hear anything they said; he didn't even listen. He was like a brick wall.

Don't be too surprised if a school-age Boffin, or a young apprentice, or a new employee receives very mixed progress reports. We Boffins tend to do very well in areas that stimulate us mentally and quite poorly in those that don't. This is not a matter of ability but of interest; it is another issue of Selection. For example, one adolescent became captivated by world music and diligently studied languages as a route into the ideas expressed in the lyrics. Meanwhile he shunned ordinary class work. Another Boffin student applied his mind, for several years, to studying Aboriginal tribal cultures following a brief school project.

UPTAKE: HOW TO LEARN IT?

I need to make intellectual sense of an idea in order to learn it. After engaging in all the preliminary screening stages, which I have described above, I only have to fit the information into a concept and it's in – for the duration. That's it! There is no need for repetition, application, contemplation, reflection, discussion or anything else. The bottleneck comes at Selection not at Uptake. This will be as true at age ninety as it is at nine.

MEMORY: HERE IS THE STEEL TRAP

Once I take in information, I do not forget it. It is completely natural for me to remember it all. An elephant is downright forgetful by comparison. If it looks as if I have forgotten something, it's more than likely that I never learned it in the first place. That piece of information probably didn't pass my qualifying test. It may have looked to you as if I were listening, nodding my head, smiling knowingly, but actually that was your mistake. You misread me. The blinds had already come down.

CHANGING? LIKE A BOLT OF LIGHTNING OR NOT AT ALL

They tell me I have an extraordinary method of shifting gears. Actually, it is not so much a change of mind or a change of opinions, but rather a full-scale revolution.

The foundation of my absolute commitment to a particular idea is my having been captivated by it in the past. There are two ways that I can become 'uncaptivated', which is essential if I am going to be released from my commitment and able to 'change my mind'. As long as the captivation lasts, so does the commitment. One route is for me to see a flaw in one of my closely held concepts. If it appears to be wrong, incorrect or blemished in some way, I will drop it instantly, like a hot potato, and will never pick it up again. So, don't bother trying to convince or cajole me into reconsidering an idea I have cast aside. It won't happen. And don't bother to seek an explanation as to why I no longer belong to the youth group, the Conservative Party or the ballroom dancing club. You may be left wondering why I traded in my calculator in favour of a slide rule or abandoned my devotion to the French horn or my flying lessons. The simple fact may be that I saw a shortcoming in my earlier perception and simply went off it. This does not happen frequently; after all I am committed to my ideas, but I have experienced some sudden, unexpected turnabouts in my career path, the value of a particular relationship or what name I wanted to go by. I didn't anticipate or plan those changes. I have learned to fasten my safety belt.

There is a second way I can become 'uncaptivated' by a previously closely held set of ideas. If new information comes my way and it's just too exciting and too right for words BUT it does not fit with a portion of my conceptual framework already in place, then the stage is set for an upheaval. I am apt to excise and discard an entire section of the framework to which I had been committed for ages – my own personal criteria against which I had measured all other new ideas.

Then, released from previous mental commitments, I can make a most unexpected leap and adopt a way of thinking which may be very, very different from what it replaced.

> " *A mental revolution like this does not happen often, but when it strikes, it strikes like lightning. This is a completely natural Boffin process.* "

I see that it can be worrying for a parent, a partner, a child, a boss or even myself, but there is nothing 'wrong' – I just changed my mind in my very own unique way.

AN OUTSIDER'S POINT OF VIEW

People who are not like me tend to describe me as stubborn, closed-minded, not listening to other people's suggestions, weird or unusually creative. But I myself flatly reject all of that. No sir, that's not me.

I do not feel closed-minded and will certainly not admit to being fixed or stubborn. I absolutely listen to what you suggest.

> " *I see nothing either weird or particularly creative about myself – I am just normal – just like everyone else. Why are you laughing?* "

Big thinkers tell me that Boffins are charged with the task of breaking the mental mould of the Normal and the Conventional in order to allow space for the New. They say that without those who quite naturally think along original lines, humanity would circle around the same traditional attitudes forever, never moving forward, never evolving. They ask if I have ever seen a revolutionary (inventor, innovator or scientist) without serious commitment to a cause. What are they on about? I am absolutely normal.

WHAT HELPS BOFFIN, THE INNOVATOR, TO LEARN?

- Mapping new ideas on paper can help me fit them into the existing conceptual framework already in my head. It can help me find common themes and connections among ideas.
- Accept that I may not choose to take in all the information that you offer to me. Do not take personally my decision to reject some topics. It's based on my choice, not your presentation.
- I like to learn in my own way and at my own pace, when no one is either pressuring or holding me back.
- Saying things aloud may help me to learn. Provide opportunities for discussion and debate.
- Encourage me to summarize my ideas after a discussion as this helps put the information into a framework.
- Ask questions to draw out my responses as this encourages conceptualization.
- Include opportunities for me to be inventive and experimental.
- Computer-aided learning may appeal to me, but don't make any assumptions.
- Metaphorical stories and drama may also help me to explore ideas in other ways.
- Encourage me to think about the ideas behind an invention.
- Provide plenty of books, audio books, recorded lectures, radio programmes, journals, magazines, newspapers, DVDs, social media and all the other information offered on the Internet.

QUOTES FROM BOFFIN, THE INNOVATOR

'I flatly refuse to believe that I am stubborn.'

'I have clear ideas on how I think things should work and see people who don't embrace equality as quite backward.'

'Unless I'm really interested in something I only half listen.'

'Some of my best work has come from being given the opportunity to be inventive.'

'Going into technology deflects away from the ideas behind the technology, which is what's really interesting.'

'I will not stand for injustice if I can do anything about it.'

'I have a dream that one day this nation will rise up and live out the true meaning of its creed: "We hold these truths to be self-evident that all men are created equal."'

DR MARTIN LUTHER KING, JR. (BOFFIN)
b. 15 JANUARY 1929

BOFFIN, THE INNOVATOR: STORIES AND STUDIES
A spot-on observation at a Mercury Model workshop
A Mercury Model workshop participant thought this dynamic sounded like her grandmother, who had suddenly decided to walk away from a 35-year smoking habit in order to use the money to buy a fur coat. The old lady never smoked again. She was right; her grandmother was a Boffin!

A cohesive group of teachers
An English city's school department decided to thank a group of head teachers who had been battling against the threat of closure notices for many years, fiercely working to keep their local primary schools open – against all odds. Their reward, a fun-filled, action-packed get-away weekend in a lovely hotel, included a Mercury Model workshop. Why was it not too surprising that nine of these eleven determined, steadfast women were Boffins?

Paula reflects on her friend Paul
'His thinking was always outside the box. In the early 1970s he took up the ancient system of hydroponics, growing plants in water and

produced vegetables in his university room.

'In the mid-1970s he started a company to manufacture solar collectors.

'And he invented an innovative noiseless audio cassette. Due to some new type of torque gauge, it didn't produce any internal background noise. When he and his brother were students, they opened the business in the back of a car wash, employed 15 staff, and couldn't keep up with the demand. Warner Brothers used them routinely, and may still be using them. It came crashing down when cheap CDs from Korea flooded the market.'

Cory gains perspective on her mental revolution

'In the past couple of years I've been going through what feels to be a full-scale mental revolution, which I feel can be attributed to a few things. I had gone to school for mechanical engineering with the concept that it would be state of the art, high calibre problem sets, creative, hands on and fulfilling once I got a job. After doing a couple of aerospace co-op internships, I found that my experience of the real work was very different than what I initially believed it would be. So, I began to ask myself questions like, "What actually fulfils me?" "Why am I even doing this degree?" "What other things can I do that allow me to bring my love and blessing into the world?"

'Since then, it has been a lot of soul searching and what I would say to be a building of a new framework from the ground up. The Boffin chapter has helped put many things into words that I was only able to feel the subtle underlying currents of. I would also like to add that travel has opened up my world to new people/places/cultures/ways of living and offered many more mental touchstones which have added to the overall conceptual revolution I'm experiencing.'

Dr Chris Lane's report on Joseph, an adolescent at the Special Education Unit

Observations: At age 14, with a reading age score of seven years nine months, Joseph's prospects were dim. Frequently truant, disruptive in school and engaged in some criminal activities outside, he was repeatedly excluded from the classroom for bad behaviour and lack of co-operation. He adamantly refused to read aloud in class, even when teachers shouted at him to do so. In fact the shouting often resulted in even worse behaviour, laced with aggression. The teachers believed the boy would never change. He was labelled 'un-teachable' and was fundamentally abandoned by the educational system, sent to the Special Education Unit labelled as a problem.

There was, however, a peculiar quality about this boy. Joseph was highly numerate, displaying mathematical ability at least equal to that of a much older and well-educated young man. His extraordinary ability was generally recognized but was not tapped or encouraged in any way.

Actions: Joseph's learning style is Boffin, The Innovator, a naturally rebellious, freedom-loving mind that chooses what it will and will not take in. Discussion revealed that Joseph never read anything whatsoever, not magazines, books, comics or newspapers. To encourage non-pressured practice in reading, a daily newspaper was available for us to read together.

Through silent reading followed by discussion of news topics Joseph began to discover the link between reading and comprehension. Reading aloud in the classroom had always been linked with shouting and humiliation, but the concept of reading in order to learn new information dawned upon him and he never looked back. Almost immediately, Joseph bought himself a paperback thriller, way beyond his reported reading ability. We moved on to geography, history and English lessons, map reading and writing exercises. It was obvious that he quickly grasped new ideas and concepts. When lack of co-operation surfaced, it was dealt with in a level way, and without shouting. Painting and drawing were very useful activities and always allowed Joseph to settle quickly.

And the ability to actually see the words clearly through a new pair of reading glasses made a world of difference. His earlier refusal to wear 'un-cool' but much-needed glasses in school may explain some of his previous difficulties with comprehension and concentration.

Within one week, Joseph was released from the negative school experience and the dangerous cycle, which he had been in for years. After two months a new reading assessment provided a figure of 14.5 years, increasing his score by 6.8 years. His gradual acceptance of his abilities and pride in the subjects where he excelled, plus real improvement in his reading age, led to a more settled response in the classroom.

The most rewarding result of my involvement with this boy was the way in which his intelligence and ability was noted by his subject teachers. They had previously been unable to see beyond the challenge presented by his behaviour. He became very successful in school and went on to 6th form college.

DR C. LANE

Dr Chris Lane's report on Jane, an adolescent at the Special Education Unit

Observations: Like so many of the boys and girls who came to the Special Education Unit, Jane had two labels, 'difficult' and 'problem'. She was referred for poor behaviour and lateness, and was threatened with permanent exclusion from the school.

This girl was not fed properly and she was always hungry. Jane did not have a meal every day and her mother was not always able to provide her with dinner money. She regularly had nothing to eat after school and went to bed hungry. One of her teachers said that 'being hungry was not an excuse for bad behaviour'.

Vulnerable, undernourished and at risk of prostitution, Jane was often out late at night and was not awake in the morning. She needed to feel cared for and valued, not neglected and rejected.

Actions: This story has a very good outcome. It was not long before Jane would be waiting at the door for the unit to open early in the morning. I managed to refer her to a social worker, that ensured that Jane had at least one full meal each day.

Having identified the areas of conflict and the subjects causing the most difficulty, the school agreed to provide Jane with a laptop computer for her to use in class. The immediate result was the completion of written work and also homework, which had not been done previously. She personalized her work with colour and illustrations.

Although Jane was a conceptual learner, the strictly chalk and talk method used to present science in particular did not engage her. I developed an approach that was unusual enough to appeal to her learning requirements and thereby to reach her. I reformatted the basic information necessary to understand the term's science course from the textbook as a set of annotated illustrations, labelled it in longhand and scanned it into her laptop.

Within three weeks of starting the programme, Jane had risen to the top group in the class and was producing work of a high standard. Constant praise and encouragement aided this transformation and her relationship with the science teacher improved enormously. Already good at maths and reading, her work in all her other subjects showed a similar improvement, only physical education proving difficult to affect. This was due to her awareness of her body as thin and unattractive. I had every hope that her increasing self-confidence would eventually solve that as well.

Through awareness of the issues that were at the root of Jane's lateness and poor behaviour, her teachers were able to be more proactive in lesson delivery. Jane's craving for attention was diverted to positive behaviour through praise and understanding. She was encouraged to take part in the lessons in the way in which she felt included. With this realisation upon her part, her general behaviour began to improve. Most importantly she came to understand how she learned and was able to take control and apply this to herself. Increased success in the classroom allowed her natural thirst for knowledge the freedom to expand. She remained in school and eventually entered the top academic stream and will lead a full and effective adult life.

In effect, *Learning Without Tears* and the Mercury Model made it possible to identify and target the particular aspects of Jane's information processing and learning style. The usual assessment methods would not have produced such a result without that very special detail.

DR C. LANE

SONAR, THE INTUITIVE

If both of us are Sonars, we will know it at a deep intuitive level. Having recognized each other, we might watch DVDs together, listen to music or perhaps just share the subtleties of silence. If not, you may be totally bewildered by me.

Using words to describe myself and my inner process, even to myself let alone to you, is an entirely unique experience. Creating a life-sized collage would have been easier.

My intuitive mind is highly visual and extraordinarily sensitive to what feels like a swirl of information around me. I receive, absorb and interpret subtle signals that others apparently miss. Ebbing and flowing like the tide, I never stay in one place very long.

While a different kind of mind might separate, dissect and analyse information as a way to understand it, I do just the opposite. I link pieces of information together – I unify and include. I take a global view – even of tiny things – and naturally see the big picture in which everything is connected and integrated. I understand a new idea by sensing how it fits into the context of the larger whole. While other minds may examine details in order to build a composite, I start from the overview. I blur the edges, which otherwise separate one thing from another. I see the forest as a whole rather than looking at individual trees, and I very much like it that way. Normally preferring abstraction, I could, but often would rather not, work my way down toward the details. I perceive quite a different reality from other minds. And, accepting this fundamental fact will help you to understand me better.

It is well known that witnesses to an event often describe it quite differently; they report widely contrasting versions of the incident. The courts are full of examples! Where, we might ask, are the actual facts in such a situation? And can they be separated from individual perception? Good questions, perhaps, but how do they relate my way of thinking and me? First, everything always relates to everything else, and beyond that, I chafe against the constraints of pure logic and refuse to be pinned down by hard facts. That which is purely rational seems cold, angular and only partially complete. It simply does not supply enough information. I could never make logic a guiding principle for life. On the contrary, I naturally connect to a different perception of reality, through the softer facts of instinct and intuition. In this way I get the whole picture – the cause as well as the effect. My familiar state of 'un-focus' can reveal the all-important but subtle energetic underpinnings upon which hard facts appear to float. Don't doubt that this is true, for me and those like me – one twelfth of the world's population – at every age.

> **Example:** A little Sonar boy called David would share his own observations about the neighbours as his contribution to the family's lively dinnertime exchanges. Without fail his sister would aggressively demand proof. The fact that he 'just knew'

was not good enough! With his intuitive feelings discredited, he gave up both talking during dinner and valuing his ability to read people's situations accurately. Having learned before reaching the age of ten that only facts were important, David detached from his best and strongest mental qualities for about 25 years in pursuit of a career that valued rational proof. But, you should see him now! As one of his grateful clients, I personally attest to his extraordinary abilities as a cranial osteopath.

I absorb information from all around, as if by osmosis, just soaking it in, without discrimination, without the opportunity of selecting what to take in and what to reject. I do not submit available information to qualifying tests, as do many other minds. I look, I see, I drink it in, filtering the impressions through my personal feelings.

" *Learning is an emotional matter, carrying an emotional impact. Mind and feelings are intertwined for all Sonars.*"

Ask us what we think and we tell you what we feel. A good idea is one that feels right. It need not be practical, timely or conceptually logical.

I am curious, I love new information! I am wide open – taking in all that's available like a clam on the ocean floor takes in seawater. The analogy does not stop there. Neither the clam nor I capture and retain everything that enters. Neither of us can absorb endlessly without damaging our capacity to be receptive. In both cases it appears that most of what flows in flows right out again. I seem to forget much of what I learn. And the analogy continues. From the stream of seawater flowing through it, the clam filters and incorporates exactly the nutrients it needs for its survival and growth. Similarly, I select the little pieces, the facts that I want from within the big mix. I can focus on particular ideas and use them for as long as I want to. But when those bits of information are no longer in active use, I discharge and return them to the sea. Facts sink below the surface of specificity into a great pool of unfocused awareness. They are forgotten.

Some minds have a natural capacity to remember facts or ideas over the long term. Part of their contribution to the larger group is to preserve and sustain thought. These people tend to be very proud of their fine memories. But, I am not one of them! On the contrary, being blessed with a short-term memory, I make quite a different contribution. As information is easy come, easy go and any unused pieces can quickly be jettisoned, I am always mentally free to approach the new. I do not run the risk of becoming clogged with rusty, old, obsolete ideas. Part of my mission is to be constantly open to new influences, to absorb them, to stir them around, adding in a pinch of this or a measure of that, and then to synthesize from the concoction something wholly original. I am adaptable and flexible, giving a new slant to old ideas. My particular kind of memory should not be viewed as a shortcoming or a defect. It's natural, and you, as my partner, parent, friend or employer, can choose to view it as a strength too.

Tip: I can benefit from coping strategies to remember what's really important – lists, paper or electronic diaries, personal phone directories, string around the finger, etc. Seasoned Sonar-types warn that novices must not only store important pieces of information, like event times and locations, but must also remember to update and to consult the lists.

I am highly visual and will naturally express myself in visually descriptive terms. I think in pictures and learn from pictures, films, DVDs, photographs, illustrations, diagrams and charts. If you provide me with a picture, or just part of a picture, I will take it in easily, often filling in the missing sections. However, if you speak to me in words and concepts, I have to translate them with the inner eye into a

Fish Can't Climb Trees

picture of what I think you have said, and then take in that picture. The same thing happens as I read a book – a picture develops, and that picture is absorbed, not the words.

> **Tip**: Ask a Sonar to draw or describe what he or she sees when reading a book or listening to music – how characters are dressed, how they talk, the action, the local scenery, etc. You may be amazed and delighted.

We Sonars often encounter difficulty with the older, more traditional styles of providing instruction. Classroom teachers, business trainers and team leaders may misread us, viewing us as diffused, drifty, vacant, unfocused or lacking concentration. We have more than our share of 'could try harder' on our school reports. In fact our authentic strengths frequently go unnoticed, our natural learning requirements neither recognized nor understood. But who would ever realize, without being told, that we experience links between simultaneous events; that the cloud formation in the sky outside the schoolroom or office window carries the same message as the speaker's words, but in a form that is more easily absorbed? Needless to say, we do not tend to test very well by ordinary methods. Our unusually creative imaginations are often undervalued.

Because I am enormously curious as well as immensely absorptive and vastly receptive, I am easily 'distracted'.

> **Example**: Here is a story from an adult Sonar. As a young child, Al was sidetracked by the intricacies of the hedgerows along his way to school. One delight led him on to another – the creatures, flowers, seeds, webs and their mutual interactions. He became enthralled, touching the beauty of creation, experiencing it, being part of it. Eventually some inner impulse guided him toward his destination, without guilt or awareness

of tardiness, only to discover that his teacher and classmates had been observing his meandering from the upper window and were all waiting there for him.

What followed was one of those pivotal moments which could have separated the Sonar child from his own genuine mental strengths, leaving him humiliated and with a commitment 'never going to do that again', as if his natural mental functions were all wrong.

At any age we Sonars can learn to work creatively with our unique brand of mental flow, to bring it into harmony with some appealing musical, artistic, verbal or conceptual structure. Is this not how poetry is born – by containing inspiration in an accepted linguistic form, a cloud in a bottle?

Example: Another Sonar reports the hardest thing for people to understand about her is that her mind never stays in one place very long – it simply flows off in another direction. She knows this exasperates others who wish she had a more structured, focused, detailed or logical mind, but she does not. She recommends that parents of young Sonars observe and appreciate the mental fluidity which naturally draws the child from idea to idea, and to celebrate this mental quality together. This can provide a sense of support, no matter what message comes from the outside world in the future. Her advice might help you to defuse potentially damaging episodes which your child might otherwise carry into adulthood.

Because learning is so closely linked to my feeling nature, I do my best work when I feel emotionally secure. Tranquillity in the workplace, the classroom or the living room is considerably more important for me than it is for many other types of minds. Consider the potential effects of a raised voice or other loud noises, powerful emotions such as anger or fear, or even a messy, unattractive or uncomfortable space. Remember the clam analogy: it snaps its shell firmly closed when it's frightened. So do I. And it might take a long time to rebuild the confidence or willingness necessary for me to reopen it. I benefit from time alone to recharge and rebalance my sensitive nervous system.

> *" The interface between reality and fantasy is comfortable territory for me, although many others would rather avoid it."*

I have a unique ability to detach from facts in order to imagine or dream. The original ideas I pluck from that unfocused place would never come just from pure logic or rationality. I enter other realms where I am able to connect with whimsical thoughts that can delight other people. My fertile and creative imagination has a wide scope of expression in any of the traditional pursuits that reward a love of fantasy, like music, film, acting, writing, entertaining. But also, I can be extremely successful in entrepreneurial activities from commerce to furniture design to computer programming. I have a most sympathetic ear and a compassionate understanding, allowing me to identify with others' problems, from the personal to the corporate and the emotional to the professional. My ability to soothe and heal with words can be uplifting to others.

In keeping with who we are, some Sonars naturally present themselves in a tender, sympathetic or even a retreating way, while others express themselves quite differently. Sometimes an active, robust confidence, an easy assertiveness completely masks our soft, intuitive qualities. Behaviour can camouflage unseen mental dynamics. Don't be fooled. What's visible on the surface only sometimes reflects what's happening deeply within. Child, adolescent or adult, we Sonars filter the outflow of communication through our particular personality or behavioural style.

My receptive nature involves a measure of permeability – I can be impressionable. Far more open to suggestion than most, I might change my views and opinions along with my associates, unknowingly sacrificing my personal thoughts. My natural fluidity can mimic absent-mindedness, confusion or indecision. Sensitive to my own suffering and to the suffering of others, I can easily be hurt by people's comments.

Generally I do not favour words as the most natural mode of communication. For me, the big picture is not restricted to data, facts and logic, but includes a large measure of sensing and feeling; it does not easily contract into words. Instead, I am apt to reference books, movies, articles, graphics, paintings and songs created by others who I think did a good job of expressing the point I wish to make. I can convey meaning in poetry, music and dance, and, like nobody else in the world, I can say it with flowers.

Did I tell you I prefer to unite rather than to separate, to include rather than to ostracize? Combining that with my naturally diffusive nature allows me to blend with other people's mental modes. I can almost always find a fragment of you within myself. I can connect with you and I can unconsciously cater to your learning requirements in conversation. They say I have an uncanny way of asking the question which is at the forefront of other people's minds. Such is the measure of my link into collective thinking. My creative imagination is high; I can be poetic, visionary and possibly psychic or even telepathic.

I have an innate refinement and gentleness, no matter how tough my exterior may appear to be. At any age, we Sonars will benefit from your kind-hearted support. With it, there is no limit to what we may achieve in this rough and tumble world.

WHAT HELPS SONAR, THE INTUITIVE, TO LEARN?

* Present the big picture first. Details do not benefit my initial learning.

- View and talk about my short-term memory as being a strength rather than a weakness. I tend to remember things that are needed for the project at hand. Letting go of the rest allows freedom for me to embrace the new.
- Emphasize that you value my mental adaptability.
- Talk about how I get the 'feeling sense' of what I want to learn.
- Devise suitable tests of how well I am progressing, tests that use an appropriate measure. Those designed for other kinds of minds do not always work well for me.
- Help me to identify choices about working consciously with the sea of information in which I am immersed and my sensitivity to it.
- Show me how to sense the onset of mental overload and to develop a number of strategies to avoid it.
- Teach me the value of relaxation and of spending time away from other people, either alone or with animals. Encourage time and space for reflection.
- Help me to create a positive, supportive study or work space.
- Engage your own emotions when presenting information to me.
- Present information visually, using gestures, images, DVDs, charts, graphs, illustrations, drawings, photographs, etc.
- Use colour to present and record information.
- Train me to use visualization and meditation techniques.
- Suggest a wide range of ways for me to express ideas.
- Encourage the use of symbols, metaphors, drama and stories.

QUOTES FROM SONAR, THE INTUITIVE

'The feeling is too big for the words.'

'How can you talk about the scientific result or see its beauty unless you know what the engineer was feeling when she designed that bridge, and her vision for the whole community.'

'I do have a fertile imagination but it is not necessarily a dreamy thing.'

'I can pick up and hold a piece of wood and know how it will sound and its qualities of resonance, when I make a guitar out of it.'

'I do not remember things for very long. They merge into a "just below awareness" wholeness from which I cannot retrieve them easily.'

'I take in information, like an action, then another action comes up and I forget the first. Not necessarily because the first action was worse than the one I noted.'

'It's absolutely horrifying to realize what percentage of my life I spent trying to negate my own natural way of learning and be someone else. I tried to get as far as possible from the absorptive receptivity in the pursuit of the facts.'

'It's not that I don't like facts. I do, the more the merrier. I am a magpie for information, useful or otherwise.'

'If everything seems under control, you're just not going fast enough.'
MARIO ANDRETTI (SONAR)
b. 28 FEBRUARY 1940

'I've learned that people will forget what you said, people will forget what you did, but people will never forget how you made them feel.'
MAYA ANGELOU (SONAR)
b. 4 APRIL 1928

SONAR, THE INTUITIVE: STORIES AND STUDIES
Bill talks about training a dog for rescue work
'This cannot be a matter of formal, structured discipline, but more about bonding with your dog. You can do some approved practices for a while and then release the dog so that the real bonding work can begin. Five minutes later you might wonder, "Where is he? Oh, over there in the woods. Where will he show up next? There he is, over by that big rock." He knows where you are and you wait for him to reveal his position. You cannot teach this to people.

'Suggesting that teachers realize that we all think and learn differently is like asking people to undergo a paradigm shift.'

Liz modified her presentation to reach all her family members

Liz was developing a lovely gift for members of her extended family – each was to receive a copy of her book about their family history. When she learned that Sonar, The Intuitive, and two of the other learning styles cannot engage and will not read big blocks of text, she began to take more care about presenting her research. Liz really wanted the copies to be cherished and read. She abandoned the dense textbook style and opted for more levity, choosing a variety of formats which nicely present the information as photos and other visuals interspersed within the text.

Deb's advice to the parents of a four-year-old Sonar

'If you hear her through the "baby speaker" talking as if to other people, just let her be. It's normal for her. And when she does a drawing, she will want to include everyone in it and it will get very large, with a dog here and a big flower there, and people and snails, and . . . everything . . . all in one drawing.'

Dr Chris Lane's report on Sasha, an adolescent at the Special Education Unit

Observations: When I first met Sasha she was very withdrawn and isolated. Her voice was childish and immature, almost 'babyish' at times. She had been placed in a secure Special School environment due to unpredictable bouts of extreme violence. Her test results indicated a very low cognitive function. She reacted badly to the slightest touch, accidental or otherwise. Sasha had been both physically and sexually abused by members of her immediate family from the age of three years.

She would play appropriately with much younger children and seemed to be more settled and secure in their company.

Actions: I observed and worked with her for the first week and made no attempt to be 'the teacher'. By sitting quietly with her and making no demands she began to include me in whatever she was doing. She enjoyed looking at comics and books with bright and colourful pictures. She was a very poor reader and resisted my gentle prompting to read aloud to me.

In order to assess her reading level I brought a wide range of children's books into school the following week and piled them on the floor next to where she was sitting. The choices that she made were significant, mainly illustrated books for five to six year olds. She particularly liked pictures of animals and I decided to arrange a visit to a farm the next day.

While I was driving she became more animated telling me about a film she had seen about a horse, it turned out to be *Black Beauty*. While at the farm she wanted to be involved with feeding the sheep and cattle. She also helped muck out the barn, getting into quite a mess in the process. The journey back to school was wonderful, she never stopped talking about the day and her voice lost its 'babyish' edge.

The following day in class, she presented me with a bar of chocolate that she had bought with her pocket money. Even more of a breakthrough, she chose to sit next to me while I read an illustrated story to her. I then asked her to read the same story to me, which she did.

I made up a series of illustrated cards and another series with names. We spent much of the following two days putting the picture card with the corresponding name. I increased the number and range of cards as the time went on. Regular breaks were taken outside in order to find things that we had seen and named with the cards.

It was around this time that I had the chance to find a learning style Profile for Sasha in *Learning Without Tears*. It was not surprising to find that she was Sonar, The Intuitive, with an emphasis on mental sensitivity, a preference for illustrations and visuals and a fondness for animals.

Using the learning strategies in the book I was able to target my efforts effectively. Sasha became more settled and relaxed, the destructive outbursts virtually disappeared. On my accidentally touching her hand when moving a card on the desk, she did not react or even seem to notice. It was like watching a flower bud open: she was more confident every day, smiled often and took more care of herself. I even found her reading aloud to a younger child sat on her knee.

After only four weeks working with this girl, I decided to set her a test to show her reading age. We had regular breaks in order to help her stay focused and she spent these drawing and painting. The final test result showed a reading age of 13.4 years.

Sasha became an interesting and creative girl with a wide range of skills and interests. She obtained a part-time 'work experience' job at a local stable and turned into a happy, well-balanced young woman.

When the time came for her to leave the residential school, much to my surprise, she hugged me and thanked me for everything that I had done for her.

DR C. LANE

Asastasja unfolds her whole self

'As a child I had a reading age of eighteen at the age of seven, but was constantly criticized and punished for being dreamy, disorganized, not paying attention and being in my own world. Although I had a lot of exceptional creative and intellectual abilities, like many people, I repressed this side of myself as I was taught it had no value. If I struggled with anything I was penalized for pretending not to be able to do it, as it was assumed that with the capabilities I had, I should be able to tackle anything.

'I ended up leaving school very early with no qualifications and doing the only jobs I was able to get in a small town, which were usually customer service orientated such as bartending and shop work. All my jobs as a young adult involved using maths and memory, which meant that I began to utilize a type of left-brained intelligence that didn't really come naturally to me at all. Early experiences of continually being punished for my true nature meant I snapped into a different way of being in order to survive in the world, and most of my artistic abilities remained dormant since leaving school.

'I later went on to achieve great things academically in my late twenties and early thirties, attaining a first class degree and straight As in a variety of subjects. Nonetheless, I worried intensely about why it was that after studying for exams and retaining vast amounts of information, my mind seemed to erase almost every detail apart from a very general picture of the subject I'd studied. Having been able to sit in an examination room and remember names, dates, reference books and all kinds of minute details about complex academic theories, it terrified me that within days I would find that virtually all the information had gone . . . so much so that I was secretly concerned I had sustained some kind of brain damage through from partying in my younger days. I wondered what would happen, as I got older, and had awful visions of premature senility and being unable to manage my life.

'When I read my Profile in *Learning Without Tears*, and discovered that my learning style is Sonar, The Intuitive, it was probably the first time I have ever been able to view some of my weaknesses as strengths. At last I understood that far from being brain damaged, my mind simply doesn't hang on to any information it doesn't need, making it easy for me to continually learn and adapt to new ideas.

'One of my best personality traits is my ability to forgive and forget much more quickly, seemingly, than others around me, yet whenever anyone praised me for it I often felt like a bit of a fraud. After all, it has never been an effort for me to discard painful memories, especially of the small details of conversations and arguments that people around me would seem to hang onto for years. Instead I have usually retained only an overall picture of the events that happened and how they shaped my life and taught me lessons. Through reading about my learning style, I now understand that this is quite typical of my Profile and is one of the positive aspects of the way my mind works.

'In recent years I have had an awareness that I have, of necessity, abandoned much of my early, right-brain or intuitive thinking in favour of the more logical, list writing, methodical ways of being that have never come remotely naturally to me. Now that I am developing an understanding of the potential of my learning style, I feel excited about starting to step into my authentic self by pursuing my creative talents and redeveloping both sides of my brain.

'*Learning Without Tears* is the only book I have ever read that has helped me make sense of some of my challenges and limitations and realize they are not so unusual after all. Most importantly, I am now faced with the question of what I can do with my life now I understand that my learning style unlocks the door to so many unique gifts I have hidden from myself and the world.'

Janey on being Sonar in the real world.

'Most other people's minds seem focused and orderly, I envy their ability to take in and regurgitate the information while I'm still waiting for a "light" to come on. If I'm to get anything from a lesson, the best scenario is one in which I sit on the periphery and listen to the whole lecture/lesson without my thoughts being interrupted by someone needing to test me on what I've gleaned "so far".

'My husband can get quite cross when he wants an immediate answer to a "What do you think?" question, I really can take ages (sometimes days) to "think". Sometimes it's because there are several scenarios to take into consideration, they have to be played out and considered. Sometimes I don't know if I've got a "think" button, it's more of a "feel".

'I am very at home in the dark, I seem to know where things are and don't bump into things . . . using my "sonar"? Then someone comes in and puts on the light, why?

'And why was I always being put front and centre in class so I couldn't look out of the window?'

Ana had a Sonar business advisor

'Being Sponge, The Sensitive, it was always my aim to make people feel comfortable, so when our Sonar business advisor came for his monthly visit I would have prepared a summary of how I saw the issue that I wanted help with. This meant I recounted how I felt about it, naturally. I may have had some facts or figures to show for it, maybe not.

'After a while a pattern was established that, try as I might, I never second-guessed in advance. I would begin the story and not far in he would cut across me with what seemed to me an irrelevant question. A bit rattled I would answer as best I could but inevitably he would want to see numbers, the balance sheet, the profit and loss account, the monthly sales statistics, etc.

'So I would be digging about in the files for this and that, exasperated because I couldn't see where he was coming from, never mind going. He never noticed, just barked out requests for more, talking to himself as he surveyed spreadsheets, made calculations and generally ignored me. I gave up speaking and waited for him to arrive at wherever he was going.

'Surprisingly we always came to a solution that made sense to me, but to get there he needed the big picture, and an entirely different approach to mine. I had a lot of respect for him, in spite of the sometimes bumpy ride.'

Mary Rose trains her sales team in a most creative way

'I decided to hold DREAM days. I'd worked on the idea that, although some can be goal motivated, the rest of us are dream inspired! For us dreamers we need a little more space than the route map formula of goal setting. This is not implying wrong or right, just a different approach.

'So I chose environments in the UK that I hoped would help us dream. They were unusual and even I was surprised that some places let us meet there! I think they loved the idea of what I was trying to do and that their "establishments" were seen as dream places, they included:

- Blenheim Palace in Woodstock, Oxfordshire, for its splendour, history, awe, other-worldliness.
- Royal Shakespeare Theatre in Stratford Upon Avon for the drama, imagination, glamour.
- Glass Boat in Bristol for a sense of adventure, togetherness of crew, unlikely venue, humour.
- A riverside picnic for its "Englishness", ladylike, summer, bygone era.
- London for city life, business, change of pace, just getting there.

'The only thing that was thematic was that you had to wear something that made you feel fabulous. So we had people wearing a variety of clothes from ball gowns to pyjamas!

'As dreams are personal, therefore only you can deem when they become reality (whereas goals you can quantify and track and achieve, or not) the activities we did were hugely varied. The outcomes were intensely personal.'

Section 3

Learning Style Groupings: Similarities and Differences

Groupings that share common characteristics can be called families. Think of the bird family. They all have wings, feet, bills and eyes. Most of them can fly. Yet they have many differences as well. Some are very large like storks and ostriches. Others are tiny like wrens. Or consider the family group we call trees. Again they have much in common – roots, trunks, branches – yet they also have many differences – some have leaves while others have needles; some drop their leaves in winter, others hold them. There are enormous size differences among trees. Yet when we spot one, we know we are looking at a tree, not a bird. There's no doubt about it!

And, of course, there is the human family. Although we come in many colours, sizes and shapes, we instantly recognize each other as human. It is unlikely we would mistake a human for either a tree or a bird.

Similarly, people's natural mental qualities form groupings, or clusters, based upon shared features. Such common ground suggests a similarity of viewpoint and fosters ease of communication. For example, those with exactly the same learning style seem to be on the same wavelength. They communicate easily and effortlessly. One person's natural mode of speaking suits the other's natural mode of receiving information. The exchange is comfortable.

On the other extreme, we all know people whose minds are so different from ours that we just cannot figure out what makes them tick. They might as well be trees – or fish. Communication is neither easy nor satisfying. This can even occur within a close human family, where individuals are naturally highly motivated to communicate with each other. Sometimes people who love each other very much, and even with the very best intentions, find it quite impossible to talk to each other. And generally, to each person the other appears to be at the root of the problem.

Most relationships fall into a middle range between these extremes of simple understanding and acute awkwardness. We can usually find at least some areas of familiarity, foundations on which to connect enjoyably with each other. This chapter arranges different sorts of minds into clusters of compatibility, the potential cornerstones of harmony.

DIVISIONS AND FAMILIES

Let's start by looking at broad areas of similarity and difference among the 12 learning styles.

Twelve is a special number. It pops up everywhere – in music, literature, mythology, religion and even in the physical sciences. It is divisible by smaller numbers and an interesting mosaic emerges when we divide our 12 learning styles into two clusters of six styles, three clusters of four styles and four clusters of three styles. Each grouping refers to a different component of how we deal with information.

The Divisions listed in the table below relate to single steps along the path to learning – A. *Polarity*, B. *Relating* and C. *Uptake* of new information. The clusters or Families within the Divisions relate to stylistic similarities and differences.

A	Polarity: How we view information – is it about sharing it or having it?	Two families, each with six learning styles
B	Relating: How we welcome and form links to new information.	Three families, each with four learning styles
C	Uptake: Is it as easy as breathing or as deliberate as wading through molasses?	Four families, each with three learning styles

A. THE POLARITY DIVISION: HOW WE 'VIEW' THIS INFORMATION

This division comprises two family clusters, each containing six of the 12 learning styles. Here we have the classic yin/yang polarity difference expressed on the mental level: the outflow and the inflow; exhalation and inhalation; active and receptive.

These two clusters hold diametrically opposed views about the nature of information and how it should be treated. There is always tension between polar opposites. They stand at 180 degrees to each other. It can be a face off, a showdown. There is one side and there is the other. If we are not together, we are opponents. Understanding this division can easily resolve the deep conflict that often arises between people in opposite camps.

THE SHARERS: SCOUT, BUZZ, REX, PROCON, FLASH AND BOFFIN
The 'Information Is To Be Shared Immediately' Family

Believing that information is made to be shared, that's exactly what these minds do. As soon as they have some, they give it away. When they read it, hear it, see it on TV or think it up, Sharers tell it all. Their mental flow is upward and outward. Incoming ideas get down to about neck level before they are retold. Overhear a bit of conversation? Repeat it. See the morning's headline? Shout it from the rooftops.

This family of minds practises outgoing spontaneity by actively pursuing information. And they are self-expressive, pouring forth their mental energies unreservedly, either by direct action or by social or verbal expression.

Example: Others may call Sharers 'blabbermouths' and wonder why they have to tell everything. 'Why didn't my friend stop and think? That was confidential! He was not supposed to say anything to anyone, ever! I wouldn't have.'

THE CONTAINERS: STEADY, SPONGE, DETAILS, SHERLOCK, EXEC AND SONAR

The 'Information Is To Be Held And Cherished For A While' Family

Believing that information is made to be held and cherished for a while that's exactly what these minds do. As soon as they have some, they tuck it away in a safe recess and look after it. If they read it, hear it, see it on TV or think it up, Containers incorporate it. Their mental flow is downward and inward. Incoming ideas are incorporated deeply into the feelings or into the cells of the body itself and are expressed only at some appropriate time. Overhear a bit of conversation? Conceal it. See the morning's headline? Keep it to yourself for a while. Consider it. Decide what it means to you. Interact with it. Make it your own. Maybe talk about it sometime, maybe not.

This family of minds practises containment and timing. In their receptive mode, they attract information to themselves. They are self-expressive, communicating thoughts and ideas at the 'right time' after a period of containing their mental energies within.

Example: Others may call Containers 'withholding and secretive', and wonder why they remain silent. 'Why didn't my sister tell me about the surprise party? I could have worn my best jeans. Certainly it was not confidential! Why does she always make a secret of everything? I wouldn't have.'

B. THE RELATING DIVISION: HOW WE 'GREET AND LINK' TO NEW INFORMATION

This division comprises three family clusters, each containing four of the 12 learning styles. Here minds are grouped according to what they do when they see some new information coming around the corner or over the far horizon. Before even knowing what it is, a mind will naturally treat an idea like a long lost friend or an archenemy, with compassion, indifference or hostility. It may wear a smile or a smirk or carry a big stick. This is fundamental, even before learning or rejecting occurs, and reflects how the mind will act upon or link to the new information.

In the Relating Division, minds form families based partly on their degree of inquisitiveness – open and evident curiosity versus an apparent initial lack of interest. In what frame of mind do we approach new information: to challenge it, change it or reject it? Does it strongly favour generating its own ideas, and challenge any others; does it tend to modify or mutate the new; does it capture only carefully selected ideas? While one of these family clusters can become downright giddy with delight in the presence of new information, another might pull the covers up over its collective head or even build a stout stone wall to keep it at bay. Some minds enthusiastically charge at the new, while others retreat.

THE INITIATORS: SCOUT, SPONGE, PROCON AND EXEC
The 'Finished That, Let's Get On To The Next Topic' Family

Four of our 12 learning styles belong to the Initiator Family, one in three of us. This family shares the natural tendency to power forward mentally. As soon as one piece of new information has been taken in, or one new idea generated, these minds are driven to move on to another, and then to another. One topic of conversation stimulates the next. One mental activity leads on to more. Fuelled by its own mental process, the Initiator mind pushes forward relentlessly. 'Great!' It says, 'What's next?'

The common ground here is the forward motion. While some Initiators might resemble an unstoppable Roman phalanx, others move like an inchworm and still others flow gracefully like a river.

One of these four learning styles organizes as it goes; another burns its way across the mental terrain. Thought feeds the forward motion whether the mind creeps along cautiously, flows across the plane or makes progress by forming discrete packets of ideas.

These minds thrive on creating original material out of nothing. Initiators start fresh ideas, new lines of thought and novel ways of viewing things. They are motivated to initiate discussions and conversations. However, while some step forward into verbal exchange, others moderate the impulse to do so. They brainstorm, generating a stack of solutions to any problem, a pile of answers to any question. This phase comes naturally. But, then they lose interest and want to hand over for others to implement. Starting is their natural strength – not completing.

Does it sound like there may be some restlessness here? Initiators are not happy staying with a single mental task past its very personally defined end point. They run out of enthusiasm and become bored. You may experience your own or observe another's mind moving on from one activity to another, with evidence of several projects figuratively strewn across the desk. And if you are not the Initiator, you might tend to misunderstand the drive and focus instead on the clutter.

THE SUSTAINERS: STEADY, REX, SHERLOCK AND BOFFIN
The 'Once An Idea Is In There, Well, It's In There' Family

Four of our 12 learning styles belong to the Sustainer Family. These minds establish either very strong links to new information, or none at all, and taking it in is a matter of choice for them. At any age, Sustainers will decide which ideas are for them and which are not.

When a new idea appears over the horizon, a Sustainer-mind will distance itself. It will hesitate without making any move toward it and may even take a giant step backward. These minds protect themselves. To gain entry, new information has to prove itself and its validity by passing a qualifying test. The four learning styles that belong to this family are distinct in this regard, with four very different sets of criteria for validation.

And why is this so important? It is because ideas that are allowed access to the mind will still be in there years, decades, lifetimes from now. The nature of the relationship Sustainers make with information is a permanent one. Collectively these are the long-term memory people of the world. Like the proverbial elephant, they are very, very good at remembering – once they have taken something on board mentally. So, they stop, look and listen carefully before capturing a new idea, otherwise they could find themselves permanently committed to a mind full of drivel.

If an idea is important enough to learn, it is important enough to retain. Why change your mind after all that effort to ensure that an idea is worthy, appealing, powerful, or unusual enough to gain access to one's mind in the first place? If you have put a new thought through its paces and it has passed the qualifying test, why reject it just because time has passed? Thoughts are made to last. Otherwise, why give them houseroom?

Mentally, Sustainers have consistency, persistence and continuity. Their thinking is not influenced by passing fads or fashions, or by what others think. They don't change their minds for the sake of it. They hold fast to their own ideas and opinions. Sustainers know a lot about mental commitment. They don't give up.

For this reason, others may see these folks as resistant to change. Well, yes, but it's their job. It's their contribution to the rest of us. Where would we be if nobody sustained long-term thinking? Sustainers are proud of their staying power and are puzzled when others view them as fixed, stubborn or stuck in the mud. It does not feel that way from the inside. Holding an unpopular view is not new to them – they are like that even as small children. We have all heard the dialogue: Oh yes you will . . . Oh no I won't!

It is probably pretty clear what happens if new information does not pass a Sustainer's criteria for acceptance. But what happens during the time lapse before the ultimate decision has been made? And what happens to information that a Sustainer needs for a specific purpose but which fails the entry test? Or what about forgetting? Well, these are interesting situations. Don't be fooled, Sustainers can appear to have taken in information; they seem to be using it, as if they have accepted it. They can even convince others that this is so. But in truth they never did embrace the idea; they rejected it, but are using it temporally. Be suspicious whenever a Sustainer claims to have forgotten something. ('Oh, sorry, Dad, I forgot you said I should return your car by 9:30 p.m.) The idea never went in. These minds are like steel traps; once a piece of information has gained entry, it stays there.

Nobody will ever force a Sustainer Family member to learn something against his or her will, decision or desire – teachers, parents, caregivers, older siblings, team leaders, spouses or anyone else for that matter might as well save their breath. If a Sustainer mind is fixed against a thought (or even an entire body of knowledge) wild horses will not change it. This is not failure on the part of a teacher and should not be taken personally! Don't bother forcing the issue, it will not work.

THE ADAPTORS: BUZZ, DETAILS, FLASH AND SONAR
The 'What Else Is There To Learn?' Family

Four of the 12 learning styles belong to the Adaptor Family. These minds are forever curious, always interested in something new. They are receptive to fresh information, without hesitation, resistance or filtration. As Adaptor minds approach the new, they do so with their little arms flung wide open. They love it – they thrive on it.

But, once the latest mountain of data has been scooped up and taken in, these minds cannot just let it be. They set about moving the ingredients around, reconstituting, reforming, reconnecting bits to other seemingly disconnected bits. This is the process of mental synthesis – of creating something very new and quite different from the original raw materials by stirring and blending. These minds adapt and extend thought.

Adaptor Family minds retain thoughts and ideas, keeping them right on the front burner, only for the duration of a project or while the information is in active or ongoing use. When there is no immediate need to hold on to some information, and often even when there is, these minds jettison it – off into the ether. Thus cleansed, the Adaptor mind is ready for the next set of interesting facts, ideas, etc. Adult Adaptors are apt to cast away the name of the author whose book they finished reading just the previous day, or perhaps its title. They may easily drop information like your phone number or your birthday, or luncheon engagement, or where you were going to meet. They are frequently late for appointments because some other very interesting and mentally stimulating situation presented itself just as they were on the way out the door – like a phone call. And the young ones are just apprentice adult Adaptors.

It is for this reason that Adaptor Family members have earned such an unfortunate reputation for forgetfulness. These folks are not strong in the area of long-term memory. And, they take a lot of abuse about it from members of other family clusters.

They have different mental strengths. They are very good at short-term memory – some very short. They can be lively conversationalists, as they tend to know something about almost everything. Besides that, they can truly enjoy being told the same joke over and over again – as they will have forgotten the punchline in the meantime. Mentally life is always exciting and new. There is so much to learn, to read, to watch to talk about, to forget, to re-read, re-watch, repeat. There are so many mental ingredients to stir together and see what comes out.

SUMMARY: THE RELATING DIVISION
Each family cluster within the Relating Division has its mental strengths and its job to do on behalf of the larger community. We cannot get along without any one of these families; each one is necessary.

The Initiators' principle task is to instigate new ideas and lines of thought – they are good at it. There are no more original and creative 'brainstormers' anywhere. On the downside, they are not good at completing. They get bored and quite naturally move on to greener mental pastures.

The Sustainers' main strengths are tenacity, persistence and perseverance. Unflappable, they preserve and contain thought over the long term on behalf of those who are mentally free to dash off to the new and different. On the downside, members of other family clusters find these folks to be stuck in the mud mentally, stubborn, inflexible, and downright resistant to new ideas. They simply will not be pushed, cajoled or coerced.

The Adaptors quite naturally and by example, inform the other families when it's time to change and move on to other possibilities. Their strength is in coping with large amounts of information over short periods of time. But, they can appear unstable or diffused to the others, as if the slightest breeze could alter their thinking.

C. THE UPTAKE DIVISION: HOW WE TAKE IN INFORMATION

This division comprises four family clusters, each containing three of the 12 learning styles. It groups minds according to the actual mode of information uptake.

Regardless of our particular mental antics when presented with new information, there is a point at which we actually do learn something new. Information, ideas, data that we didn't possess a moment ago, becomes 'ours' the next. We have taken it in, taken it on board. Learning, however, is private business; the inner activity of that moment does not show on the surface. It occurs in our deepest recesses.

Of course some people will express a visible outer response to a moment of learning – a wry smile, an uplifted eyebrow, a wahoop. It may reflect the learning moment, but it is not the learning. The 'ah-ha' moment ('Eureka! I've got it!') itself is not visible. For this reason it's open to all sorts of personal projection and interpretation. For example, this is what makes it easy to assume that learning is the same for all of us. Just because you cannot see the process happening, don't be fooled into thinking that the complex inner dynamic in your head is the same as in everyone else's head. It is not. Our modes of taking in new information are just as person-specific as our styles of approaching it, as discussed in the Relating Division above. We do this differently. It's natural!

Four primarily distinct ways of taking in new information can be grouped into family clusters. Each is comprised of three different learning styles, so cluster members bear a resemblance to each other but are not identical. Their common ground ends with the mode of information uptake. Otherwise they go their own separate ways, mentally.

A vivid naming system for these four families parallels the four 'elements' of nature: Fire, Air, Water and Earth. The Family Portraits below cover the following points:

* What the family mind needs to do to or with information in order to 'have it'.
* How deeply a mind needs to integrate information in order to 'have it'.
* What 'having it' means.
* How long this might take – the speed of uptake demystified.

FIRE FAMILY: SCOUT, REX AND FLASH

These are the liveliest of minds! They can be extremely fast moving because they need to interact so minimally with new information in order to take it in. This family breathes in information without needing to alter it in any way. No processing is necessary, no analysis, no filtering, no grounding, no repetition, no conceptualization, no mind maps, no drawings. Nothing. They look, they breathe, they have it – all in a flash! Ideas are inhaled; they are inspired, not in small pieces but fully developed. Learning occurs on the level of intuitive perception, a knowing beyond logic.

Fire minds can burn with enthusiasm – sometimes with the rapid flare of a shooting star, igniting suddenly and extinguishing quickly, and sometimes with the thermonuclear persistence of the sun. Fire Family minds identify strongly with their own thoughts and beliefs. These are positive, optimistic, active learners, who are sparked by ideas.

When speaking their minds, which they do, Fire Family members can really light up a conversation or nicely warm up a room full of people. But they can also scorch others like a raging forest fire. Their verbal delivery can be full of vitality, charged with energy and larger than life itself. With even a single Fire mind in your household, classroom or office, you are likely to have your fill of boasting, arguing, shouting or competing.

Fire minds do not place excessive demands upon a learning environment, as long as it's at least as large as the great outdoors and is not restraining. What is critically important is movement. When the body is in gear and moving, the mind can too. Fire Family members might take in new information most easily while out for a walk, riding a pedal or exercise bike, acting out the information, swimming or running. Adult Fire Family members, who need clear thinking and an active brain, have been known to go for a drive, have a quick stroll to the water cooler or take a laptop along on a train trip. Almost any kind of movement serves to quick start mental activity. Conversely, the Fire mind seems to close down when the body is stationary. Your insistence that a Fire schoolchild sits down and looks tidy may soothe your nerves but will disadvantage the child's learning ability.

This presents an obvious dilemma in the classroom, the living room, the office and so on, where different, and sometimes conflicting, learning requirements must coexist. That quandary does not alter the Fire minds' learning needs.

AIR FAMILY: BUZZ, PROCON AND BOFFIN

In order to take up new information and make it their own, members of this family need to do a little bit more than the Fire Family, but not much more. Rather than just inhaling it, these minds have to grasp the idea behind the new material. They need to give it a structure and shape it into a concept. No concept, no learning. They will not be able to take in what does not make sense – to them. For some Air Family members, new material has to fit with their currently held ideas, for example their concepts of what's interesting, of what's fair, or of what benefits society or humanity.

An Air Family mind is a logical, rational thinker who can treat thoughts and ideas as though they were tangible. Either within themselves or with each other, Air Family members play badminton with ideas. They can rapidly build and dismantle conceptual structures. They like to talk things over, within their own heads, with a computer or with other people. Some talk out loud to themselves, considering it among the best of possible conversations. Some talk to pets, plants or road signs. They love words, especially newly invented conceptual words. It would have been Air Family adults who created 'downsizing', 'skill set', and 'disbenefit'. Air minds deal and trade in concepts.

Their decisions, as well as their presentations, are based on logic and reason. Forget about an emotional appeal, the Air Family prefers intellectual detachment. An idea is a 'good' idea if it's new and makes sense conceptually, and they will only consider taking up 'good' ideas. They have a lot to go at.

The Air Family can learn readily from the written and spoken word. They easily take in information from books, lectures and conversations, without needing to process it any further. Don't be fooled into thinking that all minds learn effectively in this way, despite the fact that this belief forms the basis of much modern educational theory. It's really just the Air Family, one in four of us, that learns effortlessly from the chalk and talk teaching method. Members of the Air Family perpetuate this idea throughout the teaching profession, which they heavily populate.

THE WATER FAMILY: SPONGE, SHERLOCK AND SONAR

Following along, in order to learn something new, members of the Water Family have to draw information even more deeply into themselves than either Fire or Air Family members. Water minds absorb information from their surroundings – just as sponges take up fluid – and then filter it through their feelings. Envision a clam at ease on the ocean floor, unconcerned, shell open, ocean water flowing in, ocean water flowing out, freely absorbing what it will from the current. Information swims or glides into the Water mind, gaining access through the emotions, the intuition or the instincts. And what's taken in produces a personal emotional response, which is intertwined with learning, even if the information is purely factual.

They rely upon the link between mind and feelings not only to learn but also to evaluate the merit of ideas and to make decisions

– a good idea is one that feels right. Unlike other kinds of minds the newness, logic or practicality of an idea just does not matter.

Water Family minds are highly visual by nature and pictures, colour, diagrams, graphics and DVDs all facilitate learning. In fact they learn only through visual imagery. When presented with bare words or dry concepts, their learning process requires an additional step of translation. They have to give shape to the images behind the words, and then take in the impressions they have created. A Water Family trait is rich, active imaginations.

The optimal learning environment for the Water Family is one that feels safe. In fact these minds close down in a threatening environment just as quickly as Fire minds do when told to sit down and be still. Words are like little brush strokes and Water minds can sense the whole picture from surprisingly few lines. This is sensitive business, however, and if this mind is upset, for example by fear, loud noise, bullying, aggression, or challenge, those big emotional responses overpower the subtle vibration associated with the new information and learning does not happen. Learning is based on a delicate feeling response to new information; emotional sensitivity is the key. A learning or working environment that conveys emotional safety and security is essential to these minds, at whatever age and in whatever circumstance.

The three learning styles comprising the Water Family experience unique but collective issues in the classroom. Their learning requirements are usually not recognized or catered for in the traditional educational setting. Consequently, a high percentage of young people who leave school feeling very badly about both their educational experience and themselves, are members of this family.

THE EARTH FAMILY: STEADY, DETAILS AND EXEC

Members of the Earth Family need to do still more to make new information their own. They must integrate it right to the body's physical cellular level. These are hands-on learners who have to get involved with information to really take it in. They need to try it out for themselves – do it, taste it, touch it, practise it, dramatize it, organize it, analyse it, structure it, digest it, or dig it into the earth and let it compost. To the Earth Family an idea is a good idea if it is practical and can be applied to real life. Otherwise, why bother? Earth minds evaluate an idea's merit by its usefulness. They opt for workable techniques, bringing an idea down and containing it, giving it form, structure and a home in the world of firm practicality. Earth minds tend to value the natural world and its dynamics (rules) for providing a reliable standard.

Earth Family members find learning easier when new ideas are presented as hands-on experiences in tangible situations. They develop mental skills through analysis, practice and application. For example their minds can best embrace mathematical fractions in relation to real-life situations – like measuring cups and recipes, steel tapes and nail sizes.

These grounded, responsible thinkers may be unimpressed by abstraction, daydreaming or flights of fancy, preferring a solid surface of fact. Their thinking is rooted, deep-seated, solid, real, sound, sensible, tangible, reasonable and pragmatic.

The Earth Family's learning dynamic often requires real time and cannot be pushed. Remember that new ideas are being integrated at a cellular level. These minds are most comfortable when allowed to process information in their own time. Asking them to hurry up and learn (or turn in the report, or provide feedback, or answer the question) is like asking your intestines to hurry up and digest lunch. Learning will happen in its own time and not a moment before.

Earth minds will not often leap to conclusions or voice instant opinions like those of the Fire or the Air Family. Uncomfortable with off the cuff replies, they really do prefer to give a considered response, in order to get it right. For example, if they submit to your pressure and come up with the goods to please you, chances are they will suffer the next day. The response was offered too soon, it was half-baked, hasty, only partially analysed, not suitably structured. It was imperfect or incorrect, not the right final product. They don't feel good about themselves, and you don't have what you wanted either.

In a learning situation, Earth Family students are responsible and mentally well behaved. (Please do not confuse behaviour with mental work.) They may require more time than others, as it often takes longer to ground an idea into the body than to fit it into a concept. They would benefit from having more time for assignments – to consider, to assess, to digest, to revise, to repeat, to recopy notes, etc. In the workplace, as teachers, accountants, writers, tradespeople, doctors, business owners, gardeners, and so on, they strive toward perfection on the mental level; things have to be right, no matter how long it might take to get there.

Section 4

Getting Along with Each Other

We have looked at the 12 individual learning styles proposed by the Mercury Model in some depth, our different mental strengths and learning requirements, our different modes of taking in, considering and expressing information and ideas. Can we agree that people are wired differently and that these differences are natural? Can we let go of the thought that 'a mind is a mind and they are all pretty much the same'? Are we willing to acknowledge that fish are valuable contributors to our life on earth, despite the fact that they can't climb trees, no matter how much we might want them to do so?

If so, then we stand on the threshold of a most amazing journey, the adventure of meeting other people as they are, without expecting their minds to function like ours, but discovering the truth of their authentic mental make-up. And letting it be. This can lift inter-personal relationships to an entirely new level, to say nothing of self-awareness, self-acceptance and personal development. The point is that each of the 12 learning styles has its own strengths and blind spots, each is valuable, one is not better or worse than another, and it takes all of us to make the great earth spin in balance.

Tension inevitably arises at the interface between different learning modes and some combinations are more uncomfortable than others. This is true, even for people who love each other very much and who are highly motivated toward communicating clearly. It's true for teachers whose top priority is to educate their students. It's true for business teams with professional commitments to the success of a new product launch. However, the greater the dissimilarity in our master operating programmes, the greater the discomfort that can arise between us, but also the greater our opportunity for highly creative resolution of the tension.

We have looked at the Learning Style Groupings, which identify common ground among the 12 primary mental dynamics. These can guide us in understanding the kind of strain we may be experiencing with another person and pinpoint where we can apply understanding and effort toward resolving the issue.

Two people who share the same learning style may not be identical, but they do not struggle to understand each other. Each person's natural mode of conveying information is compatible with the other's natural way of taking it in. No stress.

A story from the Mercury Model files: Judy, the mother, and Jenny, her younger daughter, have exactly the same learning style, Buzz, The Curious. Their mental compatibility is nothing short of remarkable. Both read books, newspapers and magazines. Both attend courses, play bridge and watch TV. Chatting and laughing, they compare notes with each other several times a day, in person, by phone and email. They are more like twins than mother and daughter. Buzz, The Curious stands as a filter to both incoming and outgoing information, and the two women have the same filter. This is 'extreme similarity', as you'll see when you read the rest of the story.

We do not encounter 'extreme similarity' too often and all other combinations of learning styles can produce varying levels of unease. The question is what to do about it? The answer depends on who it is. If you experience antipathy with someone you meet casually, fine, you are free to walk away. But, in many of your relationships, you are not, and resolving the situation creatively is essential. Differences between the speaker's mouth and the listener's ears can produce tension with your children, your spouse, your parents, your business partners, bosses, employees, colleagues and friends. It can happen between teachers and students, professionals and their clients, community members and social connections.

> **Returning to our story**: As Sherlock, The Detective, Judy's
> elder daughter, Veronica, is positioned in 'extreme difference'
> to her mother and sister. Not only did she feel very left out in
> childhood, but also she couldn't fathom how her sister could
> talk to their mother, or why she would ever want to. Even the
> word 'talk' had completely different meanings to them – to
> Buzz ideas were light, logical and fun, easy come easy go, while
> to Sherlock ideas were powerful and intense, captured for the
> long term.

A creative resolution might be intuitively obvious as soon as you read the Profiles of the people involved, or you could require a strategy to apply the Mercury Model in a situation of tension. Here is a four-step process that might help. Of course you will approach this exercise according to the parameters of your own learning style. Scout, The Trailblazer, will run at it, expecting one attempt to solve the issue, while Exec, The Achiever, may need, or expect to need, a number of repetitions to perfect the practise.

1 Recognize, refocus and reframe your understanding of the situation. STOP and realize that the tension you are feeling may have arisen naturally, at the juncture of two or more different learning styles. That's all. Nobody is being intentionally 'done to'.

2 Allow, accept and acknowledge the other's master operating programme. You may be sitting comfortably in the upper branches, after an easy climb, while the other may be a fish and can't climb that tree or any other tree.

3 Discuss the situation – without judgement, condemnation or envy. Ask how the other likes to have information presented: verbally, visually, in writing, while out for a walk or over a meal? Don't just give up. Each of us has valuable mental strengths; you may benefit from what the other has to offer and vice versa.

4 Adapt to the other's learning requirements. With the other's learning style Profile in mind, look through his or her eyes and try to convey your message over again, but in a different and more suitable way. Ask for feedback and try again.

Back to Judy and her two daughters: This story has a happy ending but only because the sisters embraced the Mercury Model's principles and put them to work. Veronica offered her insightful Sherlock determination and used it to uncover solutions. Jenny contributed her mental levity, agility and adaptability. They achieved a profound understanding of the depth of difference between their natural mental styles, worked patiently together and came to genuinely enjoy each other's company. Well done!

USING THE MERCURY MODEL IN YOUR PERSONAL LIFE

Here are some of the situations we have seen – the funny, the touching, the traumatic, the total misses, the happy ending:

THE POLARITY DIVISION: SHARERS AND CONTAINERS

Half of us are Sharers; half are Containers. As common as this division
is, it accounts for enormous stress, huge misunderstandings and
colossal hurt feelings. All of this discomfort can melt away if we but
remember that Sharers share information and Containers contain it.
This is within our nature; nobody is 'doing' anything to anybody.

Trish is no longer pained by the difference

'When I finish my phone conversation with my mother or anyone
else, I tell my husband who it was I was talking to and what we talked
about. But, when he finishes a phone conversation, he just puts the
phone down. He doesn't tell me anything. It drives me mad! All that
good information going to waste. The Mercury Model says I am a
Sharer and my husband and I have talked about this. He has not
changed. I still notice what he does. I still think it's odd. But now,
rather than making a scene and tearing my hair out, I chuckle about
the natural differences between Sharers and Containers.'

Ruth's family lunch was a success.

'I used the Mercury Model at a big family Easter gathering – table
decorated, three courses planned and prepared to perfection, 12
people sat around the table, and the meal begins in total silence . . .
it's only me that feels the need to talk, a quick recollection of the
people all eating in silence and I remember I am the only Sharer at the
table, the 11 others are Containers . . . so I smile to myself and let them
enjoy their meal, the way they like . . . slowly the conversation starts,
but this time not by me and I get to enjoy my meal too . . . the Mercury
Model can even help prevent indigestion.'

A narrowly averted calamity

The wedding was nearly derailed by a difference in learning styles.
Tracy is a Sherlock and, true to form, has always engaged in personal

communication on a 'need to know' basis. Taking the Container Family characteristics to an all new level, she didn't think her intended needed to be troubled with the little details of her daily life – who she had met for lunch, if she would be home for supper that evening, that a new window washer would be coming around, that the joint account was now with a different bank, etc. Brian is ProCon who loved sharing and discussing all sorts of information, especially with his fiancé. To him this was as natural and normal as breathing. His questions about everyday life topics, like 'How was your day, dear?', were experienced as interrogation by Tracy. No kidding! Brian read her innate privacy as secrecy. He thought she must be having an affair. Why else would she be so withholding? Their life together was not off to a good start. When she discovered the truth, she was amused. Years later, he still does not see the funny side.

THE RELATING AND UPTAKE DIVISIONS

Personal interactions between Sharers and Containers can be difficult, but when the other two Divisions are added to the mix, when people also connect with information differently and/or take it in differently, the complexity is magnified. Getting along with each other can become more challenging or more fun, depending….

Flash and Details: Two Adaptors but from different Uptake Divisions – one Fire, one Earth

'Good friends and both Americans visiting London, we walked for hours, free style, sightseeing, without any time pressures at all. But then, it was suddenly late and we needed to find the theatre – fast. Neither of us knew the city. We paused at a street corner, undecided as to which way to go. Details, The Analyst, unfolded the map and tried to figure out where we were. The next step, of course, would have been to find the theatre's location and plot a sensible course. Realizing her friend was not actually looking at the map over her shoulder, Details looked up to see Flash, The Pioneer, already halfway down the next block and moving fast. Two very different learning styles, two entirely different ways of problem solving in a new situation, we both knew it instantly. We laughed and laughed and laughed, knowing it could have ended in tears.'

Sherlock and Exec: Two Containers, one Sustainer/Water and one Initiator/Earth – a grandfather's perspective

'These two boys – Jason (age 10, Sherlock, The Detective) and Athan (age 12, Exec, The Achiever) – like each other, play together, and have many friends in the neighbourhood. Both are excelling in their new (American) schools – but with quite different learning styles. Jason soaks up everything, seems to understand it, and resolves all the homework assignments almost before he gets home from school. But Athan works well into the night on his assignments – not because he doesn't understand the material, but because he is a perfectionist. Everything must be right – all commas, apostrophes and periods in the right places. You might think he is struggling with English, since his first language is Greek, but I understand he was the same way in Greece. He is the same with physical objects: he will study instructions carefully and slowly assemble a model. Jason will go by trial and error to get the assembly done as quickly as possible – then get on to something else. By the way Athan's birthday is 7 December, Jason's 6 December – different years.'

No common ground at all – one Container/Sustainer/Water and one Sharer/Adaptor/Air

'The Mercury Model was the primary tool which allowed our partnership and therefore our business to flourish, and for us to grow personally. But really, it moved us through and beyond the decades of living with the vague discomfort of being sisters with "extreme differences".

'Using the Mercury Model allowed us to know each other so well that we could actually meet on the middle ground, with mutual respect for each other's mental dynamics, without the former fear, without the earlier criticism, either veiled or overt. For the first time ever, we both experienced the power and the strength of equal partnership. The baggage we carried into our business, from decades of being uncomfortable sisters, slowly melted away. We began to see and respect each other's genuine needs, intentions and ambitions, personally and professionally. We learned to provide each other with full support and total encouragement. The Mercury Model basically transformed my life.'

USING THE MERCURY MODEL IN GROUPS AND BUSINESS TEAMS

Beyond several one-to-one relationships, groups have lives of their own, a composite of the members' assets – intellectual, emotional, financial, etc. Boards of directors, business teams, committees and organizations of all kinds can benefit tremendously by paying attention to the blending and balance of their individual mental dynamics.

We repeatedly observe that people are recruited onto teams and into small businesses based upon common ground in thinking. This is unintentional. Those with similar or identical learning styles get along more easily, communicate without difficulty and see things along similar lines. All the ducks may be in a row, but unfortunately they are all looking in exactly the same direction and a fox coming around the corner can be completely missed – until it's too late. A broad spectrum of intellectual resources covers all the bases, but produces a group that needs to deal creatively with the tensions resulting from difference.

Let's look at a few examples of business teams from the Mercury Model files, enlisting the broad-brush stroke of the divisions and family clusters detailed in the previous section.

The divisions describe specific facets of how we handle information, each referring to a step along the path to learning and communicating. Every family within each of the three divisions makes a unique contribution to a business or group.

THE RELATING DIVISION

A balanced team or business would have members from each of the three families of the Relating Division: Initiators, Sustainers and Adaptors. In that way the overall group would have the intellectual resources necessary to begin new projects, to sustain ongoing successful activities and to notice the need for and make required adjustments.

THE INITIATOR FAMILY

This family takes the lead, starts things and moves them forward with originality. If a group has too many Initiators, forward movement would dominate the culture, new products or projects being presented far too often, new business expansion, new buildings, nothing would be fully or even appropriately developed. And, if too few, the business would lack ideas for moving forward; it wouldn't start anything at all.

Two Initiators (Sponge and Exec) with different modes of uptake – one Water and one Earth

'In our family business my brother, Exec, The Achiever, was Managing Director and I was Sponge, The Sensitive. The difference between our two styles was considerable and it took years to iron out a way of working together without conflict. But good things for the business emerged and it transpired that between us we were two halves that made the whole thing work.

'I joined in the days when the workforce did as they were told, and there was quite a divide between them and management. My brother proposed changes to the shift patterns for production, to increase output. My reaction was "the men aren't going to like it". This caused him much irritation, but eventually we agreed on asking the workforce themselves to come up with a more productive shift system they would be prepared to work, and they did. As a result of saying – "but how are they going to feel?" – I was given responsibility for HR, which suited me well.

'I was also responsible for marketing and worked closely with a graphic design company to produce all our literature – a job I loved. Between us, we came up with the concept and then had to present to my brother, which was tough. He wanted to take what were still feelings and ideas about a new theme for a brochure and question them until it felt like there wasn't an ounce of imagination left, then lay the whole thing out in neat, numbered squares that he could approve. The ideas felt crushed. I just got used to it.

'But there were times when the heat of the moment meant I lost my head and overreacted, and in contrast he stood back, took in the situation and imposed pragmatic good sense and a steady, guiding hand. He was a good Managing Director and commanded much respect.'

THE SUSTAINER FAMILY

This family has genuine staying power; it keeps on keeping on. In excess no team member would consider a new view, a new product, a new way of manufacturing, advertising, or recruiting. They would want to carry on along the same lines as always, with no website, no social media, no telephone. But without Sustainers a business would lack commitment, continuity or a steadfast mission or purpose.

All Sustainers

Four people comprised the senior management team of a quango that awarded, distributed and administered business start-up and business development grants. The chief executive officer, the operations manager, the treasurer, and the HR director were all members of the Sustainer Family. Whatever went wrong, it was the other person's fault, never one's own.

Despite a buoyant customer-facing, out-of-office workforce, there was not much movement at the top. Both the atmosphere in the working space, and the office staff itself, started to contract and close down, becoming increasingly stagnant and toxic. A great deal of unexplained sickness developed. It was not a happy place to work.

THE ADAPTOR FAMILY
This family makes modifications and moves forward. It has levity, flexibility and embraces change. In excess, change for its own sake would be emphasized. Frivolity could overtake levity; diffusion could replace flexibility. Business decisions might be childish or based on deception and confusion. If lacking, ideas would not be available for modifying things that were almost but not quite right. Instead, the baby might be thrown out with the bathwater and everything would have to start again from scratch. Inability to improve on systems, designs, processes, training, etc.

Only one Adaptor – in a sea of Sustainers

Amy was the only Adaptor on the very high-level product development team at a prestigious British bank. All the other team members were Sustainers. She felt uncomfortably like a lightweight among appropriately serious long-term thinkers. Comfortable with each other's familiar ways of viewing banking, her colleagues reinforced her observation. As her ideas for entirely new styles of financial products and services were dismissed as frivolous, she began to believe she was in the wrong job, and looked elsewhere for fulfilling employment. As it turns out, that bank desperately needed the fresh new approach she could have introduced, and began to lag behind the competition's innovative products.

THE POLARITY DIVISION

A well-constituted group, team or business would have balance between the two families in this division – the Sharers and the Containers. This is about revealing or concealing information both within a company and between the company and the public. For example, if you are at the helm of the Secret Service you might want to consciously recruit from the Container Family, but not if you run a magazine.

THE UPTAKE DIVISION

This includes four family groupings based on how information is processed while being learned – from the ultra-rapid inhalation-uptake of the Fire Family and the conceptualizing Air Family to the emotional-filtration of the Water Family and the physically integrating Earth Family.

To simplify, these two divisions will be combined in the following way: the Sharers group is made up of Fire and Air minds while the Containers are the Water and the Earth.

A team or group can be unbalanced by either too many or too few minds from an element cluster. We can observe dramatic examples of this sort of thing in the natural world, and can learn from our observations and apply them to personal and professional life. Regions of the earth easily become element unbalanced, when fire, air, water or earth are in the wrong proportions or in the wrong places. Examples of excess element activity might be forest fires, gales, tidal waves, or earthquakes, while examples of lack are deep freezes, stagnant smog, barren desert or quicksand. A well-balanced Earth has the right mixture of fire, air, water and earth; a well-balanced team does too.

Let's look at the extremes of too much and too little and what to watch out for in a team or group.

THE SHARERS POLARITY COMPRISE FIRE AND AIR UPTAKE MINDS
Excess Fire is a high-spirited, super-exciting team with lots of diverse impulses, can feel like a forest fire to the public, highly combustible, leading possibly to early burn-out.

Just one may be enough
In a team of 25 people the only Fire mind is the boss – which in this case is actually more than enough. The team runs around after her, putting out fires and settling customers' nerves.

Too many Fire minds
The team ran an ice cream parlour/café – two of the ten were working owners. Forward-looking and interested in innovative team activities, they arranged for Mercury Model Training. What an awakening!
Both owners plus six staff members were Fire Family minds, all eight Sharers. For sure the café was an exciting spot, lively, energetic, bright and bubbly. Constant motion. There were only two Containers in the group: the only male in the team, the cook, Sponge, The Sensitive (Initiator, Water), the nurturer, who was possibly forgiven for wanting to keep changing the menu, and the other, a Details, The Analyst (Adaptor, Earth). Well, talk about a scapegoat. The only practical thinker on the team, down to earth – concerned about adequate supplies and clean floors. Slow moving, perfectionist Details, holding the earth plane for the others to flash across at great speed, was just about to lose her job. Viewing her as too slow and 'not up to it', the fast ones totally missed the value of her grounded contribution. 'Boring, she never says anything.'

Insufficient Fire is a flat organisation; lacking passion, spirit, enthusiasm, get up and go; risk averse and probably boring.

Excess Air is exemplified by lots of people in the office writing glossy brochures but nobody out in the field. This group is seen as mentally dispassionate, distant and cold. Plenty of words, ideas and conceptual fluff.

Insufficient Air in a business results in little or no impulse to move ideas around, or to tell the world what the business does. No impulse to write newsletters, advertising, handbooks, stories, articles. At a deeper level, there is no unifying concept or principle.

THE CONTAINERS POLARITY ARE WATER AND EARTH
Again, be mindful of the extremes.

Excess Water is very focused on customer service, however, the customers' needs can overpower all other facets of the business. Too supportive emotionally, too many snack breaks, holidays, leaves. Very soft.

Insufficient Water can be uncaring to staff and customers, unconcerned about the human factor. No warmth, not a welcoming environment.

Cool and professional but lacking warmth
We know a hotel without a receptionist. Nobody greets arriving guests or shows them to rooms. And the chill extends from there.

Excess Earth can take an overly practical and possibly picky attitude. May be focused on financial issues to the exclusion of other important features of the business. Customers feel disapproved of. Slow to respond to enquiries or return messages. Overly formal.

Earth x 4
The team was four people, four Earth Family minds (two Details and

two Steadys) which came together on a sizeable project to renovate a stately home and transform it into a conference centre. Unfortunately this team lacked Fire (passion and enthusiasm), Air (conceptualizing, getting the sense of the project, talking it up in the right places), Water (the human factor, knowing how people would respond, looking after people) and Initiators (the starter motors). They were very strong on beauty and design, persistence, good food and wine, delicious lunches, lovely fabrics, subtle colour schemes, beautiful gardens, and for a while, the money. The owner recruited the team; they saw eye to eye, in pleasant accord and without conflict. But also without sparkle and initiative. Very practical people, they made decisions to take the cautious route, paying well over-the-top fees to make sure every facet of the construction project was well accounted. It was one of the most exciting projects ever to fail.

Too much Earth

A new member of a company's IT team was referred to Norma, in her capacity as Occupational Health nurse. She meets with individuals and teams struggling with work-related health problems – often it's stress, as it was with the new team member. She uses the Mercury Model as a tool to assess a team's mental profile and obtain information about what is really going on under the surface.

In this case Norma was stunned to discover that without exception, they all had Earth Family minds. This was one practical team. Not a shooting star or a bright spark among them. No leading-edge compassion, no fancy rhetoric, not even much impulse to share ideas. There were lots of elbows on the table with everyone waiting for someone else to enliven them. This was a team going nowhere. The members did not gel as a group. But the new man was supposed to fill in all the missing pieces. Of course, he could not. Although he very much wanted to do a good job, he was Earth as well. He decided to leave the company and is much happier in his new position.

Insufficient Earth lacks grounding and stability. New ideas and directions may be quite impractical, too costly, poor value and not worthwhile. Little attention to timeframes.

In summary, a great team has members who can initiate, sustain and adapt and the generosity of spirit to admire their colleagues' special mental skills. It has members whose minds are vibrant (Fire), logical (Air), compassionate (Water) and practical (Earth). In short, a great team is balanced in all three Divisions – Polarity, Relating and Uptake.

Section 5

More Layers of Subtlety . . .

**As you have seen, the Mercury Model introduces and describes
12 fundamentally different ways of handling information; our
minds resonate with one of these vibrations and reflect one of
the 12 archetypal images. As useful and helpful as this information
may be, it does not tell the entire story and the Mercury Model
does not stop there.**

Our minds are more individual than that. The whole of humanity
does not fit into tidy classifications; we chafe against the idea that we
should do so. The first part of this book represents the Mercury Model
in a simplified form. It is a first approximation of our unique 'master
operating programmes'.

So, for the sake of completeness, for those readers who abhor
being 'pigeonholed' into one of 12 categories, for those who are
students of astrology, and for those who do not relate 100 per cent
to their Profile, let's look more deeply.

SUBTONES AND INDIVIDUAL MENTAL UNIQUENESS

Two minds that share the same primary tone learning style do pulse
at the same frequency, but they are probably not exactly the same. It
is unusual, in fact a special case, for a mind to express as an absolutely
pure example of one of the 12 learning styles. Usually people have
additional mental influences, termed 'subtones', which contribute
subtlety to the mind's overall make-up. The Mercury Model goes on
to identify these additional ingredients and their precise blend.

The scope for individual mental uniqueness is immense. A mind
can be like

- a clear solo note
- a simple musical chord involving one or two subtones combining with the primary tone
- a complex chord comprised of any combination of up to nine possible subtones

A larger number of subtones is neither better nor worse. It is the absence or presence of subtones and in specific combinations that relate to our mental uniqueness. A subtone makes its particular nature available to the overall mental make-up. For example, a subtone can supply Sustainer-style traits of persistence or stubbornness to a basically Adaptor mind, or an Earth-style practicality to an Air Family member. Subtone activity can falsely suggest that a particular mind belongs to more than one family within a division, even though it does not. But, these additional factors can contribute not only proficiencies and virtues, but blind spots and shortcomings as well.

Like a primary tone learning style, each subtone is inherently neutral, being neither good nor bad. But any of them can at certain times behave very well or badly misbehave. Some subtones harmonize nicely with a primary tone learning style, supporting it with a similar viewpoint or mode. They naturally get along well together, figuratively producing a pleasant sounding chord. But other subtones may be very, very different from each other or from a primary learning style, presenting a relationship dynamic inside one's head just as challenging as those sometimes encountered with other people. They spar with each other and vie for supremacy of worldview or style. There can be an inner struggle, even if both are on their best behaviour.

This is critical to note: the primary tone – the basic learning style as it has been described in this book – runs the show; it's the boss. Subtones are employees. They stand in the same relationship as a team does to the team leader, an orchestra to its conductor, an athletic team to its coach, soldiers to their commanding officer, and a crew to their captain. In each case the main man always has the final word.

Despite the fierceness of a subtone's possible insistence about taking in some specific new information, the primary tone makes the final decision. It has veto power and ultimately plays the hand. However, an entirely rejected subtone has an odd way of stopping us in our tracks, shutting down the system with a mutiny, paralysing the primary tone in a bid for recognition.

The dance between primary tone and subtones is an art form of personal development in which we can grow in conscious awareness of our own 'raw materials' and develop our potential into a fully functional authentic whole as you'll see from the following examples.

How a primary tone and a subtone work together

A Sonar, The Intuitive will approach new ideas with relish, gleefully swimming around in the big pool of all information, absorbing freely of its bounty. If this mind also has a Sustainer subtone (Rex), it could have an uncharacteristic but excellent long-term memory for some items – those that have contributed to shaping its personal identity. But, most things will sink below the surface of specificity sooner or later and will be 'forgotten'.

On the other hand, Rex, The Dignified will approach new ideas with reserve, perceiving which, if any, might be learned, taken to heart and kept there over the long term, adding important components to his personal identity. If this mind also has an Adaptor subtone (Sonar), it might sometimes drift toward the romantic, the poetic or the gentle, while selectively searching for worthy new ideas.

The rational/conceptual primary style meets the intuitive subtone

Michelle, who has a ProCon primary tone with an unusually strong Sonar subtone, fully identified with one half of the description of

ProCon and its primarily logical and rational consideration of any idea. ProCon examines from multiple points of view, going back and forth from its position to another's, and back and forth among a variety of conceptual points of view. However, despite wondering if accepting only half the chapter represented her being glued to a true ProCon yes-no reaction, she identified her strong Sonar subtone as responsible for her process of making most decisions intuitively (they felt right) rather than logically. She said, 'The possibilities are endless; I cannot just think my way through them.' Michelle does not welcome input from others, as it only serves to confuse her further. And yet when she does reach her own intuitive decision, she runs it past someone else she trusts, asking for help; hearing the other's opinion helps to clarify her own.

The 'primary tone' learning style relates to the astronomical/astrological placement of the planet Mercury when we were born. This data is easy and economical to present in tabular format, as in the back of this book. Mercury's position in relation to the other planets' positions can link their energies to produce subtones. The complexity of this analysis puts it beyond the scope of *Fish Can't Climb Trees*. My website provides information about individual 'in-depth' Profiles.

HOW IT ACTUALLY TICKS

Another factor supplemental to the information provided thus far, and which perhaps is more important for adults than for children, relates to the wide gulf that can exist between how the mind actually works, on the one hand, and what we wish it would do for us on the other – the attitude we have about our mind, how we think it should function. Although this gulf can easily be identified and explored with more in-depth (astrological) analysis, it's personal and beyond the scope here. This book deals with the actual mental dynamics themselves, not one's expectations.

Astrology students will recognize this as the difference between Mercury's placement – how the energy operates – and the third house of the chart – the attitude, which we carry into situations in which an exchange of ideas occurs.

INACCESSIBLE MERCURIES – FOR ASTROLOGY STUDENTS

We tend to deny ownership of planetary energies, and the qualities they represent, if they are positioned in areas of the chart, which we don't access easily: fourth, seventh, twelfth houses. The fourth house is like a deeply personal subterranean (subconscious) river; seventh house planets are disavowed through initial projection onto others; and twelfth house planets are fully denied until the 'serve or suffer' question is resolved. People with Mercury in any of those positions may not be as connected with their actual mental dynamics as other people are, and therefore less likely to identify with its description.

But the intercepted Mercury is the most difficult of all to access. In that case, the intercepted axis as a whole will need to be identified and brought into balance before the Mercury qualities become available. It is denied not only by the person him or herself, but by the person's parents, neighbours and teachers, etc., as those people contribute to the experience of the interception itself.

LEARNING VERSUS BEHAVIOUR

Another area of potential confusion is the widespread blurring of the line between mental activity and behaviour. This can be tricky as behaviour is evident, even to the casual observer, while thinking and learning are not. Which part of the person are we describing? This book does not present insights into behaviour. The mind is its own place, so here follows a few potential potholes, which really can be filled in and resurfaced.

- Mistaking a person's behavioural style (like the sun sign or star sign) for the learning style. Behaviour is what shows – what we do. Learning is invisible.
- Mistaking a person's other psychological/physical qualities (emotion, shyness, boldness, insecurity, poor hearing or vision, need to be liked or accepted etc.) for learning style.
- Wishing for another person to have a different learning style, to make your own life easier or to assert your own values.
- Requiring standards of acceptable performance, which are incompatible with another's natural mental mode.
- Judging against particular mental activities in order to deny them – 'I do not like it, therefore the book is wrong.'
- Disconnecting from one's own learning style – 'I am not as described, I have a different learning style, therefore the book is wrong.'

Section 6

The Mercury Model – What Is It and Where Does It Come From?

To address that question, let us look at the Mercury Model through two very different lenses – loosely, the art and the science: neither pure, both applied.

On the one hand, the Model blends the mythic and the archetypal:

It assesses and describes our unique mental make-up by evaluating how we each experience the *mythic theme* of the ancient god Mercury, highly skilled in learning and communicating, as that theme is cast and costumed within the *archetypal pattern* Mercury expresses in our individual life.

And, on the other, the Mercury Model is a journey into the New Physics of thought:

The New Physics looks at the energy fields or vibrations that underpin everything that exists in familiar four-dimensional time/space. There is a subtle energy principle that is observable in all things 'mercurial'. That includes my mind, your mind, all other minds, and the spaces in between.

Do you wonder what that means? Then, please read on . . .

THE ARCHETYPAL AND THE MYTHIC – TRADITIONAL WISDOM

It all started a very long time ago in the dim recesses of history. Imagine those ancient times before TV and street lighting, when our earliest ancestors might have given top billing to the starry night sky as the greatest show on earth. How else would they have occupied themselves during a long night?

With regular viewing it wouldn't have taken them too long to differentiate between planets and fixed stars. The five inner planets, Mercury, Venus, Mars, Jupiter and Saturn, all easily visible to the naked eye, move across the sky against an unchanging backdrop of the fixed stars. Interestingly, the word planet is said to come from the Greek *planasthi* meaning 'to wander'. Of course, we now know that planets are strictly confined to prescribed orbits around the sun. They are not really at liberty to wander; they have only a limited right to roam.

The fixed stars appear to be unmoving. Our early ancestors linked them into small groups, connecting the dots to form patterns, and then applied suitably descriptive names. Many are familiar to us today. Apparently, different cultures assigned the same stars to other clusters, generating a variety of meaningful images. These star clusters are the constellations.

Unrestricted by a materialist world view, and having never seen a big screen Hollywood production, our ancestors looked up and identified stage settings, lead characters and storylines, which have endured the test of time. Can you envision parents telling their children the stories of the stars, linking the dots of light for them, pointing out the pictures and the patterns? Imagine generation after generation of parents repeating these stories, building what we now call an oral tradition.

Here are some examples. One northern constellation that never drops beneath the horizon, which is always present, all night, every night is huge Orion, The Hunter. Children may have been told, and would later tell their own children, that The Hunter, big, reliable and armed, would perpetually look out for them and look after them from high above. The Warrior could provide an eternal example of courage, fearlessness and strength. The Scales might serve as a reminder of justice and fair play. Polaris, the pole star, is positioned at the motionless centre, with all the other constellations of the night sky endlessly circling around it, like the peaceful and pivotal eye of the storm, a whirling Dervish or a community flagpole. The stories undoubtedly conveyed comfort, warnings and guidance on how to live one's life, the moral principles of that age.

You will notice that the planets carry the names of ancient gods and goddesses, the big celebrities of those days. It was the elite, the larger than life immortals, who wandered hither and thither among the constellations of the night sky. Jupiter was there hurling lightning bolts, his familiar calling card, a blast of insight to attract someone's attention. With evidence like that, who would not believe him to be top god. And the attractive Venus, goddess of love, harmony and beauty, could grace any constellation into which she wandered or could incite the locals to battle. Of course, Mercury was there, managing the messages, carrying bits of communication among the others. A quick, youthful, androgynous, prankster he was the ultimate in thinking, learning and communicating, the recognized master of instant messaging.

The planets were assigned top billing as the prime movers, the central characters, the mega-celebrities of the nocturnal drama. Each 'wanderer' came to personify the qualities and mythic themes that stood behind the god it represented. And although the names may have differed, the basic themes ran right through different cultures. For example, Venus was a Roman name, but she was called Aphrodite by the Greeks, Inanna by the Sumerians, Morning and Evening Star by the Mesopotamians, and simply the Goddess elsewhere.

Now what about the stage settings – where did our ancestors place the drama? Why, in the constellations, within the fixed star patterns created by linking the light dots. The cast of mythic heroes and heroines wandered, each at his or her own pace, through the star clusters that lay along their paths. They had experiences there: fell in love, engaged in conflict or combat, expressed creatively, ate their children or inherited untold wealth. Depending upon the star picture of the constellation, they were nurtured and helped, assisted others, ordered beheadings or were betrayed. The dramatic events depended upon the interpretation our ancestors had given to the constellation, how they saw and related to the connected dot patterns.

THE ARCHETYPES, THE SYMBOLS BEYOND THE SYMBOLS, BEYOND THE SYMBOLS

We find the levels of meaning they assigned to the star patterns went way beyond the personal. Neither ordinary nor commonplace, the ideas had universal scope. We would refer to them as 'archetypal'. Let me clarify that term. The constellations identified and named by our distant forebears carry archetypal meaning for us. They represent or are examples of the big, familiar, classic, unifying ideas or standards that are evident throughout human history and also in individual lives. Archetypes have long-term continuity – themes conveyed by drawings discovered on cave walls still find expression today in musical patterns, in literature, art and film. These are notions we tend to understand without a great deal of explanation.

For example, most of us instantly know when we encounter the unmistakably nurturing energy of a woman who is an archetypal 'Earth Mother'. Similarly without needing an explanation we recognize the disciplined, authoritative, highly organized feel of a high power chief executive – a 'Suit'. We can learn to quickly identify archetypal behaviour patterns whenever we see them, in individuals, in a country's national stereotypes or on our favourite TV series. Some examples are: The Lightweight or Butterfly, The Heavyweight or Bully, The Poet, The Scientist, The Courtesan, The Warrior/Soldier, The Compassionate One or The Victim.

Perhaps these big themes have always lived within our shared humanity or race memory, even from the beginning.

Possibly the archetypes sprang fully developed from the hearts of our predecessors and were projected onto the shapes they saw in the starry night skies, where they possibly found correspondence and representation.

From there, having entered the oral tradition, the archetypes passed to us through the generations as stories.

SAFETY DEPOSIT BOXES: STAR STORAGE PREDATES CLOUD STORAGE

But, the stellar patterns not only provided a structure to help our ancestors organize their universe and beliefs, they also became long-term storage vaults for the messages and the mythologies of their cultures. The stories were placed by repetition in the night sky for safekeeping. The storage must have been reliable and sufficient. They are still there. Stellar patterns still supply a visual key through the ages to the universal truths of the human condition; archetypes still reside in the stars. And the wandering planets still represent the mythic themes of the ancient gods.

Modern people, possibly oblivious to the similarities, tend to dismiss the richness held in these ancient safety deposit boxes, having created their own more up-to-date repositories for similar kinds of information. Oddly enough the same big themes reoccur in our modern stories today. TV programmes, films, plays, literature, dance and music itself, as well as music videos and concerts, all present characters we might recognize as the Hunter, the Warrior and the Scales if we looked into it.

THE BIRTH OF ASTROLOGY AND THE BEGINNING OF THE ANCIENT DATABASE.

Returning to our predecessors. Sooner or later some astute ancestor of yours or mine would have tried to look for the practical applications of the night-time observations – to bring the sky down to earth.

For example, someone first noticed that when the position of sunset in its yearly trek toward the north began to fall back toward the south, then the long summer days would soon give way to long cold winter nights – time to migrate.

And at some point long ago an independent-minded farmer first realized a successful harvest by anticipating, awaiting and then planting according to prime-time seed sowing indicators in the night sky. Today some still follow these old ways and call it planting by the moon. Also, there would have been a first time when star-gazing coastal families correctly foresaw an extremely high tide and took appropriate safety measures.

" Those far distant ancestors had begun to observe correlations between celestial bodies above and events in their lives. They were the parents of modern astronomy and astrology."

They made the first entries in humanity's oldest database, the ancient empirical database, the body of observations, subsequently accumulated and recorded by the intellectuals of every culture on the planet, which correlate planetary positions and movements above with the natural and human worlds on earth below.

During the intervening centuries the study they initiated has been formalized as we have matured philosophically and technologically, as scholars joined the early nomadic and agrarian observers. In time, the once unified field of study diverged – astronomy now involves itself with celestial observation, measurement and speculation about origins while astrology correlates positions of celestial bodies with events on Earth, seeking interpretation and meaning.

The work by Pythagoras in ancient Babylon in the sixth century BCE is still the basis of the philosophy of astrology. Plato (*c.* 428–348 BCE) then built a great deal of astrological theory on the foundation supplied by Pythagoras. Surfing through the centuries, we find many other respected scholars who made their contribution. A notable example was Ptolemy (born 70 BCE), who lived in Alexandria and had the vast resources of its famous library available to him. He produced texts which summarized all the astrological work of the Mesopotamians and Greeks and which were the authoritative references on the sky for the next 1,500 years.

In Medieval times many scholars were also astrologers. In the 13th century Thomas Aquinas wrote about correlations between planetary positions and human nature, during times when astrology was interwoven in the fabric of Christianity. Kepler and Galileo were both astrological advisers at court. Despite the ebb and flow of popular opinion, astrology has always enjoyed a most illustrious following.

THE STARS IN THE MODERN WORLD – OUR LEGACY OF LIGHT AND LIGHT

We have refined our methods of observation and measurement since the early days. Today we need not even venture outdoors, let alone hope for a cloudless night, as we now have computer generated reference material listing precise positions of the sun, moon and planets of our solar system as well as a wealth of supporting information.

Modern astrologers have the legacy of this ancient database, accumulated over the centuries by all major cultures of the world. It provides both a foundation and a springboard for continuing research along current lines. Today's astrologers rarely advise on the likely outcome of a joust but then their ancient counterparts were seldom consulted about stock-trading trends.

The extensive body of empirical knowledge is available to support any field in which the understanding of individual human qualities is beneficial: management training, human resource development, education, psychology and counselling, health, personal growth, career and marriage guidance. Now it can benefit all of us through the Mercury Model.

THE NEW PHYSICS

Shifting now to the somewhat more scientific lens, the Mercury Model is a journey into the New Physics of thought.

The New Physics will ultimately result in a full-scale scientific paradigm shift, not unlike the one that resulted from Einstein's insights into relativity and Schrodinger's recognition of the mathematics of quantum mechanics. The New Physics is currently a ground swell of innovative re-thinking about energy. It re-envisions a host of topics through a totally different perspective: matter has an energetic component, but the space between material objects does as well.

" We are energetic beings who live in a sea of interconnected, pulsing vibrations. "

While certain practical applications of this thinking already make our modern world go around (iPods, BlackBerries and wireless technologies), some are still considered fringe in certain circles, but lifesaving or life-enhancing in others. Many look to the New Physics to explain what has previously baffled us. This includes energy medicine and alternative therapies like homeopathy and acupuncture, mind/body/spirit work like meditation, intention and prayer, and certainly astrology. The revolution is just around the corner.

We cannot see energy. We can, however, observe its effects. When Sir Isaac Newton dropped his famous apple, he observed the effects of gravity, the apple fell, but the gravitational force itself was invisible. Our senses cannot detect the energy of magnetism, but we have all learned that opposite magnetic poles attract each other while the same poles repel. And although we cannot see, hear, smell, taste or feel the energetic radiation called gamma rays, we certainly know about their powerful effects. For example, in nuclear medicine, many highly successful diagnostic procedures employ gamma radiation, and beams of these rays are used to reduce tumours, while the patient is unaware of the radiation.

We have come to understand these energies – gravity, magnetism and radioactivity – by seeing how they behave. We now accept them, no longer doubting their existence just because they are invisible to our ordinary senses. This was not always the case. As we continue to push against the frontiers of knowledge, we will certainly discover other types of energies. And if history is repetitive, it is likely that the new ones will not meet with openhearted acceptance – initially.

ESSENTIAL MERCURY – A SUBTLE ENERGY

Here is a concept, not in ordinary use at the moment – the 'subtle energy principle'. Like other energies, an energy principle is not visible to our ordinary senses, but we can demonstrate its existence by observing its behaviour. An energy principle is the subtle version of a particular theme; it is the essence common to all expressions of that theme. And themes are dynamic processes. Consider, for example, the action of alternating tension and relaxation or the activities of solidification or attraction. An unexpressed energy principle is as vague or tenuous as gravity when it has nothing to act upon. Gravity came to life and expressed itself visibly when Newton released the apple, but it was still a force prior to that instant. Similarly, a subtle energy principle becomes obvious only when it proclaims itself or 'comes to rest' by interacting with matter. Then we can see hints of its existence – energetically expressing a particular theme through the variety of different vehicles in which it settles. We can come to know the underlying principle by spotting its theme, by observing where and how it expresses in nature, and by glimpsing it in as many ways as possible. We have to peer at it.

To view the Mercury Model through the lens of the New Physics, I wish to introduce the subtle energy principle, which underpins this book, and name it '*Essential Mercury*' or *EM* for short.

To search for evidence of the elusive *EM*, let us consider 'all things mercurial', the multitude of containers in which it finds expression.

As all metals are physical forms that provide suitable grounding points for particular subtle energies, we could start with the metallic element called mercury, and examine its chemical behaviour and physical properties, its colour and appearance, the locations and the chemical forms in which it naturally occurs, the uses we have found for it in society, etc. Defining the vehicle in which the energy principle is 'comfortable' informs us about its essential nature.

In our search for evidence of *EM* we could consider the planet called Mercury. Each planet in our solar system bears a symbolic correspondence with a metallic element, a musical note, a colour, a chakra point in our bodies, and more. Furthermore, we can identify suitable vehicles which provide grounding for *EM* among animals, in plants, in the realm of biochemistry and in ourselves.

Essential Mercury is the quintessential distillate of the planet in orbit around our sun, and central to any meaning the planet has to either astronomers or astrologers. *EM* is even more transcendent than the mythic figure of the ancient god, his qualities or activities. Standing behind these evident and esoteric expressions, back behind planets and mythologies, *Essential Mercury* is a subtle energy principle which is universal, cosmic, immense and part of nature.

" *All of its expressions include the key features of levity, agility and quickness.* "

ESSENTIAL MERCURY – WHERE IT PROCLAIMS ITSELF IN NATURE

- Mercury the *planet* is the innermost wanderer in our solar system and the fastest moving, taking only 88 days to journey around the sun. Sometimes it even appears to go backward along its orbital path, when its speed matches ours on earth – three times a year for about three weeks per episode.

- Mercury the *element* is 'quicksilver', the only metal that is liquid at room temperature. As its nickname suggests it is always in motion, never stopping. It is so adventurous that if left alone in an uncovered container it leaves; it evaporates into the atmosphere. If poured from a container, quicksilver breaks into tiny balls which dash about making contact with everything from dust to dog hair. Then, with just the slightest encouragement, it will coalesce into a large pool. All the silver balls reconnect, forming something akin to a multinational union, incorporating the dust and all. In chemical reactions it is often used as a catalyst, fostering 'communication' pathways between reactants. Mercury has a rapid response to temperature and pressure fluctuations and is useful in thermometers and barometers. As mercury is a metal, it conducts electricity, and is used in scientific and electronic equipment, even in fluorescent tubes.

- Mercury in *music* is quick, light and staccato. Its sounds have short wavelengths. All wind instruments capture Mercury's essential nature as they depend on the rhythm of breath. Striking examples are Vivaldi's recorder and oboe concerti.

- Mercury *animals* have swift disconnected movements exemplified by songbirds, squirrels, monkeys, crows, parrots and all flying insects and especially butterflies.

- Mercury in *literature* is seen in adventurous characters that convey youthful and light-hearted curiosity – 'I wonder what today will bring!' Examples include the Puer theme discussed by Carl Jung, Dorothy in *The Wizard of Oz*, *The Lion, The Witch and The Wardrobe*, *Peter Pan* and *Swallows and Amazons*.

- Mercury in *esoterica* is exemplified by The Fool card of the Tarot Deck, the astrological sign of Gemini, the brow chakra at the third eye.

- Mercury in *our anatomy* has a special relationship with the brain, nervous system, lungs, oxygen and other blood gases, all the sensory organs, which are the information receptors. *EM* allows us to live, to breathe and to perceive.

ESSENTIAL MERCURY AND THE ANCIENT GOD OF COMMUNICATION
In ancient Greek mythology, Hermes was the handsome young messenger and herald of the gods. He alone had totally free mobility and access to both Zeus, his father on high, and to Pluto in the depth of the underworld. (Between the heights of the super-conscious and the depths of the sub-conscious resides our conscious awareness.) With his swiftness and agility, portrayed by a winged helmet and sandals, the quicksilver-tongued Hermes guided writers, speakers, teachers, travellers, traders and tricksters.

Renamed Mercury by the Romans, he inherited the role – god of eloquence and manager of messages. This universal mythic theme is found in many cultures, going under different names, for example the Norse Woden, the Egyptian Thoth and the Indian Ganesh.

ESSENTIAL MERCURY AND THE ASTROLOGICAL SYMBOL

In astrology, the planet Mercury symbolizes all the mental dynamics: learning, thinking, sharing, receiving, processing and communicating information. It represents conscious intelligence, our own particular logic and our pattern of consciousness.

Mercury corresponds with the uniquely human powers of reflection and speech – our ability to plan, organize, name and categorize objects. It represents our need to be understood by another person, the urge to establish contact in true give and take information exchange.

Like the breath, the inflow is perception while the outflow is the urge to express our thoughts.

ESSENTIAL MERCURY AND THE MERCURY MODEL

When it comes to exploring the New Physics, we do not have a firm foundation – yet. We are cautiously moving over the thin ice of the new. Without accepted laws or even well phrased theories, but fully aware that something important is going on here, we can return to basic scientific practice and involve ourselves in empirical observation. If we cannot see, feel, taste or measure subtle energy directly, we can still observe it in action and watch its effects. We can follow in the well-positioned footsteps of post-Newtonian students of gravity and of Marie Curie's early students of ionizing radiation. Hopefully, we too can come to understand the energy by seeing how it behaves. We can collect data, take note of evident correlations and test them.

We cannot directly measure the subtle energy principle, *Essential Mercury*. But, we can experience it as it expresses through the planet, the metal, specific animals, music, literature and ourselves.

The subtle energy principle called *Essential Mercury* resides within and proclaims itself through every one of us. It must be one of our operating programmes. *EM* contains features that are attributable to the human mind. As children and adults, we exhibit mercurial qualities – we perceive, learn, think and share information.

It's universal, but it's not uniform. We are different; we each have a learning style.

The observable fact is that an individual's learning style, the specific archetypal manner in which *EM* operates through a person, correlates with the zodiacal position of the planet Mercury at the person's birth. Does *Essential Mercury* somehow enliven or vitalize the archetypal qualities filed in the stars over the centuries? It is quite possible for many people to use the Mercury Model and the benefits it offers to modern people without further consideration of its intricacies. Others are going to need to push against the outer boundary of current human knowledge to find out why and how it works.

The Big Picture

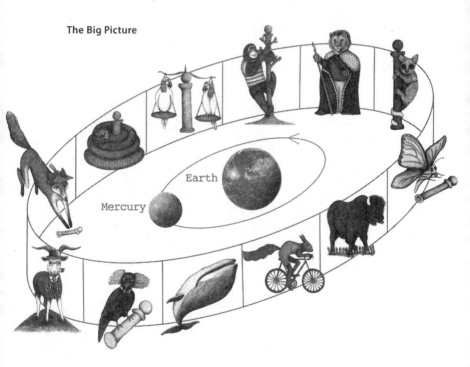

PART II

Learning Style Tables

Identify Learning Styles in Moments

Here is how to use these tables:

For each year from 1925 through 2025 the following tables show the date and time (in GMT, Greenwich Mean Time) at which the planet Mercury passed from one zodiacal sign to another, the points at which the ancient god Mercury changed his costume and his mood, and when the archetypal pattern behind the mercurial (mental) qualities shifted from one learning style to another. During the time between listings the previous learning style prevails.

For example, the learning style of anyone born between midnight 1st January 1925 and 7:16 AM on 14th January 1925 is Flash, The Pioneer. These times are in GMT.

On average, changes from one learning style to another occur on 14 days each year. To assign the learning style for a person born on one of those particular days, the time of birth would have to be taken into account. This is not necessary for people born on the other 351 days per year.

For example, the learning style of a person born on 14th January 1925 before 7:16 AM GMT, would be Flash, The Pioneer. However, if the birth occurred after 7:16 AM, we would be looking at Exec, The Achiever, which would remain the prevailing learning style for all people born until 8:12 AM on 7th February 1925. Boffin, The Innovator then takes over until 4:53 PM (GMT) on 25th February 1925.

To convert from local time at the place of birth to GMT, you would need to know the time zone at the place of birth and add or subtract the appropriate number of hours. Don't forget about Daylight Savings Time (USA), British Summer Time (UK) and any other seasonal time changes.

1925

DATE	TIME	STYLE	POLARITY	RELATING	UPTAKE
Jan 1st	0:00 AM	Flash, The Pioneer	Sharer	Adaptor	Fire
Jan 14th	7:16 AM	Exec, The Achiever	Container	Initiator	Earth
Feb 7th	8:12 AM	Boffin, The Innovator	Sharer	Sustainer	Air
Feb 25th	4:53 PM	Sonar, The Intuitive	Container	Adaptor	Water
Mar 13th	12:36 PM	Scout, The Trailblazer	Sharer	Initiator	Fire
April 1st	3:21 PM	Steady, The Vault	Container	Sustainer	Earth
April 15th	11:09 PM	Scout, The Trailblazer	Sharer	Initiator	Fire
May 17th	1:32 AM	Steady, The Vault	Container	Sustainer	Earth
June 6th	3:23 PM	Buzz, The Curious	Sharer	Adaptor	Air
June 20th	11:07 PM	Sponge, The Sensitive	Container	Initiator	Water
July 5th	5:52 PM	Rex, The Dignified	Sharer	Sustainer	Fire
July 26th	11:46 AM	Details, The Analyst	Container	Adaptor	Earth
Aug 27th	6:46 AM	Rex, The Dignified	Sharer	Sustainer	Fire
Sept 11th	5:09 AM	Details, The Analyst	Container	Adaptor	Earth
Sept 29th	6:04 PM	ProCon, The Diplomat	Sharer	Initiator	Air
Oct 17th	3:52 AM	Sherlock, The Detective	Container	Sustainer	Water
Nov 5th	6:54 PM	Flash, The Pioneer	Sharer	Adaptor	Fire

1926

DATE	TIME	STYLE	POLARITY	RELATING	UPTAKE
Jan 1st	0:00 AM	Flash, The Pioneer	Sharer	Adaptor	Fire
Jan 11th	7:27 AM	Exec, The Achiever	Container	Initiator	Earth
Jan 31st	10:04 AM	Boffin, The Innovator	Sharer	Sustainer	Air
Feb 17th	9:30 PM	Sonar, The Intuitive	Container	Adaptor	Water
Mar 6th	2:57 AM	Scout, The Trailblazer	Sharer	Initiator	Fire
May 13th	10:53 AM	Steady, The Vault	Container	Sustainer	Earth
May 29th	1:51 PM	Buzz, The Curious	Sharer	Adaptor	Air
June 12th	10:08 AM	Sponge, The Sensitive	Container	Initiator	Water
June 29th	5:01 AM	Rex, The Dignified	Sharer	Sustainer	Fire
Sept 5th	8:33 PM	Details, The Analyst	Container	Adaptor	Earth
Sept 21st	8:57 PM	ProCon, The Diplomat	Sharer	Initiator	Air
Oct 9th	9:58 PM	Sherlock, The Detective	Container	Sustainer	Water
Oct 31st	11:01 AM	Flash, The Pioneer	Sharer	Adaptor	Fire
Nov 28th	5:27 AM	Sherlock, The Detective	Container	Sustainer	Water
Dec 13th	8:38 PM	Flash, The Pioneer	Sharer	Adaptor	Fire

1927

DATE	TIME	STYLE	POLARITY	RELATING	UPTAKE
Jan 1st	0:00 AM	Flash, The Pioneer	Sharer	Adaptor	Fire
Jan 5th	1:58 AM	Exec, The Achiever	Container	Initiator	Earth
Jan 24th	1:13 AM	Boffin, The Innovator	Sharer	Sustainer	Air
Feb 10th	4:28 AM	Sonar, The Intuitive	Container	Adaptor	Water
April 17th	12:24 PM	Scout, The Trailblazer	Sharer	Initiator	Fire
May 6th	11:28 AM	Steady, The Vault	Container	Sustainer	Earth
May 21st	12:03 AM	Buzz, The Curious	Sharer	Adaptor	Air
June 4th	1:38 PM	Sponge, The Sensitive	Container	Initiator	Water
June 28th	7:33 PM	Rex, The Dignified	Sharer	Sustainer	Fire
July 14th	3:50 AM	Sponge, The Sensitive	Container	Initiator	Water
Aug 12th	3:43 AM	Rex, The Dignified	Sharer	Sustainer	Fire
Aug 28th	11:07 PM	Details, The Analyst	Container	Adaptor	Earth
Sept 14th	1:37 AM	ProCon, The Diplomat	Sharer	Initiator	Air
Oct 3rd	8:38 AM	Sherlock, The Detective	Container	Sustainer	Water
Dec 9th	9:26 AM	Flash, The Pioneer	Sharer	Adaptor	Fire
Dec 29th	1:48 AM	Exec, The Achiever	Container	Initiator	Earth

1928

DATE	TIME	STYLE	POLARITY	RELATING	UPTAKE
Jan 1st	0:00 AM	Exec, The Achiever	Container	Initiator	Earth
Jan 16th	1:35 PM	Boffin, The Innovator	Sharer	Sustainer	Air
Feb 3rd	10:22 AM	Sonar, The Intuitive	Container	Adaptor	Water
Feb 29th	6:26 AM	Boffin, The Innovator	Sharer	Sustainer	Air
Mar 18th	2:45 AM	Sonar, The Intuitive	Container	Adaptor	Water
April 11th	1:55 AM	Scout, The Trailblazer	Sharer	Initiator	Fire
April 27th	10:35 AM	Steady, The Vault	Container	Sustainer	Earth
May 11th	12:07 PM	Buzz, The Curious	Sharer	Adaptor	Air
May 28th	11:03 PM	Sponge, The Sensitive	Container	Initiator	Water
Aug 4th	8:00 PM	Rex, The Dignified	Sharer	Sustainer	Fire
Aug 19th	4:59 PM	Details, The Analyst	Container	Adaptor	Earth
Sept 5th	4:20 PM	ProCon, The Diplomat	Sharer	Initiator	Air
Sept 27th	6:12 PM	Sherlock, The Detective	Container	Sustainer	Water
Oct 24th	9:45 PM	ProCon, The Diplomat	Sharer	Initiator	Air
Nov 11th	9:05 AM	Sherlock, The Detective	Container	Sustainer	Water
Dec 1st	4:57 PM	Flash, The Pioneer	Sharer	Adaptor	Fire
Dec 20th	7:37 PM	Exec, The Achiever	Container	Initiator	Earth

1929

DATE	TIME	STYLE	POLARITY	RELATING	UPTAKE
Jan 1st	0:00 AM	Exec, The Achiever	Container	Initiator	Earth
Jan 8th	8:09 AM	Boffin, The Innovator	Sharer	Sustainer	Air
Mar 16th	1:07 AM	Sonar, The Intuitive	Container	Adaptor	Water
April 3rd	9:21 PM	Scout, The Trailblazer	Sharer	Initiator	Fire
April 19th	12:23 AM	Steady, The Vault	Container	Sustainer	Earth
May 3rd	9:34 PM	Buzz, The Curious	Sharer	Adaptor	Air
July 11th	9:07 PM	Sponge, The Sensitive	Container	Initiator	Water
July 27th	3:11 PM	Rex, The Dignified	Sharer	Sustainer	Fire
Aug 11th	2:48 PM	Details, The Analyst	Container	Adaptor	Earth
Aug 30th	6:01 AM	ProCon, The Diplomat	Sharer	Initiator	Air
Nov 5th	7:29 PM	Sherlock, The Detective	Container	Sustainer	Water
Nov 24th	12:06 PM	Flash, The Pioneer	Sharer	Adaptor	Fire
Dec 13th	2:42 PM	Exec, The Achiever	Container	Initiator	Earth

1930

DATE	TIME	STYLE	POLARITY	RELATING	UPTAKE
Jan 1st	0:00 AM	Exec, The Achiever	Container	Initiator	Earth
Jan 2nd	10:25 AM	Boffin, The Innovator	Sharer	Sustainer	Air
Jan 23rd	12:30 AM	Exec, The Achiever	Container	Initiator	Earth
Feb 15th	3:08 PM	Boffin, The Innovator	Sharer	Sustainer	Air
Mar 9th	10:39 PM	Sonar, The Intuitive	Container	Adaptor	Water
Mar 26th	11:36 PM	Scout, The Trailblazer	Sharer	Initiator	Fire
April 10th	5:05 PM	Steady, The Vault	Container	Sustainer	Earth
May 1st	5:30 AM	Buzz, The Curious	Sharer	Adaptor	Air
May 17th	10:46 AM	Steady, The Vault	Container	Sustainer	Earth
June 14th	8:09 PM	Buzz, The Curious	Sharer	Adaptor	Air
July 4th	10:10 PM	Sponge, The Sensitive	Container	Initiator	Water
July 19th	2:44 AM	Rex, The Dignified	Sharer	Sustainer	Fire
Aug 4th	2:38 AM	Details, The Analyst	Container	Adaptor	Earth
Aug 26th	6:04 PM	ProCon, The Diplomat	Sharer	Initiator	Air
Sept 20th	2:13 AM	Details, The Analyst	Container	Adaptor	Earth
Oct 11th	4:45 AM	ProCon, The Diplomat	Sharer	Initiator	Air
Oct 29th	2:35 PM	Sherlock, The Detective	Container	Sustainer	Water
Nov 17th	5:31 AM	Flash, The Pioneer	Sharer	Adaptor	Fire
Dec 6th	8:57 PM	Exec, The Achiever	Container	Initiator	Earth

1931

DATE	TIME	STYLE	POLARITY	RELATING	UPTAKE
Jan 1st	0:00 AM	Exec, The Achiever	Container	Initiator	Earth
Feb 11th	12:27 PM	Boffin, The Innovator	Sharer	Sustainer	Air
Mar 2nd	5:28 PM	Sonar, The Intuitive	Container	Adaptor	Water
Mar 18th	7:31 PM	Scout, The Trailblazer	Sharer	Initiator	Fire
April 3rd	1:38 PM	Steady, The Vault	Container	Sustainer	Earth
June 11th	7:27 AM	Buzz, The Curious	Sharer	Adaptor	Air
June 26th	1:49 PM	Sponge, The Sensitive	Container	Initiator	Water
July 10th	7:56 PM	Rex, The Dignified	Sharer	Sustainer	Fire
July 28th	11:24 PM	Details, The Analyst	Container	Adaptor	Earth
Oct 4th	6:27 PM	ProCon, The Diplomat	Sharer	Initiator	Air
Oct 22nd	2:08 AM	Sherlock, The Detective	Container	Sustainer	Water
Nov 10th	4:27 AM	Flash, The Pioneer	Sharer	Adaptor	Fire
Dec 2nd	12:00 AM	Exec, The Achiever	Container	Initiator	Earth
Dec 20th	7:47 AM	Flash, The Pioneer	Sharer	Adaptor	Fire

1932

DATE	TIME	STYLE	POLARITY	RELATING	UPTAKE
Jan 1st	0:00 AM	Flash, The Pioneer	Sharer	Adaptor	Fire
Jan 14th	12:47 PM	Exec, The Achiever	Container	Initiator	Earth
Feb 5th	2:36 AM	Boffin, The Innovator	Sharer	Sustainer	Air
Feb 23rd	12:50 AM	Sonar, The Intuitive	Container	Adaptor	Water
Mar 9th	8:21 PM	Scout, The Trailblazer	Sharer	Initiator	Fire
May 15th	10:49 PM	Steady, The Vault	Container	Sustainer	Earth
June 2nd	11:05 PM	Buzz, The Curious	Sharer	Adaptor	Air
June 16th	10:30 PM	Sponge, The Sensitive	Container	Initiator	Water
July 2nd	8:16 AM	Rex, The Dignified	Sharer	Sustainer	Fire
July 27th	8:38 PM	Details, The Analyst	Container	Adaptor	Earth
Aug 10th	6:52 AM	Rex, The Dignified	Sharer	Sustainer	Fire
Sept 9th	7:20 AM	Details, The Analyst	Container	Adaptor	Earth
Sept 26th	1:15 AM	ProCon, The Diplomat	Sharer	Initiator	Air
Oct 13th	3:41 PM	Sherlock, The Detective	Container	Sustainer	Water
Nov 2nd	8:28 PM	Flash, The Pioneer	Sharer	Adaptor	Fire

1933

DATE	TIME	STYLE	POLARITY	RELATING	UPTAKE
Jan 1st	0:00 AM	Flash, The Pioneer	Sharer	Adaptor	Fire
Jan 8th	10:25 AM	Exec, The Achiever	Container	Initiator	Earth
Jan 27th	10:39 PM	Boffin, The Innovator	Sharer	Sustainer	Air
Feb 14th	5:06 AM	Sonar, The Intuitive	Container	Adaptor	Water
Mar 3rd	10:49 AM	Scout, The Trailblazer	Sharer	Initiator	Fire
Mar 25th	9:52 PM	Sonar, The Intuitive	Container	Adaptor	Water
April 17th	3:27 PM	Scout, The Trailblazer	Sharer	Initiator	Fire
May 10th	7:42 AM	Steady, The Vault	Container	Sustainer	Earth
May 25th	2:27 PM	Buzz, The Curious	Sharer	Adaptor	Air
June 8th	2:12 PM	Sponge, The Sensitive	Container	Initiator	Water
June 27th	1:12 AM	Rex, The Dignified	Sharer	Sustainer	Fire
Sept 2nd	5:44 AM	Details, The Analyst	Container	Adaptor	Earth
Sept 18th	3:48 AM	ProCon, The Diplomat	Sharer	Initiator	Air
Oct 6th	3:04 PM	Sherlock, The Detective	Container	Sustainer	Water
Oct 30th	4:27 AM	Flash, The Pioneer	Sharer	Adaptor	Fire
Nov 16th	1:57 AM	Sherlock, The Detective	Container	Sustainer	Water
Dec 12th	3:44 AM	Flash, The Pioneer	Sharer	Adaptor	Fire

1934

DATE	TIME	STYLE	POLARITY	RELATING	UPTAKE
Jan 1st	0:00 AM	Flash, The Pioneer	Sharer	Adaptor	Fire
Jan 1st	6:40 PM	Exec, The Achiever	Container	Initiator	Earth
Jan 20th	11:44 AM	Boffin, The Innovator	Sharer	Sustainer	Air
Feb 6th	5:24 PM	Sonar, The Intuitive	Container	Adaptor	Water
April 15th	4:14 AM	Scout, The Trailblazer	Sharer	Initiator	Fire
May 2nd	6:45 PM	Steady, The Vault	Container	Sustainer	Earth
May 16th	11:43 PM	Buzz, The Curious	Sharer	Adaptor	Air
June 1st	8:22 AM	Sponge, The Sensitive	Container	Initiator	Water
Aug 9th	1:49 PM	Rex, The Dignified	Sharer	Sustainer	Fire
Aug 25th	2:18 AM	Details, The Analyst	Container	Adaptor	Earth
Sept 10th	11:29 AM	ProCon, The Diplomat	Sharer	Initiator	Air
Sept 30th	2:46 PM	Sherlock, The Detective	Container	Sustainer	Water
Dec 6th	6:42 AM	Flash, The Pioneer	Sharer	Adaptor	Fire
Dec 25th	2:59 PM	Exec, The Achiever	Container	Initiator	Earth

1935

DATE	TIME	STYLE	POLARITY	RELATING	UPTAKE
Jan 1st	0:00 AM	Exec, The Achiever	Container	Initiator	Earth
Jan 13th	1:20 AM	Boffin, The Innovator	Sharer	Sustainer	Air
Feb 1st	11:16 AM	Sonar, The Intuitive	Container	Adaptor	Water
Feb 15th	2:50 AM	Boffin, The Innovator	Sharer	Sustainer	Air
Mar 18th	9:53 PM	Sonar, The Intuitive	Container	Adaptor	Water
April 8th	6:40 PM	Scout, The Trailblazer	Sharer	Initiator	Fire
April 24th	12:29 PM	Steady, The Vault	Container	Sustainer	Earth
May 8th	5:20 PM	Buzz, The Curious	Sharer	Adaptor	Air
May 29th	7:26 PM	Sponge, The Sensitive	Container	Initiator	Water
June 20th	5:55 PM	Buzz, The Curious	Sharer	Adaptor	Air
July 13th	10:22 PM	Sponge, The Sensitive	Container	Initiator	Water
Aug 2nd	1:48 AM	Rex, The Dignified	Sharer	Sustainer	Fire
Aug 16th	8:39 PM	Details, The Analyst	Container	Adaptor	Earth
Sept 3rd	9:33 AM	ProCon, The Diplomat	Sharer	Initiator	Air
Sept 28th	3:52 PM	Sherlock, The Detective	Container	Sustainer	Water
Oct 12th	5:22 PM	ProCon, The Diplomat	Sharer	Initiator	Air
Nov 10th	1:24 AM	Sherlock, The Detective	Container	Sustainer	Water
Nov 29th	7:05 AM	Flash, The Pioneer	Sharer	Adaptor	Fire
Dec 18th	8:28 AM	Exec, The Achiever	Container	Initiator	Earth

1936

DATE	TIME	STYLE	POLARITY	RELATING	UPTAKE
Jan 1st	0:00 AM	Exec, The Achiever	Container	Initiator	Earth
Jan 6th	3:32 AM	Boffin, The Innovator	Sharer	Sustainer	Air
Mar 13th	6:40 AM	Sonar, The Intuitive	Container	Adaptor	Water
Mar 31st	5:08 AM	Scout, The Trailblazer	Sharer	Initiator	Fire
April 15th	1:45 AM	Steady, The Vault	Container	Sustainer	Earth
May 1st	1:30 AM	Buzz, The Curious	Sharer	Adaptor	Air
July 8th	8:47 PM	Sponge, The Sensitive	Container	Initiator	Water
July 23rd	3:39 PM	Rex, The Dignified	Sharer	Sustainer	Fire
Aug 7th	10:59 PM	Details, The Analyst	Container	Adaptor	Earth
Aug 27th	5:43 PM	ProCon, The Diplomat	Sharer	Initiator	Air
Nov 2nd	11:00 AM	Sherlock, The Detective	Container	Sustainer	Water
Nov 21st	12:39 AM	Flash, The Pioneer	Sharer	Adaptor	Fire
Dec 10th	6:40 AM	Exec, The Achiever	Container	Initiator	Earth

1937

DATE	TIME	STYLE	POLARITY	RELATING	UPTAKE
Jan 1st	0:00 AM	Exec, The Achiever	Container	Initiator	Earth
Jan 1st	4:44 PM	Boffin, The Innovator	Sharer	Sustainer	Air
Jan 9th	8:49 PM	Exec, The Achiever	Container	Initiator	Earth
Feb 14th	12:26 AM	Boffin, The Innovator	Sharer	Sustainer	Air
Mar 6th	2:06 PM	Sonar, The Intuitive	Container	Adaptor	Water
Mar 23rd	3:41 AM	Scout, The Trailblazer	Sharer	Initiator	Fire
April 7th	1:09 AM	Steady, The Vault	Container	Sustainer	Earth
June 13th	10:28 PM	Buzz, The Curious	Sharer	Adaptor	Air
July 1st	2:21 AM	Sponge, The Sensitive	Container	Initiator	Water
July 15th	4:11 AM	Rex, The Dignified	Sharer	Sustainer	Fire
July 31st	9:07 PM	Details, The Analyst	Container	Adaptor	Earth
Oct 8th	10:12 AM	ProCon, The Diplomat	Sharer	Initiator	Air
Oct 26th	1:14 AM	Sherlock, The Detective	Container	Sustainer	Water
Nov 13th	7:25 PM	Flash, The Pioneer	Sharer	Adaptor	Fire
Dec 3rd	11:51 PM	Exec, The Achiever	Container	Initiator	Earth

1938

DATE	TIME	STYLE	POLARITY	RELATING	UPTAKE
Jan 1st	0:00 AM	Exec, The Achiever	Container	Initiator	Earth
Jan 6th	10:16 PM	Flash, The Pioneer	Sharer	Adaptor	Fire
Jan 12th	10:30 PM	Exec, The Achiever	Container	Initiator	Earth
Feb 8th	1:17 PM	Boffin, The Innovator	Sharer	Sustainer	Air
Feb 27th	3:01 AM	Sonar, The Intuitive	Container	Adaptor	Water
Mar 15th	12:02 AM	Scout, The Trailblazer	Sharer	Initiator	Fire
April 1st	1:24 PM	Steady, The Vault	Container	Sustainer	Earth
April 23rd	2:02 PM	Scout, The Trailblazer	Sharer	Initiator	Fire
May 16th	5:46 PM	Steady, The Vault	Container	Sustainer	Earth
June 8th	12:32 AM	Buzz, The Curious	Sharer	Adaptor	Air
June 22nd	1:09 PM	Sponge, The Sensitive	Container	Initiator	Water
July 7th	3:21 AM	Rex, The Dignified	Sharer	Sustainer	Fire
July 26th	10:55 PM	Details, The Analyst	Container	Adaptor	Earth
Sept 3rd	3:40 AM	Rex, The Dignified	Sharer	Sustainer	Fire
Sept 10th	3:38 PM	Details, The Analyst	Container	Adaptor	Earth
Oct 1st	4:19 AM	ProCon, The Diplomat	Sharer	Initiator	Air
Oct 18th	12:43 PM	Sherlock, The Detective	Container	Sustainer	Water
Nov 6th	11:33 PM	Flash, The Pioneer	Sharer	Adaptor	Fire

1939

DATE	TIME	STYLE	POLARITY	RELATING	UPTAKE
Jan 1st	0:00 AM	Flash, The Pioneer	Sharer	Adaptor	Fire
Jan 12th	7:57 AM	Exec, The Achiever	Container	Initiator	Earth
Feb 1st	5:57 PM	Boffin, The Innovator	Sharer	Sustainer	Air
Feb 19th	8:09 AM	Sonar, The Intuitive	Container	Adaptor	Water
Mar 7th	9:14 AM	Scout, The Trailblazer	Sharer	Initiator	Fire
May 14th	1:43 PM	Steady, The Vault	Container	Sustainer	Earth
May 31st	2:45 AM	Buzz, The Curious	Sharer	Adaptor	Air
June 13th	11:01 PM	Sponge, The Sensitive	Container	Initiator	Water
June 30th	6:41 AM	Rex, The Dignified	Sharer	Sustainer	Fire
Sept 7th	4:58 AM	Details, The Analyst	Container	Adaptor	Earth
Sept 23rd	7:48 AM	ProCon, The Diplomat	Sharer	Initiator	Air
Oct 11th	5:20 AM	Sherlock, The Detective	Container	Sustainer	Water
Nov 1st	7:03 AM	Flash, The Pioneer	Sharer	Adaptor	Fire
Dec 3rd	8:22 AM	Sherlock, The Detective	Container	Sustainer	Water
Dec 13th	7:16 PM	Flash, The Pioneer	Sharer	Adaptor	Fire

1940

DATE	TIME	STYLE	POLARITY	RELATING	UPTAKE
Jan 1st	0:00 AM	Flash, The Pioneer	Sharer	Adaptor	Fire
Jan 6th	7:56 AM	Exec, The Achiever	Container	Initiator	Earth
Jan 25th	10:14 AM	Boffin, The Innovator	Sharer	Sustainer	Air
Feb 11th	2:01 PM	Sonar, The Intuitive	Container	Adaptor	Water
Mar 4th	10:09 AM	Scout, The Trailblazer	Sharer	Initiator	Fire
Mar 8th	12:55 AM	Sonar, The Intuitive	Container	Adaptor	Water
April 17th	4:56 AM	Scout, The Trailblazer	Sharer	Initiator	Fire
May 6th	9:14 PM	Steady, The Vault	Container	Sustainer	Earth
May 21st	1:59 PM	Buzz, The Curious	Sharer	Adaptor	Air
June 4th	10:29 PM	Sponge, The Sensitive	Container	Initiator	Water
June 26th	2:32 PM	Rex, The Dignified	Sharer	Sustainer	Fire
July 21st	1:39 AM	Sponge, The Sensitive	Container	Initiator	Water
Aug 11th	5:06 PM	Rex, The Dignified	Sharer	Sustainer	Fire
Aug 29th	11:11 AM	Details, The Analyst	Container	Adaptor	Earth
Sept 14th	11:34 AM	ProCon, The Diplomat	Sharer	Initiator	Air
Oct 3rd	12:14 PM	Sherlock, The Detective	Container	Sustainer	Water
Dec 9th	12:45 PM	Flash, The Pioneer	Sharer	Adaptor	Fire
Dec 29th	9:35 AM	Exec, The Achiever	Container	Initiator	Earth

1941

DATE	TIME	STYLE	POLARITY	RELATING	UPTAKE
Jan 1st	0:00 AM	Exec, The Achiever	Container	Initiator	Earth
Jan 16th	10:36 PM	Boffin, The Innovator	Sharer	Sustainer	Air
Feb 3rd	1:08 PM	Sonar, The Intuitive	Container	Adaptor	Water
Mar 7th	2:54 AM	Boffin, The Innovator	Sharer	Sustainer	Air
Mar 16th	12:26 PM	Sonar, The Intuitive	Container	Adaptor	Water
April 12th	7:19 AM	Scout, The Trailblazer	Sharer	Initiator	Fire
April 28th	11:09 PM	Steady, The Vault	Container	Sustainer	Earth
May 13th	12:50 AM	Buzz, The Curious	Sharer	Adaptor	Air
May 29th	5:32 PM	Sponge, The Sensitive	Container	Initiator	Water
Aug 6th	5:57 AM	Rex, The Dignified	Sharer	Sustainer	Fire
Aug 21st	5:18 AM	Details, The Analyst	Container	Adaptor	Earth
Sept 6th	11:58 PM	ProCon, The Diplomat	Sharer	Initiator	Air
Sept 28th	9:21 AM	Sherlock, The Detective	Container	Sustainer	Water
Oct 29th	8:51 PM	ProCon, The Diplomat	Sharer	Initiator	Air
Nov 11th	8:11 PM	Sherlock, The Detective	Container	Sustainer	Water
Dec 3rd	12:11 AM	Flash, The Pioneer	Sharer	Adaptor	Fire
Dec 22nd	3:54 AM	Exec, The Achiever	Container	Initiator	Earth

1942

DATE	TIME	STYLE	POLARITY	RELATING	UPTAKE
Jan 1st	0:00 AM	Exec, The Achiever	Container	Initiator	Earth
Jan 9th	3:24 PM	Boffin, The Innovator	Sharer	Sustainer	Air
Mar 17th	12:10 AM	Sonar, The Intuitive	Container	Adaptor	Water
April 5th	7:06 AM	Scout, The Trailblazer	Sharer	Initiator	Fire
April 20th	1:42 PM	Steady, The Vault	Container	Sustainer	Earth
May 5th	4:37 AM	Buzz, The Curious	Sharer	Adaptor	Air
July 12th	8:24 PM	Sponge, The Sensitive	Container	Initiator	Water
July 29th	4:24 AM	Rex, The Dignified	Sharer	Sustainer	Fire
Aug 13th	1:48 AM	Details, The Analyst	Container	Adaptor	Earth
Aug 31st	8:27 AM	ProCon, The Diplomat	Sharer	Initiator	Air
Nov 7th	1:44 AM	Sherlock, The Detective	Container	Sustainer	Water
Nov 25th	8:26 PM	Flash, The Pioneer	Sharer	Adaptor	Fire
Dec 14th	10:21 PM	Exec, The Achiever	Container	Initiator	Earth

1943

DATE	TIME	STYLE	POLARITY	RELATING	UPTAKE
Jan 1st	0:00 AM	Exec, The Achiever	Container	Initiator	Earth
Jan 3rd	8:27 AM	Boffin, The Innovator	Sharer	Sustainer	Air
Jan 27th	11:42 PM	Exec, The Achiever	Container	Initiator	Earth
Feb 15th	7:00 PM	Boffin, The Innovator	Sharer	Sustainer	Air
Mar 11th	4:59 AM	Sonar, The Intuitive	Container	Adaptor	Water
Mar 28th	11:19 AM	Scout, The Trailblazer	Sharer	Initiator	Fire
April 12th	4:56 AM	Steady, The Vault	Container	Sustainer	Earth
April 30th	3:56 PM	Buzz, The Curious	Sharer	Adaptor	Air
May 26th	10:22 AM	Steady, The Vault	Container	Sustainer	Earth
June 14th	12:46 AM	Buzz, The Curious	Sharer	Adaptor	Air
July 6th	9:05 AM	Sponge, The Sensitive	Container	Initiator	Water
July 20th	4:08 PM	Rex, The Dignified	Sharer	Sustainer	Fire
Aug 5th	10:33 AM	Details, The Analyst	Container	Adaptor	Earth
Aug 27th	12:36 AM	ProCon, The Diplomat	Sharer	Initiator	Air
Sept 25th	10:08 AM	Details, The Analyst	Container	Adaptor	Earth
Oct 11th	11:27 PM	ProCon, The Diplomat	Sharer	Initiator	Air
Oct 30th	11:37 PM	Sherlock, The Detective	Container	Sustainer	Water
Nov 18th	1:39 PM	Flash, The Pioneer	Sharer	Adaptor	Fire
Dec 8th	1:47 AM	Exec, The Achiever	Container	Initiator	Earth

1944

DATE	TIME	STYLE	POLARITY	RELATING	UPTAKE
Jan 1st	0:00 AM	Exec, The Achiever	Container	Initiator	Earth
Feb 12th	2:17 PM	Boffin, The Innovator	Sharer	Sustainer	Air
Mar 3rd	2:45 AM	Sonar, The Intuitive	Container	Adaptor	Water
Mar 19th	7:43 AM	Scout, The Trailblazer	Sharer	Initiator	Fire
April 3rd	5:29 PM	Steady, The Vault	Container	Sustainer	Earth
June 11th	11:46 AM	Buzz, The Curious	Sharer	Adaptor	Air
June 27th	3:40 AM	Sponge, The Sensitive	Container	Initiator	Water
July 11th	7:41 AM	Rex, The Dignified	Sharer	Sustainer	Fire
July 28th	11:44 PM	Details, The Analyst	Container	Adaptor	Earth
Oct 5th	3:17 AM	ProCon, The Diplomat	Sharer	Initiator	Air
Oct 22nd	11:33 AM	Sherlock, The Detective	Container	Sustainer	Water
Nov 10th	11:09 AM	Flash, The Pioneer	Sharer	Adaptor	Fire
Dec 1st	3:31 PM	Exec, The Achiever	Container	Initiator	Earth
Dec 23rd	11:21 PM	Flash, The Pioneer	Sharer	Adaptor	Fire

1945

DATE	TIME	STYLE	POLARITY	RELATING	UPTAKE
Jan 1st	0:00 AM	Flash, The Pioneer	Sharer	Adaptor	Fire
Jan 14th	3:04 AM	Exec, The Achiever	Container	Initiator	Earth
Feb 5th	9:20 AM	Boffin, The Innovator	Sharer	Sustainer	Air
Feb 23rd	11:25 AM	Sonar, The Intuitive	Container	Adaptor	Water
Mar 11th	6:45 AM	Scout, The Trailblazer	Sharer	Initiator	Fire
May 16th	3:21 PM	Steady, The Vault	Container	Sustainer	Earth
June 4th	10:30 AM	Buzz, The Curious	Sharer	Adaptor	Air
June 18th	12:27 PM	Sponge, The Sensitive	Container	Initiator	Water
July 3rd	3:39 PM	Rex, The Dignified	Sharer	Sustainer	Fire
July 26th	2:48 PM	Details, The Analyst	Container	Adaptor	Earth
Aug 17th	8:35 AM	Rex, The Dignified	Sharer	Sustainer	Fire
Sept 10th	7:21 AM	Details, The Analyst	Container	Adaptor	Earth
Sept 27th	12:08 PM	ProCon, The Diplomat	Sharer	Initiator	Air
Oct 15th	12:13 AM	Sherlock, The Detective	Container	Sustainer	Water
Nov 3rd	11:06 PM	Flash, The Pioneer	Sharer	Adaptor	Fire

1946

DATE	TIME	STYLE	POLARITY	RELATING	UPTAKE
Jan 1st	0:00 AM	Flash, The Pioneer	Sharer	Adaptor	Fire
Jan 9th	2:09 PM	Exec, The Achiever	Container	Initiator	Earth
Jan 29th	7:22 AM	Boffin, The Innovator	Sharer	Sustainer	Air
Feb 15th	3:43 PM	Sonar, The Intuitive	Container	Adaptor	Water
Mar 4th	9:26 AM	Scout, The Trailblazer	Sharer	Initiator	Fire
April 1st	6:44 PM	Sonar, The Intuitive	Container	Adaptor	Water
April 16th	2:54 PM	Scout, The Trailblazer	Sharer	Initiator	Fire
May 11th	2:29 PM	Steady, The Vault	Container	Sustainer	Earth
May 27th	4:13 AM	Buzz, The Curious	Sharer	Adaptor	Air
June 10th	2:00 AM	Sponge, The Sensitive	Container	Initiator	Water
June 27th	7:07 PM	Rex, The Dignified	Sharer	Sustainer	Fire
Sept 3rd	4:29 PM	Details, The Analyst	Container	Adaptor	Earth
Sept 19th	2:34 PM	ProCon, The Diplomat	Sharer	Initiator	Air
Oct 7th	9:21 PM	Sherlock, The Detective	Container	Sustainer	Water
Oct 30th	11:23 AM	Flash, The Pioneer	Sharer	Adaptor	Fire
Nov 20th	8:09 PM	Sherlock, The Detective	Container	Sustainer	Water
Dec 13th	12:03 AM	Flash, The Pioneer	Sharer	Adaptor	Fire

1947

DATE	TIME	STYLE	POLARITY	RELATING	UPTAKE
Jan 1st	0:00 AM	Flash, The Pioneer	Sharer	Adaptor	Fire
Jan 3rd	1:46 AM	Exec, The Achiever	Container	Initiator	Earth
Jan 21st	9:06 PM	Boffin, The Innovator	Sharer	Sustainer	Air
Feb 8th	1:31 AM	Sonar, The Intuitive	Container	Adaptor	Water
April 16th	4:31 AM	Scout, The Trailblazer	Sharer	Initiator	Fire
May 4th	6:03 AM	Steady, The Vault	Container	Sustainer	Earth
May 18th	1:33 PM	Buzz, The Curious	Sharer	Adaptor	Air
June 2nd	1:40 PM	Sponge, The Sensitive	Container	Initiator	Water
Aug 10th	5:40 PM	Rex, The Dignified	Sharer	Sustainer	Fire
Aug 26th	2:50 PM	Details, The Analyst	Container	Adaptor	Earth
Sept 11th	8:54 PM	ProCon, The Diplomat	Sharer	Initiator	Air
Oct 1st	3:26 PM	Sherlock, The Detective	Container	Sustainer	Water
Dec 7th	12:32 PM	Flash, The Pioneer	Sharer	Adaptor	Fire
Dec 26th	11:17 PM	Exec, The Achiever	Container	Initiator	Earth

1948

DATE	TIME	STYLE	POLARITY	RELATING	UPTAKE
Jan 1st	0:00 AM	Exec, The Achiever	Container	Initiator	Earth
Jan 14th	10:06 AM	Boffin, The Innovator	Sharer	Sustainer	Air
Feb 2nd	12:46 AM	Sonar, The Intuitive	Container	Adaptor	Water
Feb 20th	11:05 AM	Boffin, The Innovator	Sharer	Sustainer	Air
Mar 18th	8:14 AM	Sonar, The Intuitive	Container	Adaptor	Water
April 9th	2:26 AM	Scout, The Trailblazer	Sharer	Initiator	Fire
April 25th	1:38 AM	Steady, The Vault	Container	Sustainer	Earth
May 9th	4:38 AM	Buzz, The Curious	Sharer	Adaptor	Air
May 28th	10:50 AM	Sponge, The Sensitive	Container	Initiator	Water
June 28th	6:24 PM	Buzz, The Curious	Sharer	Adaptor	Air
July 11th	8:56 PM	Sponge, The Sensitive	Container	Initiator	Water
Aug 2nd	1:54 PM	Rex, The Dignified	Sharer	Sustainer	Fire
Aug 17th	8:44 AM	Details, The Analyst	Container	Adaptor	Earth
Sept 3rd	3:47 PM	ProCon, The Diplomat	Sharer	Initiator	Air
Sept 27th	7:19 AM	Sherlock, The Detective	Container	Sustainer	Water
Oct 17th	3:21 AM	ProCon, The Diplomat	Sharer	Initiator	Air
Nov 10th	2:19 AM	Sherlock, The Detective	Container	Sustainer	Water
Nov 29th	3:09 PM	Flash, The Pioneer	Sharer	Adaptor	Fire
Dec 18th	4:46 PM	Exec, The Achiever	Container	Initiator	Earth

1949

DATE	TIME	STYLE	POLARITY	RELATING	UPTAKE
Jan 1st	0:00 AM	Exec, The Achiever	Container	Initiator	Earth
Jan 6th	8:53 AM	Boffin, The Innovator	Sharer	Sustainer	Air
Mar 14th	9:52 AM	Sonar, The Intuitive	Container	Adaptor	Water
April 1st	4:02 PM	Scout, The Trailblazer	Sharer	Initiator	Fire
April 16th	2:55 PM	Steady, The Vault	Container	Sustainer	Earth
May 2nd	2:19 AM	Buzz, The Curious	Sharer	Adaptor	Air
July 10th	3:19 AM	Sponge, The Sensitive	Container	Initiator	Water
July 25th	5:20 AM	Rex, The Dignified	Sharer	Sustainer	Fire
Aug 9th	9:04 AM	Details, The Analyst	Container	Adaptor	Earth
Aug 28th	3:48 PM	ProCon, The Diplomat	Sharer	Initiator	Air
Nov 3rd	6:58 PM	Sherlock, The Detective	Container	Sustainer	Water
Nov 22nd	9:06 AM	Flash, The Pioneer	Sharer	Adaptor	Fire
Dec 11th	1:37 PM	Exec, The Achiever	Container	Initiator	Earth

1950

DATE	TIME	STYLE	POLARITY	RELATING	UPTAKE
Jan 1st	0:00 AM	Exec, The Achiever	Container	Initiator	Earth
Jan 1st	12:39 PM	Boffin, The Innovator	Sharer	Sustainer	Air
Jan 15th	7:08 AM	Exec, The Achiever	Container	Initiator	Earth
Feb 14th	7:12 PM	Boffin, The Innovator	Sharer	Sustainer	Air
Mar 7th	10:04 PM	Sonar, The Intuitive	Container	Adaptor	Water
Mar 24th	3:52 PM	Scout, The Trailblazer	Sharer	Initiator	Fire
April 8th	11:13 AM	Steady, The Vault	Container	Sustainer	Earth
June 14th	2:33 PM	Buzz, The Curious	Sharer	Adaptor	Air
July 2nd	2:57 PM	Sponge, The Sensitive	Container	Initiator	Water
July 16th	5:08 PM	Rex, The Dignified	Sharer	Sustainer	Fire
Aug 2nd	2:44 AM	Details, The Analyst	Container	Adaptor	Earth
Aug 27th	2:17 PM	ProCon, The Diplomat	Sharer	Initiator	Air
Sept 10th	6:41 PM	Details, The Analyst	Container	Sustainer	Water
Oct 9th	2:40 PM	ProCon, The Diplomat	Sharer	Initiator	Air
Oct 27th	10:36 AM	Sherlock, The Detective	Container	Sustainer	Water
Nov 15th	3:10 AM	Flash, The Pioneer	Sharer	Adaptor	Fire
Dec 5th	1:57 AM	Exec, The Achiever	Container	Initiator	Earth

1951

DATE	TIME	STYLE	POLARITY	RELATING	UPTAKE
Jan 1st	0:00 AM	Exec, The Achiever	Container	Initiator	Earth
Feb 9th	5:50 PM	Boffin, The Innovator	Sharer	Sustainer	Air
Feb 28th	1:04 PM	Sonar, The Intuitive	Container	Adaptor	Water
Mar 16th	11:53 AM	Scout, The Trailblazer	Sharer	Initiator	Fire
April 2nd	3:27 AM	Steady, The Vault	Container	Sustainer	Earth
May 1st	9:25 PM	Scout, The Trailblazer	Sharer	Initiator	Fire
May 15th	1:40 AM	Steady, The Vault	Container	Sustainer	Earth
June 9th	8:43 AM	Buzz, The Curious	Sharer	Adaptor	Air
June 24th	3:13 AM	Sponge, The Sensitive	Container	Initiator	Water
July 8th	1:39 PM	Rex, The Dignified	Sharer	Sustainer	Fire
July 27th	3:24 PM	Details, The Analyst	Container	Adaptor	Earth
Oct 2nd	2:25 PM	ProCon, The Diplomat	Sharer	Initiator	Air
Oct 19th	9:52 PM	Sherlock, The Detective	Container	Sustainer	Water
Nov 8th	4:59 AM	Flash, The Pioneer	Sharer	Adaptor	Fire
Dec 1st	8:41 PM	Exec, The Achiever	Container	Initiator	Earth
Dec 12th	11:32 AM	Flash, The Pioneer	Sharer	Adaptor	Fire

1952

DATE	TIME	STYLE	POLARITY	RELATING	UPTAKE
Jan 1st	0:00 AM	Flash, The Pioneer	Sharer	Adaptor	Fire
Jan 13th	6:44 AM	Exec, The Achiever	Container	Initiator	Earth
Feb 3rd	1:38 AM	Boffin, The Innovator	Sharer	Sustainer	Air
Feb 20th	6:55 PM	Sonar, The Intuitive	Container	Adaptor	Water
Mar 7th	5:10 PM	Scout, The Trailblazer	Sharer	Initiator	Fire
May 14th	2:43 PM	Steady, The Vault	Container	Sustainer	Earth
May 31st	3:26 PM	Buzz, The Curious	Sharer	Adaptor	Air
June 14th	12:22 PM	Sponge, The Sensitive	Container	Initiator	Water
June 30th	10:27 AM	Rex, The Dignified	Sharer	Sustainer	Fire
Sept 7th	12:02 PM	Details, The Analyst	Container	Adaptor	Earth
Sept 23rd	6:45 PM	ProCon, The Diplomat	Sharer	Initiator	Air
Oct 11th	1:05 PM	Sherlock, The Detective	Container	Sustainer	Water
Nov 1st	5:34 AM	Flash, The Pioneer	Sharer	Adaptor	Fire

1953

DATE	TIME	STYLE	POLARITY	RELATING	UPTAKE
Jan 1st	0:00 AM	Flash, The Pioneer	Sharer	Adaptor	Fire
Jan 6th	1:24 PM	Exec, The Achiever	Container	Initiator	Earth
Jan 25th	7:10 PM	Boffin, The Innovator	Sharer	Sustainer	Air
Feb 11th	11:57 PM	Sonar, The Intuitive	Container	Adaptor	Water
Mar 2nd	7:21 PM	Scout, The Trailblazer	Sharer	Initiator	Fire
Mar 15th	9:01 PM	Sonar, The Intuitive	Container	Adaptor	Water
April 17th	4:48 PM	Scout, The Trailblazer	Sharer	Initiator	Fire
May 8th	6:24 AM	Steady, The Vault	Container	Sustainer	Earth
May 23rd	3:58 AM	Buzz, The Curious	Sharer	Adaptor	Air
June 6th	8:23 AM	Sponge, The Sensitive	Container	Initiator	Water
June 26th	11:01 AM	Rex, The Dignified	Sharer	Sustainer	Fire
July 28th	2:09 PM	Sponge, The Sensitive	Container	Initiator	Water
Aug 11th	2:04 PM	Rex, The Dignified	Sharer	Sustainer	Fire
Aug 30th	10:59 PM	Details, The Analyst	Container	Adaptor	Earth
Sept 15th	9:45 PM	ProCon, The Diplomat	Sharer	Initiator	Air
Oct 4th	4:40 PM	Sherlock, The Detective	Container	Sustainer	Water
Oct 31st	3:49 PM	Flash, The Pioneer	Sharer	Adaptor	Fire
Nov 6th	9:36 PM	Sherlock, The Detective	Container	Sustainer	Water
Dec 10th	2:48 PM	Flash, The Pioneer	Sharer	Adaptor	Fire
Dec 30th	5:14 PM	Exec, The Achiever	Container	Initiator	Earth

1954

DATE	TIME	STYLE	POLARITY	RELATING	UPTAKE
Jan 1st	0:00 AM	Exec, The Achiever	Container	Initiator	Earth
Jan 18th	7:43 AM	Boffin, The Innovator	Sharer	Sustainer	Air
Feb 4th	6:03 PM	Sonar, The Intuitive	Container	Adaptor	Water
April 13th	11:34 AM	Scout, The Trailblazer	Sharer	Initiator	Fire
April 30th	11:26 AM	Steady, The Vault	Container	Sustainer	Earth
May 14th	1:57 PM	Buzz, The Curious	Sharer	Adaptor	Air
May 30th	4:13 PM	Sponge, The Sensitive	Container	Initiator	Water
Aug 7th	2:44 PM	Rex, The Dignified	Sharer	Sustainer	Fire
Aug 22nd	5:42 PM	Details, The Analyst	Container	Adaptor	Earth
Sept 8th	8:05 AM	ProCon, The Diplomat	Sharer	Initiator	Air
Sept 29th	4:06 AM	Sherlock, The Detective	Container	Sustainer	Water
Nov 4th	12:18 PM	ProCon, The Diplomat	Sharer	Initiator	Air
Nov 11th	10:25 AM	Sherlock, The Detective	Container	Sustainer	Water
Dec 4th	7:02 AM	Flash, The Pioneer	Sharer	Adaptor	Fire
Dec 23rd	12:10 PM	Exec, The Achiever	Container	Initiator	Earth

1955

DATE	TIME	STYLE	POLARITY	RELATING	UPTAKE
Jan 1st	0:00 AM	Exec, The Achiever	Container	Initiator	Earth
Jan 10th	11:05 PM	Boffin, The Innovator	Sharer	Sustainer	Air
Mar 17th	8:49 PM	Sonar, The Intuitive	Container	Adaptor	Water
April 6th	4:14 PM	Scout, The Trailblazer	Sharer	Initiator	Fire
April 22nd	2:57 AM	Steady, The Vault	Container	Sustainer	Earth
May 6th	1:05 PM	Buzz, The Curious	Sharer	Adaptor	Air
July 13th	2:44 PM	Sponge, The Sensitive	Container	Initiator	Water
July 30th	5:22 PM	Rex, The Dignified	Sharer	Sustainer	Fire
Aug 14th	1:08 PM	Details, The Analyst	Container	Adaptor	Earth
Sept 1st	12:06 PM	ProCon, The Diplomat	Sharer	Initiator	Air
Nov 8th	6:57 AM	Sherlock, The Detective	Container	Sustainer	Water
Nov 27th	4:34 AM	Flash, The Pioneer	Sharer	Adaptor	Fire
Dec 16th	6:06 AM	Exec, The Achiever	Container	Initiator	Earth

1956

DATE	TIME	STYLE	POLARITY	RELATING	UPTAKE
Jan 1st	0:00 AM	Exec, The Achiever	Container	Initiator	Earth
Jan 4th	9:16 AM	Boffin, The Innovator	Sharer	Sustainer	Air
Feb 2nd	1:16 PM	Exec, The Achiever	Container	Initiator	Earth
Feb 15th	6:34 AM	Boffin, The Innovator	Sharer	Sustainer	Air
Mar 11th	10:27 AM	Sonar, The Intuitive	Container	Adaptor	Water
Mar 28th	10:41 PM	Scout, The Trailblazer	Sharer	Initiator	Fire
April 12th	5:10 PM	Steady, The Vault	Container	Sustainer	Earth
April 29th	10:41 PM	Buzz, The Curious	Sharer	Adaptor	Air
July 6th	7:02 PM	Sponge, The Sensitive	Container	Initiator	Water
July 21st	5:35 AM	Rex, The Dignified	Sharer	Sustainer	Fire
Aug 5th	7:06 PM	Details, The Analyst	Container	Adaptor	Earth
Aug 26th	1:30 PM	ProCon, The Diplomat	Sharer	Initiator	Air
Sept 29th	9:40 PM	Details, The Analyst	Container	Sustainer	Water
Oct 11th	7:30 AM	ProCon, The Diplomat	Sharer	Initiator	Air
Oct 31st	8:19 AM	Sherlock, The Detective	Container	Sustainer	Water
Nov 18th	9:42 PM	Flash, The Pioneer	Sharer	Adaptor	Fire
Dec 8th	7:11 AM	Exec, The Achiever	Container	Initiator	Earth

1957

DATE	TIME	STYLE	POLARITY	RELATING	UPTAKE
Jan 1st	0:00 AM	Exec, The Achiever	Container	Initiator	Earth
Feb 12th	2:30 PM	Boffin, The Innovator	Sharer	Sustainer	Air
Mar 4th	11:34 AM	Sonar, The Intuitive	Container	Adaptor	Water
Mar 20th	7:48 PM	Scout, The Trailblazer	Sharer	Initiator	Fire
April 4th	11:37 PM	Steady, The Vault	Container	Sustainer	Earth
June 12th	1:40 PM	Buzz, The Curious	Sharer	Adaptor	Air
June 28th	5:08 PM	Sponge, The Sensitive	Container	Initiator	Water
July 12th	7:41 PM	Rex, The Dignified	Sharer	Sustainer	Fire
July 30th	1:44 AM	Details, The Analyst	Container	Adaptor	Earth
Oct 6th	11:08 AM	ProCon, The Diplomat	Sharer	Initiator	Air
Oct 23rd	8:50 PM	Sherlock, The Detective	Container	Sustainer	Water
Nov 11th	6:00 PM	Flash, The Pioneer	Sharer	Adaptor	Fire
Dec 2nd	11:19 AM	Exec, The Achiever	Container	Initiator	Earth
Dec 28th	5:55 PM	Flash, The Pioneer	Sharer	Adaptor	Fire

1958

DATE	TIME	STYLE	POLARITY	RELATING	UPTAKE
Jan 1st	0:00 AM	Flash, The Pioneer	Sharer	Adaptor	Fire
Jan 14th	10:03 AM	Exec, The Achiever	Container	Initiator	Earth
Feb 6th	3:21 PM	Boffin, The Innovator	Sharer	Sustainer	Air
Feb 24th	9:44 PM	Sonar, The Intuitive	Container	Adaptor	Water
Mar 12th	5:31 PM	Scout, The Trailblazer	Sharer	Initiator	Fire
April 2nd	7:20 PM	Steady, The Vault	Container	Sustainer	Earth
April 10th	12:35 PM	Scout, The Trailblazer	Sharer	Initiator	Fire
May 17th	1:53 AM	Steady, The Vault	Container	Sustainer	Earth
June 5th	8:59 PM	Buzz, The Curious	Sharer	Adaptor	Air
June 20th	2:20 AM	Sponge, The Sensitive	Container	Initiator	Water
July 4th	11:46 PM	Rex, The Dignified	Sharer	Sustainer	Fire
July 26th	10:08 AM	Details, The Analyst	Container	Adaptor	Earth
Aug 23rd	2:36 PM	Rex, The Dignified	Sharer	Sustainer	Fire
Sept 11th	1:10 AM	Details, The Analyst	Container	Adaptor	Earth
Sept 28th	10:45 PM	ProCon, The Diplomat	Sharer	Initiator	Air
Oct 16th	8:52 AM	Sherlock, The Detective	Container	Sustainer	Water
Nov 5th	2:36 AM	Flash, The Pioneer	Sharer	Adaptor	Fire

1959

DATE	TIME	STYLE	POLARITY	RELATING	UPTAKE
Jan 1st	0:00 AM	Flash, The Pioneer	Sharer	Adaptor	Fire
Jan 10th	4:47 PM	Exec, The Achiever	Container	Initiator	Earth
Jan 30th	3:41 PM	Boffin, The Innovator	Sharer	Sustainer	Air
Feb 17th	2:15 AM	Sonar, The Intuitive	Container	Adaptor	Water
Mar 5th	11:52 AM	Scout, The Trailblazer	Sharer	Initiator	Fire
May 12th	7:48 PM	Steady, The Vault	Container	Sustainer	Earth
May 28th	5:35 PM	Buzz, The Curious	Sharer	Adaptor	Air
June 11th	2:11 PM	Sponge, The Sensitive	Container	Initiator	Water
June 28th	4:31 PM	Rex, The Dignified	Sharer	Sustainer	Fire
Sept 5th	2:28 AM	Details, The Analyst	Container	Adaptor	Earth
Sept 21st	1:20 AM	ProCon, The Diplomat	Sharer	Initiator	Air
Oct 9th	4:02 AM	Sherlock, The Detective	Container	Sustainer	Water
Oct 31st	1:16 AM	Flash, The Pioneer	Sharer	Adaptor	Fire
Nov 25th	12:07 PM	Sherlock, The Detective	Container	Sustainer	Water
Dec 13th	3:42 PM	Flash, The Pioneer	Sharer	Adaptor	Fire

1960

DATE	TIME	STYLE	POLARITY	RELATING	UPTAKE
Jan 1st	0:00 AM	Flash, The Pioneer	Sharer	Adaptor	Fire
Jan 4th	8:24 AM	Exec, The Achiever	Container	Initiator	Earth
Jan 23rd	6:16 AM	Boffin, The Innovator	Sharer	Sustainer	Air
Feb 9th	10:13 AM	Sonar, The Intuitive	Container	Adaptor	Water
April 16th	2:22 AM	Scout, The Trailblazer	Sharer	Initiator	Fire
May 4th	4:45 PM	Steady, The Vault	Container	Sustainer	Earth
May 19th	3:27 AM	Buzz, The Curious	Sharer	Adaptor	Air
June 2nd	8:31 PM	Sponge, The Sensitive	Container	Initiator	Water
July 1st	1:08 AM	Rex, The Dignified	Sharer	Sustainer	Fire
July 6th	12:59 AM	Sponge, The Sensitive	Container	Initiator	Water
Aug 10th	5:49 PM	Rex, The Dignified	Sharer	Sustainer	Fire
Aug 27th	3:11 AM	Details, The Analyst	Container	Adaptor	Earth
Sept 12th	6:29 AM	ProCon, The Diplomat	Sharer	Initiator	Air
Oct 1st	5:17 PM	Sherlock, The Detective	Container	Sustainer	Water
Dec 7th	5:30 PM	Flash, The Pioneer	Sharer	Adaptor	Fire
Dec 27th	7:21 AM	Exec, The Achiever	Container	Initiator	Earth

1961

DATE	TIME	STYLE	POLARITY	RELATING	UPTAKE
Jan 1st	0:00 AM	Exec, The Achiever	Container	Initiator	Earth
Jan 14th	6:58 PM	Boffin, The Innovator	Sharer	Sustainer	Air
Feb 1st	9:39 PM	Sonar, The Intuitive	Container	Adaptor	Water
Feb 24th	8:31 PM	Boffin, The Innovator	Sharer	Sustainer	Air
Mar 18th	10:16 AM	Sonar, The Intuitive	Container	Adaptor	Water
April 10th	9:22 AM	Scout, The Trailblazer	Sharer	Initiator	Fire
April 26th	2:34 PM	Steady, The Vault	Container	Sustainer	Earth
May 10th	4:34 PM	Buzz, The Curious	Sharer	Adaptor	Air
May 28th	5:23 PM	Sponge, The Sensitive	Container	Initiator	Water
Aug 4th	1:15 AM	Rex, The Dignified	Sharer	Sustainer	Fire
Aug 18th	8:52 PM	Details, The Analyst	Container	Adaptor	Earth
Sept 4th	10:32 PM	ProCon, The Diplomat	Sharer	Initiator	Air
Sept 27th	12:16 PM	Sherlock, The Detective	Container	Sustainer	Water
Oct 22nd	2:29 AM	ProCon, The Diplomat	Sharer	Initiator	Air
Nov 10th	11:53 PM	Sherlock, The Detective	Container	Sustainer	Water
Nov 30th	10:54 PM	Flash, The Pioneer	Sharer	Adaptor	Fire
Dec 20th	1:04 AM	Exec, The Achiever	Container	Initiator	Earth

1962

DATE	TIME	STYLE	POLARITY	RELATING	UPTAKE
Jan 1st	0:00 AM	Exec, The Achiever	Container	Initiator	Earth
Jan 7th	3:08 PM	Boffin, The Innovator	Sharer	Sustainer	Air
Mar 15th	11:43 AM	Sonar, The Intuitive	Container	Adaptor	Water
April 3rd	2:32 AM	Scout, The Trailblazer	Sharer	Initiator	Fire
April 18th	4:10 AM	Steady, The Vault	Container	Sustainer	Earth
May 3rd	6:05 AM	Buzz, The Curious	Sharer	Adaptor	Air
July 11th	7:36 AM	Sponge, The Sensitive	Container	Initiator	Water
July 26th	6:50 PM	Rex, The Dignified	Sharer	Sustainer	Fire
Aug 10th	7:29 PM	Details, The Analyst	Container	Adaptor	Earth
Aug 29th	3:48 PM	ProCon, The Diplomat	Sharer	Initiator	Air
Nov 5th	2:20 AM	Sherlock, The Detective	Container	Sustainer	Water
Nov 23rd	5:31 PM	Flash, The Pioneer	Sharer	Adaptor	Fire
Dec 12th	8:51 PM	Exec, The Achiever	Container	Initiator	Earth

1963

DATE	TIME	STYLE	POLARITY	RELATING	UPTAKE
Jan 1st	0:00 AM	Exec, The Achiever	Container	Initiator	Earth
Jan 2nd	1:10 AM	Boffin, The Innovator	Sharer	Sustainer	Air
Jan 20th	4:56 AM	Exec, The Achiever	Container	Initiator	Earth
Feb 15th	10:08 AM	Boffin, The Innovator	Sharer	Sustainer	Air
Mar 9th	5:26 AM	Sonar, The Intuitive	Container	Adaptor	Water
Mar 26th	3:52 AM	Scout, The Trailblazer	Sharer	Initiator	Fire
April 9th	10:03 PM	Steady, The Vault	Container	Sustainer	Earth
May 3rd	4:14 AM	Buzz, The Curious	Sharer	Adaptor	Air
May 10th	7:56 PM	Steady, The Vault	Container	Sustainer	Earth
June 14th	11:20 PM	Buzz, The Curious	Sharer	Adaptor	Air
July 4th	3:00 AM	Sponge, The Sensitive	Container	Initiator	Water
July 18th	6:19 AM	Rex, The Dignified	Sharer	Sustainer	Fire
Aug 3rd	9:20 AM	Details, The Analyst	Container	Adaptor	Earth
Aug 26th	8:33 PM	ProCon, The Diplomat	Sharer	Initiator	Air
Sept 16th	8:17 PM	Details, The Analyst	Container	Adaptor	Earth
Oct 10th	4:44 PM	ProCon, The Diplomat	Sharer	Initiator	Air
Oct 28th	7:54 PM	Sherlock, The Detective	Container	Sustainer	Water
Nov 16th	11:07 AM	Flash, The Pioneer	Sharer	Adaptor	Fire
Dec 6th	5:17 AM	Exec, The Achiever	Container	Initiator	Earth

1964

DATE	TIME	STYLE	POLARITY	RELATING	UPTAKE
Jan 1st	0:00 AM	Exec, The Achiever	Container	Initiator	Earth
Feb 10th	9:30 PM	Boffin, The Innovator	Sharer	Sustainer	Air
Feb 29th	10:50 PM	Sonar, The Intuitive	Container	Adaptor	Water
Mar 16th	11:54 PM	Scout, The Trailblazer	Sharer	Initiator	Fire
April 2nd	12:57 AM	Steady, The Vault	Container	Sustainer	Earth
June 9th	3:45 PM	Buzz, The Curious	Sharer	Adaptor	Air
June 24th	5:17 PM	Sponge, The Sensitive	Container	Initiator	Water
July 9th	12:38 AM	Rex, The Dignified	Sharer	Sustainer	Fire
July 27th	11:35 AM	Details, The Analyst	Container	Adaptor	Earth
Oct 3rd	12:12 AM	ProCon, The Diplomat	Sharer	Initiator	Air
Oct 20th	7:11 AM	Sherlock, The Detective	Container	Sustainer	Water
Nov 8th	11:02 AM	Flash, The Pioneer	Sharer	Adaptor	Fire
Nov 30th	7:30 PM	Exec, The Achiever	Container	Initiator	Earth
Dec 16th	2:01 PM	Flash, The Pioneer	Sharer	Adaptor	Fire

1965

DATE	TIME	STYLE	POLARITY	RELATING	UPTAKE
Jan 1st	0:00 AM	Flash, The Pioneer	Sharer	Adaptor	Fire
Jan 13th	3:12 AM	Exec, The Achiever	Container	Initiator	Earth
Feb 3rd	9:02 AM	Boffin, The Innovator	Sharer	Sustainer	Air
Feb 21st	5:40 AM	Sonar, The Intuitive	Container	Adaptor	Water
Mar 9th	2:19 AM	Scout, The Trailblazer	Sharer	Initiator	Fire
May 15th	1:19 PM	Steady, The Vault	Container	Sustainer	Earth
June 2nd	3:47 AM	Buzz, The Curious	Sharer	Adaptor	Air
June 16th	2:04 AM	Sponge, The Sensitive	Container	Initiator	Water
July 1st	3:55 PM	Rex, The Dignified	Sharer	Sustainer	Fire
July 31st	11:23 AM	Details, The Analyst	Container	Adaptor	Earth
Aug 3rd	4:57 AM	Rex, The Dignified	Sharer	Sustainer	Fire
Sept 8th	5:14 PM	Details, The Analyst	Container	Adaptor	Earth
Sept 25th	5:49 AM	ProCon, The Diplomat	Sharer	Initiator	Air
Oct 12th	9:15 PM	Sherlock, The Detective	Container	Sustainer	Water
Nov 2nd	6:04 AM	Flash, The Pioneer	Sharer	Adaptor	Fire

1966

DATE	TIME	STYLE	POLARITY	RELATING	UPTAKE
Jan 1st	0:00 AM	Flash, The Pioneer	Sharer	Adaptor	Fire
Jan 7th	6:26 PM	Exec, The Achiever	Container	Initiator	Earth
Jan 27th	4:10 AM	Boffin, The Innovator	Sharer	Sustainer	Air
Feb 13th	10:17 AM	Sonar, The Intuitive	Container	Adaptor	Water
Mar 3rd	2:57 AM	Scout, The Trailblazer	Sharer	Initiator	Fire
Mar 22nd	2:34 AM	Sonar, The Intuitive	Container	Adaptor	Water
April 17th	9:31 PM	Scout, The Trailblazer	Sharer	Initiator	Fire
May 9th	2:48 PM	Steady, The Vault	Container	Sustainer	Earth
May 24th	5:59 PM	Buzz, The Curious	Sharer	Adaptor	Air
June 7th	7:11 PM	Sponge, The Sensitive	Container	Initiator	Water
June 26th	7:05 PM	Rex, The Dignified	Sharer	Sustainer	Fire
Sept 1st	10:35 AM	Details, The Analyst	Container	Adaptor	Earth
Sept 17th	8:19 AM	ProCon, The Diplomat	Sharer	Initiator	Air
Oct 5th	10:03 PM	Sherlock, The Detective	Container	Sustainer	Water
Oct 30th	7:38 AM	Flash, The Pioneer	Sharer	Adaptor	Fire
Nov 13th	3:03 AM	Sherlock, The Detective	Container	Sustainer	Water
Dec 11th	3:27 PM	Flash, The Pioneer	Sharer	Adaptor	Fire

1967

DATE	TIME	STYLE	POLARITY	RELATING	UPTAKE
Jan 1st	0:00 AM	Flash, The Pioneer	Sharer	Adaptor	Fire
Jan 1st	12:52 AM	Exec, The Achiever	Container	Initiator	Earth
Jan 19th	5:05 PM	Boffin, The Innovator	Sharer	Sustainer	Air
Feb 6th	12:38 AM	Sonar, The Intuitive	Container	Adaptor	Water
April 14th	2:38 PM	Scout, The Trailblazer	Sharer	Initiator	Fire
May 1st	11:26 PM	Steady, The Vault	Container	Sustainer	Earth
May 16th	3:27 AM	Buzz, The Curious	Sharer	Adaptor	Air
May 31st	6:02 PM	Sponge, The Sensitive	Container	Initiator	Water
Aug 8th	10:09 PM	Rex, The Dignified	Sharer	Sustainer	Fire
Aug 24th	6:17 AM	Details, The Analyst	Container	Adaptor	Earth
Sept 9th	4:53 PM	ProCon, The Diplomat	Sharer	Initiator	Air
Sept 30th	1:46 AM	Sherlock, The Detective	Container	Sustainer	Water
Dec 5th	1:41 PM	Flash, The Pioneer	Sharer	Adaptor	Fire
Dec 24th	8:33 PM	Exec, The Achiever	Container	Initiator	Earth

1968

DATE	TIME	STYLE	POLARITY	RELATING	UPTAKE
Jan 1st	0:00 AM	Exec, The Achiever	Container	Initiator	Earth
Jan 12th	7:19 AM	Boffin, The Innovator	Sharer	Sustainer	Air
Feb 1st	12:57 PM	Sonar, The Intuitive	Container	Adaptor	Water
Feb 11th	6:13 PM	Boffin, The Innovator	Sharer	Sustainer	Air
Mar 17th	2:45 PM	Sonar, The Intuitive	Container	Adaptor	Water
April 7th	1:01 AM	Scout, The Trailblazer	Sharer	Initiator	Fire
April 22nd	4:18 PM	Steady, The Vault	Container	Sustainer	Earth
May 6th	10:56 PM	Buzz, The Curious	Sharer	Adaptor	Air
May 29th	10:42 PM	Sponge, The Sensitive	Container	Initiator	Water
June 13th	10:26 PM	Buzz, The Curious	Sharer	Adaptor	Air
July 13th	1:30 AM	Sponge, The Sensitive	Container	Initiator	Water
July 31st	6:11 AM	Rex, The Dignified	Sharer	Sustainer	Fire
Aug 15th	12:53 AM	Details, The Analyst	Container	Adaptor	Earth
Sept 1st	4:59 PM	ProCon, The Diplomat	Sharer	Initiator	Air
Sept 28th	2:40 PM	Sherlock, The Detective	Container	Sustainer	Water
Oct 7th	10:25 PM	ProCon, The Diplomat	Sharer	Initiator	Air
Nov 8th	11:00 AM	Sherlock, The Detective	Container	Sustainer	Water
Nov 27th	12:47 PM	Flash, The Pioneer	Sharer	Adaptor	Fire
Dec 16th	2:11 PM	Exec, The Achiever	Container	Initiator	Earth

1969

DATE	TIME	STYLE	POLARITY	RELATING	UPTAKE
Jan 1st	0:00 AM	Exec, The Achiever	Container	Initiator	Earth
Jan 4th	12:18 PM	Boffin, The Innovator	Sharer	Sustainer	Air
Mar 12th	3:19 PM	Sonar, The Intuitive	Container	Adaptor	Water
Mar 30th	9:59 AM	Scout, The Trailblazer	Sharer	Initiator	Fire
April 14th	5:55 AM	Steady, The Vault	Container	Sustainer	Earth
April 30th	3:18 PM	Buzz, The Curious	Sharer	Adaptor	Air
July 8th	3:58 AM	Sponge, The Sensitive	Container	Initiator	Water
July 22nd	7:11 PM	Rex, The Dignified	Sharer	Sustainer	Fire
Aug 7th	4:21 AM	Details, The Analyst	Container	Adaptor	Earth
Aug 27th	6:50 AM	ProCon, The Diplomat	Sharer	Initiator	Air
Oct 7th	6:23 AM	Details, The Analyst	Container	Adaptor	Earth
Oct 9th	5:13 PM	ProCon, The Diplomat	Sharer	Initiator	Air
Nov 1st	4:53 PM	Sherlock, The Detective	Container	Sustainer	Water
Nov 20th	6:00 AM	Flash, The Pioneer	Sharer	Adaptor	Fire
Dec 9th	1:21 PM	Exec, The Achiever	Container	Initiator	Earth

1970

DATE	TIME	STYLE	POLARITY	RELATING	UPTAKE
Jan 1st	0:00 AM	Exec, The Achiever	Container	Initiator	Earth
Feb 13th	1:08 PM	Boffin, The Innovator	Sharer	Sustainer	Air
Mar 5th	8:10 PM	Sonar, The Intuitive	Container	Adaptor	Water
Mar 22nd	7:59 AM	Scout, The Trailblazer	Sharer	Initiator	Fire
April 6th	7:40 AM	Steady, The Vault	Container	Sustainer	Earth
June 13th	12:46 PM	Buzz, The Curious	Sharer	Adaptor	Air
June 30th	6:22 AM	Sponge, The Sensitive	Container	Initiator	Water
July 14th	8:06 AM	Rex, The Dignified	Sharer	Sustainer	Fire
July 31st	5:21 AM	Details, The Analyst	Container	Adaptor	Earth
Oct 7th	6:04 PM	ProCon, The Diplomat	Sharer	Initiator	Air
Oct 25th	6:16 AM	Sherlock, The Detective	Container	Sustainer	Water
Nov 13th	1:16 AM	Flash, The Pioneer	Sharer	Adaptor	Fire
Dec 3rd	10:14 AM	Exec, The Achiever	Container	Initiator	Earth

1971

DATE	TIME	STYLE	POLARITY	RELATING	UPTAKE
Jan 1st	0:00 AM	Exec, The Achiever	Container	Initiator	Earth
Jan 2nd	11:40 PM	Flash, The Pioneer	Sharer	Adaptor	Fire
Jan 14th	2:16 AM	Exec, The Achiever	Container	Initiator	Earth
Feb 7th	8:51 PM	Boffin, The Innovator	Sharer	Sustainer	Air
Feb 26th	7:57 AM	Sonar, The Intuitive	Container	Adaptor	Water
Mar 14th	4:46 AM	Scout, The Trailblazer	Sharer	Initiator	Fire
April 1st	2:11 PM	Steady, The Vault	Container	Sustainer	Earth
April 18th	9:47 PM	Scout, The Trailblazer	Sharer	Initiator	Fire
May 17th	3:32 AM	Steady, The Vault	Container	Sustainer	Earth
June 7th	6:45 AM	Buzz, The Curious	Sharer	Adaptor	Air
June 21st	4:25 PM	Sponge, The Sensitive	Container	Initiator	Water
July 6th	8:53 AM	Rex, The Dignified	Sharer	Sustainer	Fire
July 26th	5:03 PM	Details, The Analyst	Container	Adaptor	Earth
Aug 29th	8:57 PM	Rex, The Dignified	Sharer	Sustainer	Fire
Sept 11th	6:45 AM	Details, The Analyst	Container	Adaptor	Earth
Sept 30th	9:19 AM	ProCon, The Diplomat	Sharer	Initiator	Air
Oct 17th	5:49 PM	Sherlock, The Detective	Container	Sustainer	Water
Nov 6th	6:58 AM	Flash, The Pioneer	Sharer	Adaptor	Fire

1972

DATE	TIME	STYLE	POLARITY	RELATING	UPTAKE
Jan 1st	0:00 AM	Flash, The Pioneer	Sharer	Adaptor	Fire
Jan 11th	6:18 PM	Exec, The Achiever	Container	Initiator	Earth
Jan 31st	11:46 PM	Boffin, The Innovator	Sharer	Sustainer	Air
Feb 18th	12:53 PM	Sonar, The Intuitive	Container	Adaptor	Water
Mar 5th	4:59 PM	Scout, The Trailblazer	Sharer	Initiator	Fire
May 12th	11:45 PM	Steady, The Vault	Container	Sustainer	Earth
May 29th	6:46 AM	Buzz, The Curious	Sharer	Adaptor	Air
June 12th	2:56 AM	Sponge, The Sensitive	Container	Initiator	Water
June 28th	4:52 PM	Rex, The Dignified	Sharer	Sustainer	Fire
Sept 5th	11:36 AM	Details, The Analyst	Container	Adaptor	Earth
Sept 21st	12:11 PM	ProCon, The Diplomat	Sharer	Initiator	Air
Oct 9th	11:11 AM	Sherlock, The Detective	Container	Sustainer	Water
Oct 30th	7:27 PM	Flash, The Pioneer	Sharer	Adaptor	Fire
Nov 29th	7:46 AM	Sherlock, The Detective	Container	Sustainer	Water
Dec 12th	11:20 PM	Flash, The Pioneer	Sharer	Adaptor	Fire

1973

DATE	TIME	STYLE	POLARITY	RELATING	UPTAKE
Jan 1st	0:00 AM	Flash, The Pioneer	Sharer	Adaptor	Fire
Jan 4th	2:41 PM	Exec, The Achiever	Container	Initiator	Earth
Jan 23rd	3:23 PM	Boffin, The Innovator	Sharer	Sustainer	Air
Feb 9th	7:30 PM	Sonar, The Intuitive	Container	Adaptor	Water
April 16th	9:17 PM	Scout, The Trailblazer	Sharer	Initiator	Fire
May 6th	2:55 AM	Steady, The Vault	Container	Sustainer	Earth
May 20th	5:24 PM	Buzz, The Curious	Sharer	Adaptor	Air
June 4th	4:42 AM	Sponge, The Sensitive	Container	Initiator	Water
June 27th	6:42 AM	Rex, The Dignified	Sharer	Sustainer	Fire
July 16th	7:47 AM	Sponge, The Sensitive	Container	Initiator	Water
Aug 11th	12:21 PM	Rex, The Dignified	Sharer	Sustainer	Fire
Aug 28th	3:22 PM	Details, The Analyst	Container	Adaptor	Earth
Sept 13th	4:16 PM	ProCon, The Diplomat	Sharer	Initiator	Air
Oct 2nd	8:12 PM	Sherlock, The Detective	Container	Sustainer	Water
Dec 8th	9:29 PM	Flash, The Pioneer	Sharer	Adaptor	Fire
Dec 28th	3:14 PM	Exec, The Achiever	Container	Initiator	Earth

1974

DATE	TIME	STYLE	POLARITY	RELATING	UPTAKE
Jan 1st	0:00 AM	Exec, The Achiever	Container	Initiator	Earth
Jan 16th	3:56 AM	Boffin, The Innovator	Sharer	Sustainer	Air
Feb 2nd	10:42 PM	Sonar, The Intuitive	Container	Adaptor	Water
Mar 2nd	6:20 PM	Boffin, The Innovator	Sharer	Sustainer	Air
Mar 17th	8:11 PM	Sonar, The Intuitive	Container	Adaptor	Water
April 11th	3:20 PM	Scout, The Trailblazer	Sharer	Initiator	Fire
April 28th	3:10 AM	Steady, The Vault	Container	Sustainer	Earth
May 12th	4:55 AM	Buzz, The Curious	Sharer	Adaptor	Air
May 29th	8:03 AM	Sponge, The Sensitive	Container	Initiator	Water
Aug 5th	11:42 AM	Rex, The Dignified	Sharer	Sustainer	Fire
Aug 20th	9:04 AM	Details, The Analyst	Container	Adaptor	Earth
Sept 6th	5:48 AM	ProCon, The Diplomat	Sharer	Initiator	Air
Sept 28th	12:20 AM	Sherlock, The Detective	Container	Sustainer	Water
Oct 26th	11:21 PM	ProCon, The Diplomat	Sharer	Initiator	Air
Nov 11th	4:05 PM	Sherlock, The Detective	Container	Sustainer	Water
Dec 2nd	6:17 AM	Flash, The Pioneer	Sharer	Adaptor	Fire
Dec 21st	9:16 AM	Exec, The Achiever	Container	Initiator	Earth

1975

DATE	TIME	STYLE	POLARITY	RELATING	UPTAKE
Jan 1st	0:00 AM	Exec, The Achiever	Container	Initiator	Earth
Jan 8th	9:58 PM	Boffin, The Innovator	Sharer	Sustainer	Air
Mar 16th	11:50 AM	Sonar, The Intuitive	Container	Adaptor	Water
April 4th	12:28 PM	Scout, The Trailblazer	Sharer	Initiator	Fire
April 19th	5:20 PM	Steady, The Vault	Container	Sustainer	Earth
May 4th	11:55 AM	Buzz, The Curious	Sharer	Adaptor	Air
July 12th	8:56 AM	Sponge, The Sensitive	Container	Initiator	Water
July 28th	8:05 AM	Rex, The Dignified	Sharer	Sustainer	Fire
Aug 12th	6:12 AM	Details, The Analyst	Container	Adaptor	Earth
Aug 30th	5:20 PM	ProCon, The Diplomat	Sharer	Initiator	Air
Nov 6th	8:58 AM	Sherlock, The Detective	Container	Sustainer	Water
Nov 25th	1:44 AM	Flash, The Pioneer	Sharer	Adaptor	Fire
Dec 14th	4:10 AM	Exec, The Achiever	Container	Initiator	Earth

1976

DATE	TIME	STYLE	POLARITY	RELATING	UPTAKE
Jan 1st	0:00 AM	Exec, The Achiever	Container	Initiator	Earth
Jan 2nd	8:22 PM	Boffin, The Innovator	Sharer	Sustainer	Air
Jan 25th	1:34 AM	Exec, The Achiever	Container	Initiator	Earth
Feb 15th	7:03 PM	Boffin, The Innovator	Sharer	Sustainer	Air
Mar 9th	12:02 PM	Sonar, The Intuitive	Container	Adaptor	Water
Mar 26th	3:36 PM	Scout, The Trailblazer	Sharer	Initiator	Fire
April 10th	9:29 AM	Steady, The Vault	Container	Sustainer	Earth
April 29th	11:11 PM	Buzz, The Curious	Sharer	Adaptor	Air
May 19th	7:17 PM	Steady, The Vault	Container	Sustainer	Earth
June 13th	7:20 PM	Buzz, The Curious	Sharer	Adaptor	Air
July 4th	2:18 PM	Sponge, The Sensitive	Container	Initiator	Water
July 18th	7:35 PM	Rex, The Dignified	Sharer	Sustainer	Fire
Aug 3rd	4:41 PM	Details, The Analyst	Container	Adaptor	Earth
Aug 25th	8:52 PM	ProCon, The Diplomat	Sharer	Initiator	Air
Sept 21st	7:15 AM	Details, The Analyst	Container	Adaptor	Earth
Oct 10th	2:47 PM	ProCon, The Diplomat	Sharer	Initiator	Air
Oct 29th	4:55 AM	Sherlock, The Detective	Container	Sustainer	Water
Nov 16th	7:02 PM	Flash, The Pioneer	Sharer	Adaptor	Fire
Dec 6th	9:25 AM	Exec, The Achiever	Container	Initiator	Earth

1977

DATE	TIME	STYLE	POLARITY	RELATING	UPTAKE
Jan 1st	0:00 AM	Exec, The Achiever	Container	Initiator	Earth
Feb 10th	11:55 PM	Boffin, The Innovator	Sharer	Sustainer	Air
Mar 2nd	8:09 AM	Sonar, The Intuitive	Container	Adaptor	Water
Mar 18th	11:56 AM	Scout, The Trailblazer	Sharer	Initiator	Fire
April 3rd	2:46 AM	Steady, The Vault	Container	Sustainer	Earth
June 10th	9:07 PM	Buzz, The Curious	Sharer	Adaptor	Air
June 26th	7:07 AM	Sponge, The Sensitive	Container	Initiator	Water
July 10th	12:00 PM	Rex, The Dignified	Sharer	Sustainer	Fire
July 28th	10:15 AM	Details, The Analyst	Container	Adaptor	Earth
Oct 4th	9:16 AM	ProCon, The Diplomat	Sharer	Initiator	Air
Oct 21st	4:23 PM	Sherlock, The Detective	Container	Sustainer	Water
Nov 9th	5:20 PM	Flash, The Pioneer	Sharer	Adaptor	Fire
Dec 1st	6:43 AM	Exec, The Achiever	Container	Initiator	Earth
Dec 21st	7:15 AM	Flash, The Pioneer	Sharer	Adaptor	Fire

1978

DATE	TIME	STYLE	POLARITY	RELATING	UPTAKE
Jan 1st	0:00 AM	Flash, The Pioneer	Sharer	Adaptor	Fire
Jan 13th	10:07 PM	Exec, The Achiever	Container	Initiator	Earth
Feb 4th	3:54 PM	Boffin, The Innovator	Sharer	Sustainer	Air
Feb 22nd	4:11 PM	Sonar, The Intuitive	Container	Adaptor	Water
Mar 10th	12:10 PM	Scout, The Trailblazer	Sharer	Initiator	Fire
May 16th	8:20 AM	Steady, The Vault	Container	Sustainer	Earth
June 3rd	3:26 PM	Buzz, The Curious	Sharer	Adaptor	Air
June 17th	3:49 PM	Sponge, The Sensitive	Container	Initiator	Water
July 2nd	10:28 PM	Rex, The Dignified	Sharer	Sustainer	Fire
July 27th	6:10 AM	Details, The Analyst	Container	Adaptor	Earth
Aug 13th	6:40 AM	Rex, The Dignified	Sharer	Sustainer	Fire
Sept 9th	7:23 PM	Details, The Analyst	Container	Adaptor	Earth
Sept 26th	4:40 PM	ProCon, The Diplomat	Sharer	Initiator	Air
Oct 14th	5:30 AM	Sherlock, The Detective	Container	Sustainer	Water
Nov 3rd	7:48 AM	Flash, The Pioneer	Sharer	Adaptor	Fire

1979

DATE	TIME	STYLE	POLARITY	RELATING	UPTAKE
Jan 1st	0:00 AM	Flash, The Pioneer	Sharer	Adaptor	Fire
Jan 8th	10:33 PM	Exec, The Achiever	Container	Initiator	Earth
Jan 28th	12:49 PM	Boffin, The Innovator	Sharer	Sustainer	Air
Feb 14th	8:38 PM	Sonar, The Intuitive	Container	Adaptor	Water
Mar 3rd	9:32 PM	Scout, The Trailblazer	Sharer	Initiator	Fire
Mar 28th	11:01 AM	Sonar, The Intuitive	Container	Adaptor	Water
April 17th	12:48 PM	Scout, The Trailblazer	Sharer	Initiator	Fire
May 10th	10:03 PM	Steady, The Vault	Container	Sustainer	Earth
May 26th	7:44 AM	Buzz, The Curious	Sharer	Adaptor	Air
June 9th	6:32 AM	Sponge, The Sensitive	Container	Initiator	Water
June 27th	9:51 AM	Rex, The Dignified	Sharer	Sustainer	Fire
Sept 2nd	9:39 PM	Details, The Analyst	Container	Adaptor	Earth
Sept 18th	6:59 PM	ProCon, The Diplomat	Sharer	Initiator	Air
Oct 7th	3:55 AM	Sherlock, The Detective	Container	Sustainer	Water
Oct 30th	7:06 AM	Flash, The Pioneer	Sharer	Adaptor	Fire
Nov 18th	2:59 AM	Sherlock, The Detective	Container	Sustainer	Water
Dec 12th	1:34 PM	Flash, The Pioneer	Sharer	Adaptor	Fire

1980

DATE	TIME	STYLE	POLARITY	RELATING	UPTAKE
Jan 1st	0:00 AM	Flash, The Pioneer	Sharer	Adaptor	Fire
Jan 2nd	8:02 AM	Exec, The Achiever	Container	Initiator	Earth
Jan 21st	2:18 AM	Boffin, The Innovator	Sharer	Sustainer	Air
Feb 7th	8:07 AM	Sonar, The Intuitive	Container	Adaptor	Water
April 14th	3:58 PM	Scout, The Trailblazer	Sharer	Initiator	Fire
May 2nd	10:56 AM	Steady, The Vault	Container	Sustainer	Earth
May 16th	5:06 PM	Buzz, The Curious	Sharer	Adaptor	Air
May 31st	10:05 PM	Sponge, The Sensitive	Container	Initiator	Water
Aug 9th	3:31 AM	Rex, The Dignified	Sharer	Sustainer	Fire
Aug 24th	6:47 PM	Details, The Analyst	Container	Adaptor	Earth
Sept 10th	2:00 AM	ProCon, The Diplomat	Sharer	Initiator	Air
Sept 30th	1:16 AM	Sherlock, The Detective	Container	Sustainer	Water
Dec 5th	7:45 PM	Flash, The Pioneer	Sharer	Adaptor	Fire
Dec 25th	4:46 AM	Exec, The Achiever	Container	Initiator	Earth

1981

DATE	TIME	STYLE	POLARITY	RELATING	UPTAKE
Jan 1st	0:00 AM	Exec, The Achiever	Container	Initiator	Earth
Jan 12th	3:48 PM	Boffin, The Innovator	Sharer	Sustainer	Air
Jan 31st	5:35 PM	Sonar, The Intuitive	Container	Adaptor	Water
Feb 16th	7:48 AM	Boffin, The Innovator	Sharer	Sustainer	Air
Mar 18th	4:33 AM	Sonar, The Intuitive	Container	Adaptor	Water
April 8th	9:11 AM	Scout, The Trailblazer	Sharer	Initiator	Fire
April 24th	5:31 AM	Steady, The Vault	Container	Sustainer	Earth
May 8th	9:42 AM	Buzz, The Curious	Sharer	Adaptor	Air
May 28th	5:04 PM	Sponge, The Sensitive	Container	Initiator	Water
June 22nd	10:51 PM	Buzz, The Curious	Sharer	Adaptor	Air
July 12th	9:08 PM	Sponge, The Sensitive	Container	Initiator	Water
Aug 1st	6:30 PM	Rex, The Dignified	Sharer	Sustainer	Fire
Aug 16th	12:47 PM	Details, The Analyst	Container	Adaptor	Earth
Sept 2nd	10:40 PM	ProCon, The Diplomat	Sharer	Initiator	Air
Sept 27th	11:02 AM	Sherlock, The Detective	Container	Sustainer	Water
Oct 14th	1:56 AM	ProCon, The Diplomat	Sharer	Initiator	Air
Nov 9th	1:14 PM	Sherlock, The Detective	Container	Sustainer	Water
Nov 28th	8:52 PM	Flash, The Pioneer	Sharer	Adaptor	Fire
Dec 17th	10:21 PM	Exec, The Achiever	Container	Initiator	Earth

1982

DATE	TIME	STYLE	POLARITY	RELATING	UPTAKE
Jan 1st	0:00 AM	Exec, The Achiever	Container	Initiator	Earth
Jan 5th	4:49 PM	Boffin, The Innovator	Sharer	Sustainer	Air
Mar 13th	7:11 PM	Sonar, The Intuitive	Container	Adaptor	Water
Mar 31st	8:59 PM	Scout, The Trailblazer	Sharer	Initiator	Fire
April 15th	6:54 PM	Steady, The Vault	Container	Sustainer	Earth
May 1st	1:29 PM	Buzz, The Curious	Sharer	Adaptor	Air
July 9th	11:26 AM	Sponge, The Sensitive	Container	Initiator	Water
July 24th	8:48 AM	Rex, The Dignified	Sharer	Sustainer	Fire
Aug 8th	2:06 PM	Details, The Analyst	Container	Adaptor	Earth
Aug 28th	3:22 AM	ProCon, The Diplomat	Sharer	Initiator	Air
Nov 3rd	1:10 AM	Sherlock, The Detective	Container	Sustainer	Water
Nov 21st	2:28 PM	Flash, The Pioneer	Sharer	Adaptor	Fire
Dec 10th	8:04 PM	Exec, The Achiever	Container	Initiator	Earth

1983

DATE	TIME	STYLE	POLARITY	RELATING	UPTAKE
Jan 1st	0:00 AM	Exec, The Achiever	Container	Initiator	Earth
Jan 1st	1:32 PM	Boffin, The Innovator	Sharer	Sustainer	Air
Jan 12th	6:10 AM	Exec, The Achiever	Container	Initiator	Earth
Feb 14th	9:36 AM	Boffin, The Innovator	Sharer	Sustainer	Air
Mar 7th	4:24 AM	Sonar, The Intuitive	Container	Adaptor	Water
Mar 23rd	8:09 PM	Scout, The Trailblazer	Sharer	Initiator	Fire
April 7th	5:04 PM	Steady, The Vault	Container	Sustainer	Earth
June 14th	8:06 AM	Buzz, The Curious	Sharer	Adaptor	Air
July 1st	7:18 PM	Sponge, The Sensitive	Container	Initiator	Water
July 15th	8:57 PM	Rex, The Dignified	Sharer	Sustainer	Fire
Aug 1st	10:22 AM	Details, The Analyst	Container	Adaptor	Earth
Aug 29th	6:07 AM	ProCon, The Diplomat	Sharer	Initiator	Air
Sept 6th	1:59 AM	Details, The Analyst	Container	Adaptor	Earth
Oct 8th	11:44 PM	ProCon, The Diplomat	Sharer	Initiator	Air
Oct 26th	3:47 PM	Sherlock, The Detective	Container	Sustainer	Water
Nov 14th	8:56 AM	Flash, The Pioneer	Sharer	Adaptor	Fire
Dec 4th	11:22 AM	Exec, The Achiever	Container	Initiator	Earth

1984

DATE	TIME	STYLE	POLARITY	RELATING	UPTAKE
Jan 1st	0:00 AM	Exec, The Achiever	Container	Initiator	Earth
Feb 9th	1:50 AM	Boffin, The Innovator	Sharer	Sustainer	Air
Feb 27th	6:07 PM	Sonar, The Intuitive	Container	Adaptor	Water
Mar 14th	4:27 PM	Scout, The Trailblazer	Sharer	Initiator	Fire
Mar 31st	8:25 PM	Steady, The Vault	Container	Sustainer	Earth
April 25th	12:06 PM	Scout, The Trailblazer	Sharer	Initiator	Fire
May 15th	12:33 PM	Steady, The Vault	Container	Sustainer	Earth
June 7th	3:45 PM	Buzz, The Curious	Sharer	Adaptor	Air
June 22nd	6:39 AM	Sponge, The Sensitive	Container	Initiator	Water
July 6th	6:56 PM	Rex, The Dignified	Sharer	Sustainer	Fire
July 26th	6:49 AM	Details, The Analyst	Container	Adaptor	Earth
Sept 30th	7:44 PM	ProCon, The Diplomat	Sharer	Initiator	Air
Oct 18th	3:01 AM	Sherlock, The Detective	Container	Sustainer	Water
Nov 6th	12:09 PM	Flash, The Pioneer	Sharer	Adaptor	Fire
Dec 1st	4:32 PM	Exec, The Achiever	Container	Initiator	Earth
Dec 7th	8:52 PM	Flash, The Pioneer	Sharer	Adaptor	Fire

1985

DATE	TIME	STYLE	POLARITY	RELATING	UPTAKE
Jan 1st	0:00 AM	Flash, The Pioneer	Sharer	Adaptor	Fire
Jan 11th	6:25 PM	Exec, The Achiever	Container	Initiator	Earth
Feb 1st	7:43 AM	Boffin, The Innovator	Sharer	Sustainer	Air
Feb 18th	11:41 PM	Sonar, The Intuitive	Container	Adaptor	Water
Mar 7th	12:07 AM	Scout, The Trailblazer	Sharer	Initiator	Fire
May 14th	2:10 AM	Steady, The Vault	Container	Sustainer	Earth
May 30th	7:44 PM	Buzz, The Curious	Sharer	Adaptor	Air
June 13th	4:11 PM	Sponge, The Sensitive	Container	Initiator	Water
June 29th	7:34 PM	Rex, The Dignified	Sharer	Sustainer	Fire
Sept 6th	7:39 PM	Details, The Analyst	Container	Adaptor	Earth
Sept 22nd	11:13 PM	ProCon, The Diplomat	Sharer	Initiator	Air
Oct 10th	6:50 PM	Sherlock, The Detective	Container	Sustainer	Water
Oct 31st	4:44 PM	Flash, The Pioneer	Sharer	Adaptor	Fire
Dec 4th	8:16 PM	Sherlock, The Detective	Container	Sustainer	Water
Dec 12th	11:05 AM	Flash, The Pioneer	Sharer	Adaptor	Fire

1986

DATE	TIME	STYLE	POLARITY	RELATING	UPTAKE
Jan 1st	0:00 AM	Flash, The Pioneer	Sharer	Adaptor	Fire
Jan 5th	8:42 PM	Exec, The Achiever	Container	Initiator	Earth
Jan 25th	12:33 AM	Boffin, The Innovator	Sharer	Sustainer	Air
Feb 11th	5:21 AM	Sonar, The Intuitive	Container	Adaptor	Water
Mar 3rd	7:22 AM	Scout, The Trailblazer	Sharer	Initiator	Fire
Mar 11th	4:37 PM	Sonar, The Intuitive	Container	Adaptor	Water
April 17th	12:33 PM	Scout, The Trailblazer	Sharer	Initiator	Fire
May 7th	12:33 PM	Steady, The Vault	Container	Sustainer	Earth
May 22nd	7:26 AM	Buzz, The Curious	Sharer	Adaptor	Air
June 5th	2:06 PM	Sponge, The Sensitive	Container	Initiator	Water
June 26th	2:13 PM	Rex, The Dignified	Sharer	Sustainer	Fire
July 23rd	9:51 PM	Sponge, The Sensitive	Container	Initiator	Water
Aug 11th	9:09 PM	Rex, The Dignified	Sharer	Sustainer	Fire
Aug 30th	3:28 AM	Details, The Analyst	Container	Adaptor	Earth
Sept 15th	2:28 AM	ProCon, The Diplomat	Sharer	Initiator	Air
Oct 4th	12:19 AM	Sherlock, The Detective	Container	Sustainer	Water
Dec 10th	12:34 AM	Flash, The Pioneer	Sharer	Adaptor	Fire
Dec 29th	11:09 PM	Exec, The Achiever	Container	Initiator	Earth

1987

DATE	TIME	STYLE	POLARITY	RELATING	UPTAKE
Jan 1st	0:00 AM	Exec, The Achiever	Container	Initiator	Earth
Jan 17th	1:08 PM	Boffin, The Innovator	Sharer	Sustainer	Air
Feb 4th	2:31 AM	Sonar, The Intuitive	Container	Adaptor	Water
Mar 11th	11:03 PM	Boffin, The Innovator	Sharer	Sustainer	Air
Mar 13th	10:23 PM	Sonar, The Intuitive	Container	Adaptor	Water
April 12th	8:23 PM	Scout, The Trailblazer	Sharer	Initiator	Fire
April 29th	3:39 PM	Steady, The Vault	Container	Sustainer	Earth
May 13th	5:30 PM	Buzz, The Curious	Sharer	Adaptor	Air
May 30th	4:21 AM	Sponge, The Sensitive	Container	Initiator	Water
Aug 6th	9:20 PM	Rex, The Dignified	Sharer	Sustainer	Fire
Aug 21st	9:36 PM	Details, The Analyst	Container	Adaptor	Earth
Sept 7th	1:52 PM	ProCon, The Diplomat	Sharer	Initiator	Air
Sept 28th	5:21 PM	Sherlock, The Detective	Container	Sustainer	Water
Nov 1st	2:16 AM	ProCon, The Diplomat	Sharer	Initiator	Air
Nov 11th	9:57 PM	Sherlock, The Detective	Container	Sustainer	Water
Dec 3rd	1:33 PM	Flash, The Pioneer	Sharer	Adaptor	Fire
Dec 22nd	5:40 PM	Exec, The Achiever	Container	Initiator	Earth

1988

DATE	TIME	STYLE	POLARITY	RELATING	UPTAKE
Jan 1st	0:00 AM	Exec, The Achiever	Container	Initiator	Earth
Jan 10th	5:28 AM	Boffin, The Innovator	Sharer	Sustainer	Air
Mar 16th	10:09 AM	Sonar, The Intuitive	Container	Adaptor	Water
April 4th	10:04 PM	Scout, The Trailblazer	Sharer	Initiator	Fire
April 20th	6:42 AM	Steady, The Vault	Container	Sustainer	Earth
May 4th	7:40 PM	Buzz, The Curious	Sharer	Adaptor	Air
July 12th	6:42 AM	Sponge, The Sensitive	Container	Initiator	Water
July 28th	9:19 PM	Rex, The Dignified	Sharer	Sustainer	Fire
Aug 12th	5:29 PM	Details, The Analyst	Container	Adaptor	Earth
Aug 30th	8:25 PM	ProCon, The Diplomat	Sharer	Initiator	Air
Nov 6th	2:57 PM	Sherlock, The Detective	Container	Sustainer	Water
Nov 25th	10:04 AM	Flash, The Pioneer	Sharer	Adaptor	Fire
Dec 14th	11:53 AM	Exec, The Achiever	Container	Initiator	Earth

1989

DATE	TIME	STYLE	POLARITY	RELATING	UPTAKE
Jan 1st	0:00 AM	Exec, The Achiever	Container	Initiator	Earth
Jan 2nd	7:41 PM	Boffin, The Innovator	Sharer	Sustainer	Air
Jan 29th	4:30 AM	Exec, The Achiever	Container	Initiator	Earth
Feb 14th	6:11 PM	Boffin, The Innovator	Sharer	Sustainer	Air
Mar 10th	6:07 PM	Sonar, The Intuitive	Container	Adaptor	Water
Mar 28th	3:16 AM	Scout, The Trailblazer	Sharer	Initiator	Fire
April 11th	9:36 PM	Steady, The Vault	Container	Sustainer	Earth
April 29th	7:53 PM	Buzz, The Curious	Sharer	Adaptor	Air
May 28th	10:59 PM	Steady, The Vault	Container	Sustainer	Earth
June 12th	8:56 AM	Buzz, The Curious	Sharer	Adaptor	Air
July 6th	12:55 AM	Sponge, The Sensitive	Container	Initiator	Water
July 20th	9:04 AM	Rex, The Dignified	Sharer	Sustainer	Fire
Aug 5th	12:54 AM	Details, The Analyst	Container	Adaptor	Earth
Aug 26th	6:14 AM	ProCon, The Diplomat	Sharer	Initiator	Air
Sept 26th	3:48 PM	Details, The Analyst	Container	Adaptor	Earth
Oct 11th	6:11 AM	ProCon, The Diplomat	Sharer	Initiator	Air
Oct 30th	1:53 PM	Sherlock, The Detective	Container	Sustainer	Water
Nov 18th	3:10 AM	Flash, The Pioneer	Sharer	Adaptor	Fire
Dec 7th	2:30 PM	Exec, The Achiever	Container	Initiator	Earth

1990

DATE	TIME	STYLE	POLARITY	RELATING	UPTAKE
Jan 1st	0:00 AM	Exec, The Achiever	Container	Initiator	Earth
Feb 12th	1:11 AM	Boffin, The Innovator	Sharer	Sustainer	Air
Mar 3rd	5:14 PM	Sonar, The Intuitive	Container	Adaptor	Water
Mar 20th	12:04 AM	Scout, The Trailblazer	Sharer	Initiator	Fire
April 4th	7:35 AM	Steady, The Vault	Container	Sustainer	Earth
June 12th	12:29 AM	Buzz, The Curious	Sharer	Adaptor	Air
June 27th	8:46 PM	Sponge, The Sensitive	Container	Initiator	Water
July 11th	11:48 PM	Rex, The Dignified	Sharer	Sustainer	Fire
July 29th	11:10 AM	Details, The Analyst	Container	Adaptor	Earth
Oct 5th	5:44 PM	ProCon, The Diplomat	Sharer	Initiator	Air
Oct 23rd	1:46 AM	Sherlock, The Detective	Container	Sustainer	Water
Nov 11th	12:06 AM	Flash, The Pioneer	Sharer	Adaptor	Fire
Dec 2nd	12:13 AM	Exec, The Achiever	Container	Initiator	Earth
Dec 25th	11:00 PM	Flash, The Pioneer	Sharer	Adaptor	Fire

1991

DATE	TIME	STYLE	POLARITY	RELATING	UPTAKE
Jan 1st	0:00 AM	Flash, The Pioneer	Sharer	Adaptor	Fire
Jan 14th	8:02 AM	Exec, The Achiever	Container	Initiator	Earth
Feb 5th	10:20 PM	Boffin, The Innovator	Sharer	Sustainer	Air
Feb 24th	2:35 AM	Sonar, The Intuitive	Container	Adaptor	Water
Mar 11th	10:40 PM	Scout, The Trailblazer	Sharer	Initiator	Fire
May 16th	10:45 PM	Steady, The Vault	Container	Sustainer	Earth
June 5th	2:24 AM	Buzz, The Curious	Sharer	Adaptor	Air
June 19th	5:40 AM	Sponge, The Sensitive	Container	Initiator	Water
July 4th	6:05 AM	Rex, The Dignified	Sharer	Sustainer	Fire
July 26th	1:00 PM	Details, The Analyst	Container	Adaptor	Earth
Aug 19th	9:40 PM	Rex, The Dignified	Sharer	Sustainer	Fire
Sept 10th	5:14 PM	Details, The Analyst	Container	Adaptor	Earth
Sept 28th	3:26 AM	ProCon, The Diplomat	Sharer	Initiator	Air
Oct 15th	2:01 PM	Sherlock, The Detective	Container	Sustainer	Water
Nov 4th	10:41 AM	Flash, The Pioneer	Sharer	Adaptor	Fire

1992

DATE	TIME	STYLE	POLARITY	RELATING	UPTAKE
Jan 1st	0:00 AM	Flash, The Pioneer	Sharer	Adaptor	Fire
Jan 10th	1:46 AM	Exec, The Achiever	Container	Initiator	Earth
Jan 29th	9:15 PM	Boffin, The Innovator	Sharer	Sustainer	Air
Feb 16th	7:04 AM	Sonar, The Intuitive	Container	Adaptor	Water
Mar 3rd	9:45 PM	Scout, The Trailblazer	Sharer	Initiator	Fire
April 3rd	11:52 PM	Sonar, The Intuitive	Container	Adaptor	Water
April 14th	5:35 PM	Scout, The Trailblazer	Sharer	Initiator	Fire
May 11th	4:10 AM	Steady, The Vault	Container	Sustainer	Earth
May 26th	9:16 PM	Buzz, The Curious	Sharer	Adaptor	Air
June 9th	6:27 PM	Sponge, The Sensitive	Container	Initiator	Water
June 27th	5:11 AM	Rex, The Dignified	Sharer	Sustainer	Fire
Sept 3rd	8:03 AM	Details, The Analyst	Container	Adaptor	Earth
Sept 19th	5:41 AM	ProCon, The Diplomat	Sharer	Initiator	Air
Oct 7th	10:13 AM	Sherlock, The Detective	Container	Sustainer	Water
Oct 29th	5:02 PM	Flash, The Pioneer	Sharer	Adaptor	Fire
Nov 21st	7:44 PM	Sherlock, The Detective	Container	Sustainer	Water
Dec 12th	8:05 AM	Flash, The Pioneer	Sharer	Adaptor	Fire

1993

DATE	TIME	STYLE	POLARITY	RELATING	UPTAKE
Jan 1st	0:00 AM	Flash, The Pioneer	Sharer	Adaptor	Fire
Jan 2nd	2:47 PM	Exec, The Achiever	Container	Initiator	Earth
Jan 21st	11:25 AM	Boffin, The Innovator	Sharer	Sustainer	Air
Feb 7th	4:19 PM	Sonar, The Intuitive	Container	Adaptor	Water
April 15th	3:18 PM	Scout, The Trailblazer	Sharer	Initiator	Fire
May 3rd	9:54 PM	Steady, The Vault	Container	Sustainer	Earth
May 18th	6:53 AM	Buzz, The Curious	Sharer	Adaptor	Air
June 2nd	3:54 AM	Sponge, The Sensitive	Container	Initiator	Water
Aug 10th	5:51 AM	Rex, The Dignified	Sharer	Sustainer	Fire
Aug 26th	7:06 AM	Details, The Analyst	Container	Adaptor	Earth
Sept 11th	11:18 AM	ProCon, The Diplomat	Sharer	Initiator	Air
Oct 1st	2:09 AM	Sherlock, The Detective	Container	Sustainer	Water
Dec 7th	1:04 AM	Flash, The Pioneer	Sharer	Adaptor	Fire
Dec 26th	12:47 PM	Exec, The Achiever	Container	Initiator	Earth

1994

DATE	TIME	STYLE	POLARITY	RELATING	UPTAKE
Jan 1st	0:00 AM	Exec, The Achiever	Container	Initiator	Earth
Jan 14th	12:25 AM	Boffin, The Innovator	Sharer	Sustainer	Air
Feb 1st	10:28 AM	Sonar, The Intuitive	Container	Adaptor	Water
Feb 21st	3:20 PM	Boffin, The Innovator	Sharer	Sustainer	Air
Mar 18th	12:04 PM	Sonar, The Intuitive	Container	Adaptor	Water
April 9th	4:30 PM	Scout, The Trailblazer	Sharer	Initiator	Fire
April 25th	6:27 PM	Steady, The Vault	Container	Sustainer	Earth
May 9th	9:08 PM	Buzz, The Curious	Sharer	Adaptor	Air
May 28th	2:52 PM	Sponge, The Sensitive	Container	Initiator	Water
July 2nd	11:27 PM	Buzz, The Curious	Sharer	Adaptor	Air
July 10th	12:41 PM	Sponge, The Sensitive	Container	Initiator	Water
Aug 3rd	6:09 AM	Rex, The Dignified	Sharer	Sustainer	Fire
Aug 18th	12:44 AM	Details, The Analyst	Container	Adaptor	Earth
Sept 4th	4:55 AM	ProCon, The Diplomat	Sharer	Initiator	Air
Sept 27th	8:51 AM	Sherlock, The Detective	Container	Sustainer	Water
Oct 19th	6:09 AM	ProCon, The Diplomat	Sharer	Initiator	Air
Nov 10th	12:46 PM	Sherlock, The Detective	Container	Sustainer	Water
Nov 30th	4:38 AM	Flash, The Pioneer	Sharer	Adaptor	Fire
Dec 19th	6:26 AM	Exec, The Achiever	Container	Initiator	Earth

1995

DATE	TIME	STYLE	POLARITY	RELATING	UPTAKE
Jan 1st	0:00 AM	Exec, The Achiever	Container	Initiator	Earth
Jan 6th	10:17 PM	Boffin, The Innovator	Sharer	Sustainer	Air
Mar 14th	9:35 PM	Sonar, The Intuitive	Container	Adaptor	Water
April 2nd	7:29 AM	Scout, The Trailblazer	Sharer	Initiator	Fire
April 17th	7:54 AM	Steady, The Vault	Container	Sustainer	Earth
May 2nd	3:18 PM	Buzz, The Curious	Sharer	Adaptor	Air
July 10th	4:58 PM	Sponge, The Sensitive	Container	Initiator	Water
July 25th	10:19 PM	Rex, The Dignified	Sharer	Sustainer	Fire
Aug 10th	12:13 AM	Details, The Analyst	Container	Adaptor	Earth
Aug 29th	2:07 AM	ProCon, The Diplomat	Sharer	Initiator	Air
Nov 4th	8:50 AM	Sherlock, The Detective	Container	Sustainer	Water
Nov 22nd	10:46 PM	Flash, The Pioneer	Sharer	Adaptor	Fire
Dec 12th	2:57 AM	Exec, The Achiever	Container	Initiator	Earth

1996

DATE	TIME	STYLE	POLARITY	RELATING	UPTAKE
Jan 1st	0:00 AM	Exec, The Achiever	Container	Initiator	Earth
Jan 1st	6:06 PM	Boffin, The Innovator	Sharer	Sustainer	Air
Jan 17th	9:17 AM	Exec, The Achiever	Container	Initiator	Earth
Feb 15th	2:44 AM	Boffin, The Innovator	Sharer	Sustainer	Air
Mar 7th	11:53 AM	Sonar, The Intuitive	Container	Adaptor	Water
Mar 24th	8:03 AM	Scout, The Trailblazer	Sharer	Initiator	Fire
April 8th	3:16 AM	Steady, The Vault	Container	Sustainer	Earth
June 13th	9:45 PM	Buzz, The Curious	Sharer	Adaptor	Air
July 2nd	7:36 AM	Sponge, The Sensitive	Container	Initiator	Water
July 16th	9:56 AM	Rex, The Dignified	Sharer	Sustainer	Fire
Aug 1st	4:17 PM	Details, The Analyst	Container	Adaptor	Earth
Aug 26th	5:17 AM	ProCon, The Diplomat	Sharer	Initiator	Air
Sept 12th	8:58 AM	Details, The Analyst	Container	Adaptor	Earth
Oct 9th	3:13 AM	ProCon, The Diplomat	Sharer	Initiator	Air
Oct 27th	1:01 AM	Sherlock, The Detective	Container	Sustainer	Water
Nov 14th	4:36 PM	Flash, The Pioneer	Sharer	Adaptor	Fire
Dec 4th	1:48 PM	Exec, The Achiever	Container	Initiator	Earth

1997

DATE	TIME	STYLE	POLARITY	RELATING	UPTAKE
Jan 1st	0:00 AM	Exec, The Achiever	Container	Initiator	Earth
Feb 9th	5:53 AM	Boffin, The Innovator	Sharer	Sustainer	Air
Feb 28th	3:54 AM	Sonar, The Intuitive	Container	Adaptor	Water
Mar 16th	4:13 AM	Scout, The Trailblazer	Sharer	Initiator	Fire
April 1st	1:45 PM	Steady, The Vault	Container	Sustainer	Earth
May 5th	2:21 AM	Scout, The Trailblazer	Sharer	Initiator	Fire
May 12th	10:25 AM	Steady, The Vault	Container	Sustainer	Earth
June 8th	11:25 PM	Buzz, The Curious	Sharer	Adaptor	Air
June 23rd	8:41 PM	Sponge, The Sensitive	Container	Initiator	Water
July 8th	5:28 AM	Rex, The Dignified	Sharer	Sustainer	Fire
July 27th	12:42 AM	Details, The Analyst	Container	Adaptor	Earth
Oct 2nd	5:38 AM	ProCon, The Diplomat	Sharer	Initiator	Air
Oct 19th	12:08 PM	Sherlock, The Detective	Container	Sustainer	Water
Nov 7th	5:42 PM	Flash, The Pioneer	Sharer	Adaptor	Fire
Nov 30th	7:11 PM	Exec, The Achiever	Container	Initiator	Earth
Dec 13th	5:26 PM	Flash, The Pioneer	Sharer	Adaptor	Fire

1998

DATE	TIME	STYLE	POLARITY	RELATING	UPTAKE
Jan 1st	0:00 AM	Flash, The Pioneer	Sharer	Adaptor	Fire
Jan 12th	4:20 PM	Exec, The Achiever	Container	Initiator	Earth
Feb 2nd	3:15 PM	Boffin, The Innovator	Sharer	Sustainer	Air
Feb 20th	10:22 AM	Sonar, The Intuitive	Container	Adaptor	Water
Mar 8th	8:28 AM	Scout, The Trailblazer	Sharer	Initiator	Fire
May 15th	2:10 AM	Steady, The Vault	Container	Sustainer	Earth
June 1st	8:07 AM	Buzz, The Curious	Sharer	Adaptor	Air
June 15th	5:33 AM	Sponge, The Sensitive	Container	Initiator	Water
June 30th	11:52 PM	Rex, The Dignified	Sharer	Sustainer	Fire
Sept 8th	1:58 AM	Details, The Analyst	Container	Adaptor	Earth
Sept 24th	10:12 AM	ProCon, The Diplomat	Sharer	Initiator	Air
Oct 12th	2:44 AM	Sherlock, The Detective	Container	Sustainer	Water
Nov 1st	4:02 PM	Flash, The Pioneer	Sharer	Adaptor	Fire

1999

DATE	TIME	STYLE	POLARITY	RELATING	UPTAKE
Jan 1st	0:00 AM	Flash, The Pioneer	Sharer	Adaptor	Fire
Jan 7th	2:03 AM	Exec, The Achiever	Container	Initiator	Earth
Jan 26th	9:32 AM	Boffin, The Innovator	Sharer	Sustainer	Air
Feb 12th	3:28 PM	Sonar, The Intuitive	Container	Adaptor	Water
Mar 2nd	10:50 PM	Scout, The Trailblazer	Sharer	Initiator	Fire
Mar 18th	9:06 AM	Sonar, The Intuitive	Container	Adaptor	Water
April 17th	10:09 PM	Scout, The Trailblazer	Sharer	Initiator	Fire
May 8th	9:22 PM	Steady, The Vault	Container	Sustainer	Earth
May 23rd	9:22 PM	Buzz, The Curious	Sharer	Adaptor	Air
June 7th	12:18 AM	Sponge, The Sensitive	Container	Initiator	Water
June 26th	3:39 PM	Rex, The Dignified	Sharer	Sustainer	Fire
July 31st	7:16 PM	Sponge, The Sensitive	Container	Initiator	Water
Aug 11th	4:25 AM	Rex, The Dignified	Sharer	Sustainer	Fire
Aug 31st	3:15 PM	Details, The Analyst	Container	Adaptor	Earth
Sept 16th	12:53 PM	ProCon, The Diplomat	Sharer	Initiator	Air
Oct 5th	5:12 AM	Sherlock, The Detective	Container	Sustainer	Water
Oct 30th	8:08 PM	Flash, The Pioneer	Sharer	Adaptor	Fire
Nov 9th	7:25 PM	Sherlock, The Detective	Container	Sustainer	Water
Dec 11th	2:09 AM	Flash, The Pioneer	Sharer	Adaptor	Fire
Dec 31st	6:48 AM	Exec, The Achiever	Container	Initiator	Earth

2000

DATE	TIME	STYLE	POLARITY	RELATING	UPTAKE
Jan 1st	0:00 AM	Exec, The Achiever	Container	Initiator	Earth
Jan 18th	10:21 PM	Boffin, The Innovator	Sharer	Sustainer	Air
Feb 5th	8:10 AM	Sonar, The Intuitive	Container	Adaptor	Water
April 13th	12:18 AM	Scout, The Trailblazer	Sharer	Initiator	Fire
April 30th	3:54 AM	Steady, The Vault	Container	Sustainer	Earth
May 14th	7:11 AM	Buzz, The Curious	Sharer	Adaptor	Air
May 30th	4:28 AM	Sponge, The Sensitive	Container	Initiator	Water
Aug 7th	5:43 AM	Rex, The Dignified	Sharer	Sustainer	Fire
Aug 22nd	10:12 AM	Details, The Analyst	Container	Adaptor	Earth
Sept 7th	10:23 PM	ProCon, The Diplomat	Sharer	Initiator	Air
Sept 28th	1:29 PM	Sherlock, The Detective	Container	Sustainer	Water
Nov 7th	7:29 AM	ProCon, The Diplomat	Sharer	Initiator	Air
Nov 8th	9:43 PM	Sherlock, The Detective	Container	Sustainer	Water
Dec 3rd	8:27 PM	Flash, The Pioneer	Sharer	Adaptor	Fire
Dec 23rd	2:04 AM	Exec, The Achiever	Container	Initiator	Earth

2001

DATE	TIME	STYLE	POLARITY	RELATING	UPTAKE
Jan 1st	0:00 AM	Exec, The Achiever	Container	Initiator	Earth
Jan 10th	1:27 PM	Boffin, The Innovator	Sharer	Sustainer	Air
Feb 1st	7:14 AM	Sonar, The Intuitive	Container	Adaptor	Water
Feb 6th	7:58 PM	Boffin, The Innovator	Sharer	Sustainer	Air
Mar 17th	6:06 AM	Sonar, The Intuitive	Container	Adaptor	Water
April 6th	7:15 AM	Scout, The Trailblazer	Sharer	Initiator	Fire
April 21st	8:09 PM	Steady, The Vault	Container	Sustainer	Earth
May 6th	4:54 AM	Buzz, The Curious	Sharer	Adaptor	Air
July 12th	10:48 PM	Sponge, The Sensitive	Container	Initiator	Water
July 30th	10:19 AM	Rex, The Dignified	Sharer	Sustainer	Fire
Aug 14th	5:05 AM	Details, The Analyst	Container	Adaptor	Earth
Sept 1st	12:38 AM	ProCon, The Diplomat	Sharer	Initiator	Air
Nov 7th	7:54 PM	Sherlock, The Detective	Container	Sustainer	Water
Nov 26th	6:25 PM	Flash, The Pioneer	Sharer	Adaptor	Fire
Dec 15th	7:56 PM	Exec, The Achiever	Container	Initiator	Earth

2002

DATE	TIME	STYLE	POLARITY	RELATING	UPTAKE
Jan 1st	0:00 AM	Exec, The Achiever	Container	Initiator	Earth
Jan 3rd	9:39 PM	Boffin, The Innovator	Sharer	Sustainer	Air
Feb 4th	4:20 AM	Exec, The Achiever	Container	Initiator	Earth
Feb 13th	5:21 PM	Boffin, The Innovator	Sharer	Sustainer	Air
Mar 11th	11:35 PM	Sonar, The Intuitive	Container	Adaptor	Water
Mar 29th	2:45 PM	Scout, The Trailblazer	Sharer	Initiator	Fire
April 13th	10:12 AM	Steady, The Vault	Container	Sustainer	Earth
April 30th	7:17 AM	Buzz, The Curious	Sharer	Adaptor	Air
July 7th	10:37 AM	Sponge, The Sensitive	Container	Initiator	Water
July 21st	10:42 PM	Rex, The Dignified	Sharer	Sustainer	Fire
Aug 6th	9:52 AM	Details, The Analyst	Container	Adaptor	Earth
Aug 26th	9:11 PM	ProCon, The Diplomat	Sharer	Initiator	Air
Oct 2nd	9:27 AM	Details, The Analyst	Container	Adaptor	Earth
Oct 11th	5:57 AM	ProCon, The Diplomat	Sharer	Initiator	Air
Oct 31st	10:44 PM	Sherlock, The Detective	Container	Sustainer	Water
Nov 19th	11:30 AM	Flash, The Pioneer	Sharer	Adaptor	Fire
Dec 8th	8:22 PM	Exec, The Achiever	Container	Initiator	Earth

2003

DATE	TIME	STYLE	POLARITY	RELATING	UPTAKE
Jan 1st	0:00 AM	Exec, The Achiever	Container	Initiator	Earth
Feb 13th	1:01 AM	Boffin, The Innovator	Sharer	Sustainer	Air
Mar 5th	2:05 AM	Sonar, The Intuitive	Container	Adaptor	Water
Mar 21st	12:17 PM	Scout, The Trailblazer	Sharer	Initiator	Fire
April 5th	2:38 PM	Steady, The Vault	Container	Sustainer	Earth
June 13th	1:35 AM	Buzz, The Curious	Sharer	Adaptor	Air
June 29th	10:18 AM	Sponge, The Sensitive	Container	Initiator	Water
July 13th	12:11 PM	Rex, The Dignified	Sharer	Sustainer	Fire
July 30th	2:06 PM	Details, The Analyst	Container	Adaptor	Earth
Oct 7th	1:29 AM	ProCon, The Diplomat	Sharer	Initiator	Air
Oct 24th	11:21 AM	Sherlock, The Detective	Container	Sustainer	Water
Nov 12th	7:20 AM	Flash, The Pioneer	Sharer	Adaptor	Fire
Dec 2nd	9:35 PM	Exec, The Achiever	Container	Initiator	Earth
Dec 30th	7:54 PM	Flash, The Pioneer	Sharer	Adaptor	Fire

2004

DATE	TIME	STYLE	POLARITY	RELATING	UPTAKE
Jan 1st	0:00 AM	Flash, The Pioneer	Sharer	Adaptor	Fire
Jan 14th	11:03 AM	Exec, The Achiever	Container	Initiator	Earth
Feb 7th	4:21 AM	Boffin, The Innovator	Sharer	Sustainer	Air
Feb 25th	12:59 PM	Sonar, The Intuitive	Container	Adaptor	Water
Mar 12th	9:45 AM	Scout, The Trailblazer	Sharer	Initiator	Fire
April 1st	2:29 AM	Steady, The Vault	Container	Sustainer	Earth
April 13th	1:24 AM	Scout, The Trailblazer	Sharer	Initiator	Fire
May 16th	6:55 AM	Steady, The Vault	Container	Sustainer	Earth
June 5th	12:49 PM	Buzz, The Curious	Sharer	Adaptor	Air
June 19th	7:51 PM	Sponge, The Sensitive	Container	Initiator	Water
July 4th	2:53 PM	Rex, The Dignified	Sharer	Sustainer	Fire
July 25th	1:59 PM	Details, The Analyst	Container	Adaptor	Earth
Aug 25th	1:34 AM	Rex, The Dignified	Sharer	Sustainer	Fire
Sept 10th	7:39 AM	Details, The Analyst	Container	Adaptor	Earth
Sept 28th	2:14 PM	ProCon, The Diplomat	Sharer	Initiator	Air
Oct 1st	10:58 PM	Sherlock, The Detective	Container	Sustainer	Water
Nov 4th	2:41 PM	Flash, The Pioneer	Sharer	Adaptor	Fire

2005

DATE	TIME	STYLE	POLARITY	RELATING	UPTAKE
Jan 1st	0:00 AM	Flash, The Pioneer	Sharer	Adaptor	Fire
Jan 10th	4:10 AM	Exec, The Achiever	Container	Initiator	Earth
Jan 30th	5:38 AM	Boffin, The Innovator	Sharer	Sustainer	Air
Feb 16th	5:47 PM	Sonar, The Intuitive	Container	Adaptor	Water
Mar 5th	1:35 AM	Scout, The Trailblazer	Sharer	Initiator	Fire
May 12th	9:15 AM	Steady, The Vault	Container	Sustainer	Earth
May 28th	10:45 AM	Buzz, The Curious	Sharer	Adaptor	Air
June 11th	7:04 AM	Sponge, The Sensitive	Container	Initiator	Water
June 28th	4:02 AM	Rex, The Dignified	Sharer	Sustainer	Fire
Sept 4th	5:54 PM	Details, The Analyst	Container	Adaptor	Earth
Sept 20th	4:41 PM	ProCon, The Diplomat	Sharer	Initiator	Air
Oct 8th	5:16 PM	Sherlock, The Detective	Container	Sustainer	Water
Oct 30th	9:03 AM	Flash, The Pioneer	Sharer	Adaptor	Fire
Nov 26th	11:55 AM	Sherlock, The Detective	Container	Sustainer	Water
Dec 12th	9:20 PM	Flash, The Pioneer	Sharer	Adaptor	Fire

2006

DATE	TIME	STYLE	POLARITY	RELATING	UPTAKE
Jan 1st	0:00 AM	Flash, The Pioneer	Sharer	Adaptor	Fire
Jan 3rd	9:27 PM	Exec, The Achiever	Container	Initiator	Earth
Jan 22nd	8:43 PM	Boffin, The Innovator	Sharer	Sustainer	Air
Feb 9th	1:23 AM	Sonar, The Intuitive	Container	Adaptor	Water
April 16th	12:21 PM	Scout, The Trailblazer	Sharer	Initiator	Fire
May 5th	8:29 AM	Steady, The Vault	Container	Sustainer	Earth
May 19th	8:53 PM	Buzz, The Curious	Sharer	Adaptor	Air
June 3rd	11:22 AM	Sponge, The Sensitive	Container	Initiator	Water
June 28th	7:58 PM	Rex, The Dignified	Sharer	Sustainer	Fire
July 10th	8:19 PM	Sponge, The Sensitive	Container	Initiator	Water
Aug 11th	4:11 AM	Rex, The Dignified	Sharer	Sustainer	Fire
Aug 27th	7:32 PM	Details, The Analyst	Container	Adaptor	Earth
Sept 12th	9:09 PM	ProCon, The Diplomat	Sharer	Initiator	Air
Oct 2nd	4:39 AM	Sherlock, The Detective	Container	Sustainer	Water
Dec 8th	5:53 AM	Flash, The Pioneer	Sharer	Adaptor	Fire
Dec 27th	8:56 PM	Exec, The Achiever	Container	Initiator	Earth

2007

DATE	TIME	STYLE	POLARITY	RELATING	UPTAKE
Jan 1st	0:00 AM	Exec, The Achiever	Container	Initiator	Earth
Jan 15th	9:26 AM	Boffin, The Innovator	Sharer	Sustainer	Air
Feb 2nd	9:21 AM	Sonar, The Intuitive	Container	Adaptor	Water
Feb 27th	3:02 AM	Boffin, The Innovator	Sharer	Sustainer	Air
Mar 18th	9:36 AM	Sonar, The Intuitive	Container	Adaptor	Water
April 10th	11:08 PM	Scout, The Trailblazer	Sharer	Initiator	Fire
April 27th	7:17 AM	Steady, The Vault	Container	Sustainer	Earth
May 11th	9:18 AM	Buzz, The Curious	Sharer	Adaptor	Air
May 29th	12:57 AM	Sponge, The Sensitive	Container	Initiator	Water
Aug 4th	5:16 PM	Rex, The Dignified	Sharer	Sustainer	Fire
Aug 19th	1:02 PM	Details, The Analyst	Container	Adaptor	Earth
Sept 5th	12:03 PM	ProCon, The Diplomat	Sharer	Initiator	Air
Sept 27th	5:19 PM	Sherlock, The Detective	Container	Sustainer	Water
Oct 24th	3:38 AM	ProCon, The Diplomat	Sharer	Initiator	Air
Nov 11th	8:42 AM	Sherlock, The Detective	Container	Sustainer	Water
Dec 1st	12:22 PM	Flash, The Pioneer	Sharer	Adaptor	Fire
Dec 20th	2:44 PM	Exec, The Achiever	Container	Initiator	Earth

2008

DATE	TIME	STYLE	POLARITY	RELATING	UPTAKE
Jan 1st	0:00 AM	Exec, The Achiever	Container	Initiator	Earth
Jan 8th	4:47 AM	Boffin, The Innovator	Sharer	Sustainer	Air
Mar 14th	10:47 PM	Sonar, The Intuitive	Container	Adaptor	Water
April 2nd	5:46 PM	Scout, The Trailblazer	Sharer	Initiator	Fire
April 17th	9:08 PM	Steady, The Vault	Container	Sustainer	Earth
May 2nd	8:01 PM	Buzz, The Curious	Sharer	Adaptor	Air
July 10th	8:18 PM	Sponge, The Sensitive	Container	Initiator	Water
July 26th	11:49 AM	Rex, The Dignified	Sharer	Sustainer	Fire
Aug 10th	10:52 AM	Details, The Analyst	Container	Adaptor	Earth
Aug 29th	2:51 AM	ProCon, The Diplomat	Sharer	Initiator	Air
Nov 4th	4:01 PM	Sherlock, The Detective	Container	Sustainer	Water
Nov 23rd	7:10 AM	Flash, The Pioneer	Sharer	Adaptor	Fire
Dec 12th	10:14 AM	Exec, The Achiever	Container	Initiator	Earth

2009

DATE	TIME	STYLE	POLARITY	RELATING	UPTAKE
Jan 1st	0:00 AM	Exec, The Achiever	Container	Initiator	Earth
Jan 1st	9:52 AM	Boffin, The Innovator	Sharer	Sustainer	Air
Jan 21st	5:37 AM	Exec, The Achiever	Container	Initiator	Earth
Feb 14th	3:40 PM	Boffin, The Innovator	Sharer	Sustainer	Air
Mar 8th	6:57 PM	Sonar, The Intuitive	Container	Adaptor	Water
Mar 25th	7:56 PM	Scout, The Trailblazer	Sharer	Initiator	Fire
April 9th	2:22 PM	Steady, The Vault	Container	Sustainer	Earth
April 30th	10:30 PM	Buzz, The Curious	Sharer	Adaptor	Air
May 13th	11:54 PM	Steady, The Vault	Container	Sustainer	Earth
June 14th	2:48 AM	Buzz, The Curious	Sharer	Adaptor	Air
July 3rd	7:21 PM	Sponge, The Sensitive	Container	Initiator	Water
July 17th	11:09 PM	Rex, The Dignified	Sharer	Sustainer	Fire
Aug 2nd	11:08 PM	Details, The Analyst	Container	Adaptor	Earth
Aug 25th	8:19 PM	ProCon, The Diplomat	Sharer	Initiator	Air
Sept 18th	3:27 AM	Details, The Analyst	Container	Adaptor	Earth
Oct 10th	3:47 AM	ProCon, The Diplomat	Sharer	Initiator	Air
Oct 28th	10:10 AM	Sherlock, The Detective	Container	Sustainer	Water
Nov 16th	12:29 AM	Flash, The Pioneer	Sharer	Adaptor	Fire
Dec 5th	5:25 PM	Exec, The Achiever	Container	Initiator	Earth

2010

DATE	TIME	STYLE	POLARITY	RELATING	UPTAKE
Jan 1st	0:00 AM	Exec, The Achiever	Container	Initiator	Earth
Feb 10th	9:07 AM	Boffin, The Innovator	Sharer	Sustainer	Air
Mar 1st	1:29 PM	Sonar, The Intuitive	Container	Adaptor	Water
Mar 17th	4:13 PM	Scout, The Trailblazer	Sharer	Initiator	Fire
April 2nd	1:07 PM	Steady, The Vault	Container	Sustainer	Earth
June 10th	5:42 AM	Buzz, The Curious	Sharer	Adaptor	Air
June 25th	10:33 AM	Sponge, The Sensitive	Container	Initiator	Water
July 9th	4:30 PM	Rex, The Dignified	Sharer	Sustainer	Fire
July 27th	9:44 PM	Details, The Analyst	Container	Adaptor	Earth
Oct 3rd	3:05 PM	ProCon, The Diplomat	Sharer	Initiator	Air
Oct 20th	9:20 PM	Sherlock, The Detective	Container	Sustainer	Water
Nov 8th	11:44 PM	Flash, The Pioneer	Sharer	Adaptor	Fire
Dec 1st	12:12 AM	Exec, The Achiever	Container	Initiator	Earth
Dec 18th	2:54 PM	Flash, The Pioneer	Sharer	Adaptor	Fire

2011

DATE	TIME	STYLE	POLARITY	RELATING	UPTAKE
Jan 1st	0:00 AM	Flash, The Pioneer	Sharer	Adaptor	Fire
Jan 13th	11:26 AM	Exec, The Achiever	Container	Initiator	Earth
Feb 3rd	10:20 PM	Boffin, The Innovator	Sharer	Sustainer	Air
Feb 21st	8:54 PM	Sonar, The Intuitive	Container	Adaptor	Water
Mar 9th	5:48 PM	Scout, The Trailblazer	Sharer	Initiator	Fire
May 15th	11:19 PM	Steady, The Vault	Container	Sustainer	Earth
June 2nd	8:04 PM	Buzz, The Curious	Sharer	Adaptor	Air
June 16th	7:10 PM	Sponge, The Sensitive	Container	Initiator	Water
July 2nd	5:39 AM	Rex, The Dignified	Sharer	Sustainer	Fire
July 28th	6:00 PM	Details, The Analyst	Container	Adaptor	Earth
Aug 8th	9:47 AM	Rex, The Dignified	Sharer	Sustainer	Fire
Sept 9th	6:00 AM	Details, The Analyst	Container	Adaptor	Earth
Sept 25th	9:10 PM	ProCon, The Diplomat	Sharer	Initiator	Air
Oct 13th	10:53 AM	Sherlock, The Detective	Container	Sustainer	Water
Nov 2nd	4:55 PM	Flash, The Pioneer	Sharer	Adaptor	Fire

2012

DATE	TIME	STYLE	POLARITY	RELATING	UPTAKE
Jan 1st	0:00 AM	Flash, The Pioneer	Sharer	Adaptor	Fire
Jan 8th	6:35 AM	Exec, The Achiever	Container	Initiator	Earth
Jan 27th	6:13 PM	Boffin, The Innovator	Sharer	Sustainer	Air
Feb 14th	1:39 AM	Sonar, The Intuitive	Container	Adaptor	Water
Mar 2nd	11:42 AM	Scout, The Trailblazer	Sharer	Initiator	Fire
Mar 23rd	1:23 PM	Sonar, The Intuitive	Container	Adaptor	Water
April 16th	10:43 PM	Scout, The Trailblazer	Sharer	Initiator	Fire
May 9th	5:16 AM	Steady, The Vault	Container	Sustainer	Earth
May 24th	11:13 AM	Buzz, The Curious	Sharer	Adaptor	Air
June 7th	11:17 AM	Sponge, The Sensitive	Container	Initiator	Water
June 26th	2:25 AM	Rex, The Dignified	Sharer	Sustainer	Fire
Sept 1st	2:33 AM	Details, The Analyst	Container	Adaptor	Earth
Sept 16th	11:23 PM	ProCon, The Diplomat	Sharer	Initiator	Air
Oct 5th	10:36 AM	Sherlock, The Detective	Container	Sustainer	Water
Oct 29th	6:19 AM	Flash, The Pioneer	Sharer	Adaptor	Fire
Nov 14th	7:43 AM	Sherlock, The Detective	Container	Sustainer	Water
Dec 11th	1:41 AM	Flash, The Pioneer	Sharer	Adaptor	Fire
Dec 31st	2:04 PM	Exec, The Achiever	Container	Initiator	Earth

2013

DATE	TIME	STYLE	POLARITY	RELATING	UPTAKE
Jan 1st	0:00 AM	Exec, The Achiever	Container	Initiator	Earth
Jan 19th	7:26 AM	Boffin, The Innovator	Sharer	Sustainer	Air
Feb 5th	2:57 PM	Sonar, The Intuitive	Container	Adaptor	Water
April 14th	2:38 AM	Scout, The Trailblazer	Sharer	Initiator	Fire
May 1st	3:38 PM	Steady, The Vault	Container	Sustainer	Earth
May 15th	8:42 PM	Buzz, The Curious	Sharer	Adaptor	Air
May 31st	7:08 AM	Sponge, The Sensitive	Container	Initiator	Water
Aug 8th	12:14 PM	Rex, The Dignified	Sharer	Sustainer	Fire
Aug 23rd	10:39 PM	Details, The Analyst	Container	Adaptor	Earth
Sept 9th	7:08 AM	ProCon, The Diplomat	Sharer	Initiator	Air
Sept 29th	11:39 AM	Sherlock, The Detective	Container	Sustainer	Water
Dec 5th	2:43 AM	Flash, The Pioneer	Sharer	Adaptor	Fire
Dec 24th	10:13 AM	Exec, The Achiever	Container	Initiator	Earth

2014

DATE	TIME	STYLE	POLARITY	RELATING	UPTAKE
Jan 1st	0:00 AM	Exec, The Achiever	Container	Initiator	Earth
Jan 11th	9:36 PM	Boffin, The Innovator	Sharer	Sustainer	Air
Jan 31st	2:30 PM	Sonar, The Intuitive	Container	Adaptor	Water
Feb 13th	3:31 AM	Boffin, The Innovator	Sharer	Sustainer	Air
Mar 17th	10:25 PM	Sonar, The Intuitive	Container	Adaptor	Water
April 7th	3:36 PM	Scout, The Trailblazer	Sharer	Initiator	Fire
April 23rd	9:17 AM	Steady, The Vault	Container	Sustainer	Earth
May 7th	2:58 PM	Buzz, The Curious	Sharer	Adaptor	Air
May 29th	9:13 AM	Sponge, The Sensitive	Container	Initiator	Water
June 17th	10:06 AM	Buzz, The Curious	Sharer	Adaptor	Air
July 13th	4:46 AM	Sponge, The Sensitive	Container	Initiator	Water
July 31st	10:47 PM	Rex, The Dignified	Sharer	Sustainer	Fire
Aug 15th	4:45 PM	Details, The Analyst	Container	Adaptor	Earth
Sept 2nd	5:39 AM	ProCon, The Diplomat	Sharer	Initiator	Air
Sept 27th	10:40 PM	Sherlock, The Detective	Container	Sustainer	Water
Oct 10th	5:28 PM	ProCon, The Diplomat	Sharer	Initiator	Air
Nov 8th	11:10 PM	Sherlock, The Detective	Container	Sustainer	Water
Nov 28th	2:27 AM	Flash, The Pioneer	Sharer	Adaptor	Fire
Dec 17th	3:54 AM	Exec, The Achiever	Container	Initiator	Earth

2015

DATE	TIME	STYLE	POLARITY	RELATING	UPTAKE
Jan 1st	0:00 AM	Exec, The Achiever	Container	Initiator	Earth
Jan 5th	1:09 AM	Boffin, The Innovator	Sharer	Sustainer	Air
Mar 13th	3:53 AM	Sonar, The Intuitive	Container	Adaptor	Water
Mar 31st	1:45 AM	Scout, The Trailblazer	Sharer	Initiator	Fire
Apr 14th	10:53 PM	Steady - The Vault	Container	Sustainer	Earth
May 1st	2:01 AM	Buzz - The Curious	Sharer	Adaptor	Air
Jul 8th	6:53 PM	Sponge - The Sensitive	Container	Initiator	Water
Jul 23rd	12:15 PM	Rex - The Dignified	Sharer	Sustainer	Fire
Aug 7th	7:16 PM	Details - The Analyst	Container	Adaptor	Earth
Aug 27th	3:46 PM	ProCon - The Diplomat	Sharer	Initiator	Air
Nov 2nd	7:07 AM	Sherlock, The Detective	Container	Sustainer	Water
Nov 20th	7:44 PM	Flash - The Pioneer	Sharer	Adaptor	Fire
Dec 10th	2:35 AM	Exec - The Achiever	Container	Initiator	Earth

2016

DATE	TIME	STYLE	POLARITY	RELATING	UPTAKE
Jan 1st	0:00 AM	Exec, The Achiever	Container	Initiator	Earth
Jan 2nd	2:21 AM	Boffin, The Innovator	Sharer	Sustainer	Air
Jan 8th	7:37 PM	Exec, The Achiever	Container	Initiator	Earth
Feb 13th	10:44 PM	Boffin, The Innovator	Sharer	Sustainer	Air
Mar 5th	10:25 AM	Sonar, The Intuitive	Container	Adaptor	Water
Mar 22nd	0:20 AM	Scout, The Trailblazer	Sharer	Initiator	Fire
Apr 5th	11:10 PM	Steady, The Vault	Container	Sustainer	Earth
Jun 12th	11:24 PM	Buzz, The Curious	Sharer	Adaptor	Air
Jun 29th	11:25 PM	Sponge, The Sensitive	Container	Initiator	Water
Jul 14th	0:48 AM	Rex, The Dignified	Sharer	Sustainer	Fire
Jul 30th	6:19 PM	Details, The Analyst	Container	Adaptor	Earth
Oct 7th	7:57 AM	ProCon, The Diplomat	Sharer	Initiator	Air
Oct 24th	8:47 PM	Sherlock, The Detective	Container	Sustainer	Water
Nov 12th	2:41 PM	Flash, The Pioneer	Sharer	Adaptor	Fire
Dec 2nd	9:19 PM	Exec, The Achiever	Container	Initiator	Earth

2017

DATE	TIME	STYLE	POLARITY	RELATING	UPTAKE
Jan 1st	0:00 AM	Exec, The Achiever	Container	Initiator	Earth
Jan 4th	2:18 PM	Flash, The Pioneer	Sharer	Adaptor	Fire
Jan 12th	2:04 PM	Exec, The Achiever	Container	Initiator	Earth
Feb 7th	9:36 AM	Boffin, The Innovator	Sharer	Sustainer	Air
Feb 25th	11:08 PM	Sonar, The Intuitive	Container	Adaptor	Water
Mar 13th	9:08 PM	Scout, The Trailblazer	Sharer	Initiator	Fire
Mar 31st	5:32 PM	Steady, The Vault	Container	Sustainer	Earth
Apr 20th	5:38 PM	Scout, The Trailblazer	Sharer	Initiator	Fire
May 16th	4:08 AM	Steady, The Vault	Container	Sustainer	Earth
Jun 6th	10:16 PM	Buzz, The Curious	Sharer	Adaptor	Air
Jun 21st	9:59 AM	Sponge, The Sensitive	Container	Initiator	Water
Jul 6th	0:21 AM	Rex, The Dignified	Sharer	Sustainer	Fire
Jul 25th	11:42 PM	Details, The Analyst	Container	Adaptor	Earth
Aug 31st	3:29 PM	Rex, The Dignified	Sharer	Sustainer	Fire
Sept 10th	2:53 AM	Details, The Analyst	Container	Adaptor	Earth
Sept 30th	0:43 AM	ProCon, The Diplomat	Sharer	Initiator	Air
Oct 17th	8:00 AM	Sherlock, The Detective	Container	Sustainer	Water
Nov 5th	7:20 PM	Flash, The Pioneer	Sharer	Adaptor	Fire

2018

DATE	TIME	STYLE	POLARITY	RELATING	UPTAKE
Jan 1st	0:00 AM	Flash, The Pioneer	Sharer	Adaptor	Fire
Jan 11th	5:10 AM	Exec, The Achiever	Container	Initiator	Earth
Jan 31st	1:40 PM	Boffin, The Innovator	Sharer	Sustainer	Air
Feb 18th	4:29 AM	Sonar, The Intuitive	Container	Adaptor	Water
Mar 6th	7:35 AM	Scout, The Trailblazer	Sharer	Initiator	Fire
May 13th	12:41 PM	Steady, The Vault	Container	Sustainer	Earth
May 29th	11:50 PM	Buzz, The Curious	Sharer	Adaptor	Air
Jun 12th	8:01 PM	Sponge, The Sensitive	Container	Initiator	Water
Jun 29th	5:17 AM	Rex, The Dignified	Sharer	Sustainer	Fire
Sept 6th	2:40 AM	Details, The Analyst	Container	Adaptor	Earth
Sept 22nd	3:41 AM	ProCon, The Diplomat	Sharer	Initiator	Air
Oct 10th	0:41 AM	Sherlock, The Detective	Container	Sustainer	Water
Oct 31st	4:39 AM	Flash, The Pioneer	Sharer	Adaptor	Fire
Dec 1st	11:13 AM	Sherlock, The Detective	Container	Sustainer	Water
Dec 12th	11:44 PM	Flash, The Pioneer	Sharer	Adaptor	Fire

2019

DATE	TIME	STYLE	POLARITY	RELATING	UPTAKE
Jan 1st	0:00 AM	Flash, The Pioneer	Sharer	Adaptor	Fire
Jan 5th	3:41 AM	Exec, The Achiever	Container	Initiator	Earth
Jan 24th	5:50 AM	Boffin, The Innovator	Sharer	Sustainer	Air
Feb 10th	10:52 AM	Sonar, The Intuitive	Container	Adaptor	Water
Apr 17th	6:02 AM	Scout, The Trailblazer	Sharer	Initiator	Fire
May 6th	6:26 PM	Steady, The Vault	Container	Sustainer	Earth
May 21st	10:53 AM	Buzz, The Curious	Sharer	Adaptor	Air
Jun 4th	8:06 PM	Sponge, The Sensitive	Container	Initiator	Water
Jun 27th	0:21 AM	Rex, The Dignified	Sharer	Sustainer	Fire
Jul 19th	7:07 AM	Sponge, The Sensitive	Container	Initiator	Water
Aug 11th	7:47 PM	Rex, The Dignified	Sharer	Sustainer	Fire
Aug 29th	7:49 AM	Details, The Analyst	Container	Adaptor	Earth
Sept 14th	7:16 AM	ProCon, The Diplomat	Sharer	Initiator	Air
Oct 3rd	8:15 AM	Sherlock, The Detective	Container	Sustainer	Water
Dec 9th	9:43 AM	Flash, The Pioneer	Sharer	Adaptor	Fire
Dec 29th	4:56 AM	Exec, The Achiever	Container	Initiator	Earth

2020

DATE	TIME	STYLE	POLARITY	RELATING	UPTAKE
Jan 1st	0:00 AM	Exec, The Achiever	Container	Initiator	Earth
Jan 16th	6:32 PM	Boffin, The Innovator	Sharer	Sustainer	Air
Feb 3rd	11:39 AM	Sonar, The Intuitive	Container	Adaptor	Water
Mar 4th	11:09 AM	Boffin, The Innovator	Sharer	Sustainer	Air
Mar 16th	7:44 AM	Sonar, The Intuitive	Container	Adaptor	Water
Apr 11th	4:49 AM	Scout, The Trailblazer	Sharer	Initiator	Fire
Apr 27th	7:54 PM	Steady, The Vault	Container	Sustainer	Earth
May 11th	9:59 PM	Buzz, The Curious	Sharer	Adaptor	Air
May 28th	6:10 PM	Sponge, The Sensitive	Container	Initiator	Water
Aug 5th	3:33 AM	Rex, The Dignified	Sharer	Sustainer	Fire
Aug 20th	1:31 AM	Details, The Analyst	Container	Adaptor	Earth
Sept 5th	7:47 PM	ProCon, The Diplomat	Sharer	Initiator	Air
Sept 27th	7:42 AM	Sherlock, The Detective	Container	Sustainer	Water
Oct 28th	1:35 AM	ProCon, The Diplomat	Sharer	Initiator	Air
Nov 10th	09:57 PM	Sherlock, The Detective	Container	Sustainer	Water
Dec 1st	7:52 PM	Flash, The Pioneer	Sharer	Adaptor	Fire
Dec 20th	11:08 PM	Exec, The Achiever	Container	Initiator	Earth

2021

DATE	TIME	STYLE	POLARITY	RELATING	UPTAKE
Jan 1st	0:00 AM	Exec, The Achiever	Container	Initiator	Earth
Jan 8th	12:01 PM	Boffin, The Innovator	Sharer	Sustainer	Air
Mar 15th	10:28 PM	Sonar, The Intuitive	Container	Adaptor	Water
Apr 4th	3:42 AM	Scout, The Trailblazer	Sharer	Initiator	Fire
Apr 19th	10:30 AM	Steady, The Vault	Container	Sustainer	Earth
May 4th	2:50 AM	Buzz, The Curious	Sharer	Adaptor	Air
Jul 11th	8:36 PM	Sponge, The Sensitive	Container	Initiator	Water
Jul 28th	1:13 AM	Rex, The Dignified	Sharer	Sustainer	Fire
Aug 11th	9:58 PM	Details, The Analyst	Container	Adaptor	Earth
Aug 30th	5:11 AM	ProCon, The Diplomat	Sharer	Initiator	Air
Nov 5th	10:36 PM	Sherlock, The Detective	Container	Sustainer	Water
Nov 24th	3:38 PM	Flash, The Pioneer	Sharer	Adaptor	Fire
Dec 13th	5:53 PM	Exec, The Achiever	Container	Initiator	Earth

2022

DATE	TIME	STYLE	POLARITY	RELATING	UPTAKE
Jan 1st	0:00 AM	Exec, The Achiever	Container	Initiator	Earth
Jan 2nd	7:11 AM	Boffin, The Innovator	Sharer	Sustainer	Air
Jan 26th	3:06 AM	Exec, The Achiever	Container	Initiator	Earth
Feb 14th	9:56 PM	Boffin, The Innovator	Sharer	Sustainer	Air
Mar 10th	1:33 AM	Sonar, The Intuitive	Container	Adaptor	Water
Mar 27th	7:46 AM	Scout, The Trailblazer	Sharer	Initiator	Fire
Apr 11th	2:11 AM	Steady, The Vault	Container	Sustainer	Earth
Apr 29th	10:24 PM	Buzz, The Curious	Sharer	Adaptor	Air
May 23rd	1:16 AM	Steady, The Vault	Container	Sustainer	Earth
Jun 13th	3:28 PM	Buzz, The Curious	Sharer	Adaptor	Air
Jul 5th	6:26 AM	Sponge, The Sensitive	Container	Initiator	Water
Jul 19th	12:36 PM	Rex, The Dignified	Sharer	Sustainer	Fire
Aug 4th	6:59 AM	Details, The Analyst	Container	Adaptor	Earth
Aug 26th	1:04 AM	ProCon, The Diplomat	Sharer	Initiator	Air
Sept 23rd	12:06 PM	Details, The Analyst	Container	Adaptor	Earth
Oct 10th	11:52 PM	ProCon, The Diplomat	Sharer	Initiator	Air
Oct 29th	7:23 PM	Sherlock, The Detective	Container	Sustainer	Water
Nov 17th	8:43 AM	Flash, The Pioneer	Sharer	Adaptor	Fire
Dec 6th	10:09 PM	Exec, The Achiever	Container	Initiator	Earth

2023

DATE	TIME	STYLE	POLARITY	RELATING	UPTAKE
Jan 1st	0:00 AM	Exec, The Achiever	Container	Initiator	Earth
Feb 11th	11:23 AM	Boffin, The Innovator	Sharer	Sustainer	Air
Mar 2nd	10:53 PM	Sonar, The Intuitive	Container	Adaptor	Water
Mar 19th	4:25 AM	Scout, The Trailblazer	Sharer	Initiator	Fire
Apr 3rd	4:23 PM	Steady, The Vault	Container	Sustainer	Earth
Jun 11th	10:28 AM	Buzz, The Curious	Sharer	Adaptor	Air
Jun 27th	00:25 AM	Sponge, The Sensitive	Container	Initiator	Water
Jul 11th	4:12 AM	Rex, The Dignified	Sharer	Sustainer	Fire
Jul 28th	9:32 PM	Details, The Analyst	Container	Adaptor	Earth
Oct 5th	0:10 AM	ProCon, The Diplomat	Sharer	Initiator	Air
Oct 22nd	6:50 AM	Sherlock, The Detective	Container	Sustainer	Water
Nov 10th	6:26 AM	Flash, The Pioneer	Sharer	Adaptor	Fire
Dec 1st	2:33 PM	Exec, The Achiever	Container	Initiator	Earth
Dec 23rd	6:19 AM	Flash, The Pioneer	Sharer	Adaptor	Fire

2024

DATE	TIME	STYLE	POLARITY	RELATING	UPTAKE
Jan 1st	0:00 AM	Flash, The Pioneer	Sharer	Adaptor	Fire
Jan 14th	2:51 AM	Exec, The Achiever	Container	Initiator	Earth
Feb 5th	5:11 AM	Boffin, The Innovator	Sharer	Sustainer	Air
Feb 23rd	7:30 AM	Sonar, The Intuitive	Container	Adaptor	Water
Mar 10th	4:04 AM	Scout, The Trailblazer	Sharer	Initiator	Fire
May 15th	5:06 PM	Steady, The Vault	Container	Sustainer	Earth
Jun 3rd	7:38 AM	Buzz, The Curious	Sharer	Adaptor	Air
Jun 17th	9:08 AM	Sponge, The Sensitive	Container	Initiator	Water
Jul 2nd	12:51 PM	Rex, The Dignified	Sharer	Sustainer	Fire
Jul 25th	10:43 PM	Details, The Analyst	Container	Adaptor	Earth
Aug 15th	0:17 AM	Rex, The Dignified	Sharer	Sustainer	Fire
Sept 9th	6:51 AM	Details, The Analyst	Container	Adaptor	Earth
Sept 26th	8:10 AM	ProCon, The Diplomat	Sharer	Initiator	Air
Oct 13th	7:25 PM	Sherlock, The Detective	Container	Sustainer	Water
Nov 2nd	7:19 PM	Flash, The Pioneer	Sharer	Adaptor	Fire

2025

DATE	TIME	STYLE	POLARITY	RELATING	UPTAKE
Jan 1st	0:00 AM	Flash, The Pioneer	Sharer	Adaptor	Fire
Jan 8th	10:31 AM	Exec, The Achiever	Container	Initiator	Earth
Jan 28th	2:54 AM	Boffin, The Innovator	Sharer	Sustainer	Air
Feb 14th	12:08 PM	Sonar, The Intuitive	Container	Adaptor	Water
Mar 3rd	9:05 AM	Scout, The Trailblazer	Sharer	Initiator	Fire
Mar 30th	2:19 AM	Sonar, The Intuitive	Container	Adaptor	Water
Apr 16th	6:26 AM	Scout, The Trailblazer	Sharer	Initiator	Fire
May 10th	12:16 PM	Steady, The Vault	Container	Sustainer	Earth
May 26th	1:00 AM	Buzz, The Curious	Sharer	Adaptor	Air
Jun 8th	10:59 PM	Sponge, The Sensitive	Container	Initiator	Water
Jun 26th	7:10 PM	Rex, The Dignified	Sharer	Sustainer	Fire
Sept 2nd	1:24 PM	Details, The Analyst	Container	Adaptor	Earth
Sept 18th	10:07 AM	ProCon, The Diplomat	Sharer	Initiator	Air
Oct 6th	4:42 PM	Sherlock, The Detective	Container	Sustainer	Water
Oct 29th	11:03 AM	Flash, The Pioneer	Sharer	Adaptor	Fire
Nov 19th	3:21 AM	Sherlock, The Detective	Container	Sustainer	Water
Dec 11th	10:41 PM	Flash, The Pioneer	Sharer	Adaptor	Fire

The fleet-footed courier of information has been represented artistically over the centuries, in stylized drawings, classic paintings and elegant sculptures. Even a simple feather has conveyed the image of thought taking flight.

WATKINS

Sharing Wisdom Since 1893

The story of Watkins Publishing dates back to March 1893, when John M. Watkins, a scholar of esotericism, overheard his friend and teacher Madame Blavatsky lamenting the fact that there was nowhere in London to buy books on mysticism, occultism or metaphysics. At that moment Watkins was born, soon to become the home of many of the leading lights of spiritual literature, including Carl Jung, Rudolf Steiner, Alice Bailey and Chögyam Trungpa.

Today our passion for vigorous questioning is still resolute. With over 350 titles on our list, Watkins Publishing reflects the development of spiritual thinking and new science over the past 120 years. We remain at the cutting edge, committed to publishing books that change lives.

DISCOVER MORE ...

Read our blog   Watch and listen to   Sign up to
                   our authors in action   our mailing list

JOIN IN THE CONVERSATION

WatkinsPublishing   @watkinswisdom

WatkinsPublishingLtd   +watkinspublishing1893

Our books celebrate conscious, passionate, wise and happy living.
Be part of the community by visiting

www.watkinspublishing.com